Liquidity Risk Management

The Wiley Finance series contains books written specifically for finance and investment professionals as well as sophisticated individual investors and their financial advisors. Book topics range from portfolio management to e-commerce, risk management, financial engineering, valuation and financial instrument analysis, as well as much more. For a list of available titles, visit our Web site at www.WileyFinance.com.

Founded in 1807, John Wiley & Sons is the oldest independent publishing company in the United States. With offices in North America, Europe, Australia and Asia, Wiley is globally committed to developing and marketing print and electronic products and services for our customers' professional and personal knowledge and understanding.

Liquidity Risk Management

A Practitioner's Perspective

SHYAM VENKAT
STEPHEN BAIRD

WILEY

Published by John Wiley & Sons, Inc., Hoboken, New Jersey.

Published simultaneously in Canada.

For general information on our other products and services or for technical support, please contact our Customer Care Department within the United States at (800) 762-2974, outside the United States at (317) 572-3993 or fax (317) 572-4002.

Wiley publishes in a variety of print and electronic formats and by print-on-demand. Some material included with standard print versions of this book may not be included in e-books or in print-on-demand. If this book refers to media such as a CD or DVD that is not included in the version you purchased, you may download this material at http://booksupport.wiley.com. For more information about Wiley products, visit www.wiley.com.

Library of Congress Cataloging-in-Publication Data

Names: Venkat, Shyam, 1962– author. | Baird, Stephen, 1966– author.
Title: Liquidity risk management : a practitioner's perspective / Shyam Venkat, Stephen Baird.
Description: Hoboken : Wiley, 2016. | Series: Wiley finance | Includes index.
Identifiers: LCCN 2016001879 (print) | LCCN 2016006247 (ebook) | ISBN 9781118881927 (hardback) | ISBN 9781118918791 (ePDF) | ISBN 9781118918784 (ePub) | ISBN 9781118918791 (pdf) | ISBN 9781118918784 (epub)
Subjects: LCSH: Bank liquidity—Management. | Banks and banking—Risk management. | Financial risk management. | BISAC: BUSINESS & ECONOMICS / Banks & Banking.
Classification: LCC HG1656.A3 V46 2016 (print) | LCC HG1656.A3 (ebook) | DDC 332.1068/1—dc23
LC record available at http://lccn.loc.gov/2016001879

Cover Design: Wiley
Cover Image: Lost in the middle © iStock.com/3dts

Printed in the United States of America

10 9 8 7 6 5 4 3 2 1

Contents

CHAPTER 14

Alejandro Johnston

CHAPTER 1

Introduction

Shyam Venkat and Stephen Baird[1]

The global financial crisis began as fears over credit losses and counterparty insolvency eroded market confidence and quickly led to a full-fledged liquidity crisis. As early as August 2007, institutions were seeing a fundamental shift in the liquidity of markets, well before the depth of the mortgage crisis was understood. Today, over eight years later, we stand in the midst of a risk management and regulatory transformation that is touching every aspect of how financial institutions manage their risks and is far from complete. Liquidity risk—one among a very long list of worries for banks, asset managers, regulators, and customers—nevertheless stands apart as it addresses the lifeblood of an institution and liquidity can dry up suddenly if not properly managed. While the credit profile of a loan portfolio can take months or even years to deteriorate, liquidity can disappear in a matter of hours. Liquidity is unpredictable, difficult to measure, and often opaque. In a crisis, market participants are more likely to rely on the media and the rumor mill rather than earnings releases to evaluate the risk of providing liquidity to a trading partner.

Despite these challenges, or perhaps because of them, and also due to the excess liquidity in the financial markets during much of the 1990s and early 2000s, liquidity risk has in many respects held a lower position on the risk management and regulatory agenda than many other key risk types—particularly credit, market, and overall capital adequacy. As described in the chapters that follow, we believe that industry and regulatory focus is shifting rapidly to liquidity risk, and that banks will need to significantly upgrade their capabilities over the next several years. These improvements will touch every aspect of liquidity risk management—framework design, process management and oversight, and technology capabilities all will need to be upgraded to meet both the demands of the marketplace as well as regulatory expectations. Meeting this

---

[1]Shyam Venkat is a principal in PwC's New York Office, and Stephen Baird is a director in PwC's Chicago office.

challenge successfully will require an agenda, and the principal objective of this book is to suggest the details and approaches to meeting that agenda.

A PRACTITIONER'S PERSPECTIVE

The subtitle of this book is "A Practitioner's Perspective." What is a practitioner's perspective? In our view, practitioners—treasurers and risk managers charged with actually managing and monitoring the bank's liquidity risk—benefit most from information that:

- **Reflects industry practices:** The practitioners seek to understand how liquidity risk is managed outside of their institution. Where are other firms ahead of them? Where are they leading the pack?
- **Brings a regulatory perspective:** More than ever, the regulatory agenda is shaping the risk agenda. In this environment, understanding what regulators expect—both today and in the future—is an important aspect of building the most effective risk management framework. Arguably though, a well-conceived, robust, and effectively implemented set of liquidity risk management capabilities will generally align with, and even inform, supervisory expectations.
- **Is forward-looking:** The practitioner not only lives in the world of what is possible, but also understands the need to keep moving forward. Understanding emerging trends in liquidity risk management is an important aspect for practitioners.

We also note what this book is not—a theoretical view of how liquidity risk management should be performed in a world of costless analytics and unlimited access to real-time data across the enterprise. We leave that perspective to academia.

OUTLINE OF THE BOOK

This book is organized into three sections. The first section, "Measuring and Managing Liquidity Risk," lays out the building blocks of a liquidity risk program in a series of chapters dedicated to key topics. We begin with Chapter 2, "A New Era of Liquidity Risk Management," by outlining a set of leading practices that can be garnered from each of the chapters in this book. Our chapters—addressing stress testing, intraday liquidity risk management, collateral management, early warning indicators, contingency funding planning, liquidity risk information systems, and the liquidity implications of recovery and resolution planning—are designed to assist practitioners in honing their knowledge of these areas and creating a forward-looking improvement agenda.

The second section, "The Regulatory Environment of Liquidity Risk Supervision," describes recent and upcoming developments on the all-important regulatory front. This landscape includes a focus not only on recent standards in liquidity proposed by the Basel Committee of Banking Supervisors (referred to as Basel III) but other developments in the areas of stress testing and reporting.

The third and final section, "Optimizing Business Practices," considers how this transformation of liquidity risk management practices will impact business activities and how banks should respond. Clearly, with liquidity risk receiving more attention than ever before, sticky money will be more valuable than hot money. The question is: How will banks meet the challenges of aligning their business activities—through product design, funds transfer pricing, management incentives, and other mechanisms—to reflect this new priority?

CORE THEMES

Before we delve into the details, we highlight three core themes that you will see throughout the chapters in this book. These themes represent the fundamental characteristics of today's liquidity risk environment and where we see the future direction. As you read these chapters, please keep an eye out for:

- **The intertwining of the regulatory and management agendas.** The importance of the regulatory agenda in driving liquidity risk transformation is, and will continue to be, a key feature of liquidity risk management. While this agenda is driving banks to improve their practices, practitioners should remain mindful of the importance of an internal management-driven agenda aimed at continuous improvement of the firm's capabilities.
- **The challenge of automation.** In many respects, the challenge of raising the liquidity risk management bar will be less about measurement frameworks and policies and more about implementing a robust set of capabilities that will be underpinned both by effective governance and technology-enabled solutions. Building an infrastructure that captures, stores, and transforms data in an automated and controlled fashion may be the most daunting challenge.
- **The drive to integration.** Despite all of the advances in risk management since the financial crisis, banks' risk management frameworks

remain largely fragmented, with the management of various risks often being addressed in siloed fashion, and with risk management processes themselves often being delinked from other business activities such as strategic planning, incentives, and profitability measurement. Integrating liquidity considerations into how the bank is run will be a key priority.

ACKNOWLEDGMENTS

As this book is a practitioner's guide, we thought it useful to have our team of practitioners that specialize in the risk management arena share their perspectives and insights. We would like to acknowledge not only these contributors, but many dedicated current and former PwC professionals that worked behind the scenes to make this publication happen. They include: Vishal Arora, Lee Bachouros, Michelle Berman, Jon Borer, Rahul Dawra, Amiya Dharmadhikari, Jaime Garza, William Gibbons, Alison Gilmore, Mayur Java, Shahbaz Junani, Emily Lam, Fleur Meijs, Agatha Pontiki, Manan Shah, Dan Weiss, Jon Paul Wynne, Scott Yocum, and Yuanyuan (Tania) Yue.

Our special thanks go to Chi Lai and Richard Tuosto, who not only served as contributing authors but also helped us extensively with reviewing and developing content in other areas of this book. Finally, we are deeply indebted to Tina Sutorius without whom this book would not have been possible—she kept us focused on the mission at hand and helped stitch the different pieces together, both large and small.

Measuring and Managing Liquidity Risk

A New Era of Liquidity Risk Management

Shyam Venkat[1]

INTRODUCTION

Liquidity risk management is a core competency for all types of financial institutions, from "sell-side" firms, like banks, to "buy-side" institutions such as insurance companies. Banks typically engage in maturity transformation by funding themselves with deposits and other short-term liabilities and investing in assets with longer-dated maturities, while continuing to meet liability obligations as they come due. Capital markets trading businesses provide market liquidity in various asset classes by facilitating order flow between buyers and sellers of financial assets and maintaining inventory through positions using their firms' own capital.

The period from the mid-1990s to the mid-2000s saw relatively few advancements in the discipline of liquidity risk management, even as approaches for measuring and managing credit, market, and operational risks were gaining in sophistication and infrastructure. The Asian currency contagion of the late 1990s, dotcom bust in early 2000, terrorist attacks of 9/11, and subsequent commencement of two major wars in Iraq and Afghanistan did little to heighten concerns outside of regulatory circles around liquidity risk management or spur significant advances in the risk management discipline. Robust global economic growth, fueled by easy credit, looked poised to remain the new normal as industry insiders, pundits, and regulators touted the benefits of the "great moderation," pushing concerns for liquidity risk into the background.

The global financial crisis began in mid-2007, spurred on by the onset of several liquidity events, and brought on dramatic and rapid change. The dramatic increase in systemic risk made almost all financial institutions—even

---

[1] Shyam Venkat is a principal in PwC's New York Office.

those few leading firms that had upgraded their liquidity risk management practices and infrastructure over the preceding decade and made some astute market calls—unprepared for the crisis. Company treasurers and their treasury functions, tasked with managing enterprise funding and liquidity, were now immediately center stage under the spotlight, and worked feverishly to help keep their institutions afloat even as financial markets and peer institutions faltered around them. Suddenly, client cash and secured financing, long considered safe sources of funding, were evaporating; deposits, even those guaranteed by the Federal Deposit Insurance Corporation (FDIC), were being withdrawn, giving rise to concerns of runs on banks. Previously liquid asset markets with readily transactable quotes experienced significant disruptions as market makers and buy-side customers were unsure how far the contagion would spread and became risk adverse. Consequently, the ensuing erosion of balance sheet strength and earnings power among financial services firms brought forth a renewed focus on the importance of liquidity risk management. The raft of new rules and regulations that shortly followed the financial crisis also prompted financial firms, particularly banks and capital markets institutions, to significantly enhance their capital and liquidity positions and related risk management capabilities. Much of the market scrutiny in the United States, United Kingdom, and Europe directed banks and other financial services firms to concentrate on de-risking balance sheets and enhancing capital management capabilities with respect to risk governance, stress testing, capital planning, and capital actions.

In the aftermath of the crisis, liquidity risk management practices have continued to evolve and the pace of that change has quickened as regulatory guidance continues to raise the standards on what are considered "strong" capabilities. Given the relatively early stage and continuing evolution of capabilities in this area, some of these practices may even be viewed as "leading" in nature. The discussion in this chapter on leading practices for liquidity risk management is, by no means, exhaustive; we acknowledge preemptively the contrary to be true. Moreover, there are several additional sources of excellent guidance on this topic that have been issued by various experts, industry practitioners, supervisory agencies, and other regulatory regimes around the world.

The focus of the compendium of fundamental and leading practices summarized in this chapter is more methodological and practical, rather than the principles-based guidance that is often offered by supervisors and regulators. Accordingly, we offer these views on such leading practices in the hope of giving liquidity risk managers and architects additional insights and considerations that may be helpful in their continued efforts to build best-in-class liquidity risk management capabilities. Such considerations of these leading practices should be made within the context of an institution's business model, size, scale, and complexity, as well as tailored appropriately to fit within the organization's structure, cultural and social norms, operating processes, and supporting infrastructure.

We have organized our views on leading practices along the following areas: (i) Governance and organization, (ii) measuring and managing liquidity risk, and (iii) optimizing business practices. Each of these areas is further discussed in greater detail in the individual chapters of this book. We conclude this chapter by summarizing additional considerations for institutions to ponder as they chart their paths forward and advance their capabilities in this critical risk management discipline.

GOVERNANCE AND ORGANIZATION

Liquidity Risk Management Oversight and Accountability

Strengthen Board Knowledge, Capabilities, and Reporting The events leading up to and stemming from the financial crisis highlighted the need for improved awareness and reporting of liquidity risk at the board of directors and executive management levels within financial institutions. Strong governance is critical in effectively managing all aspects of an enterprise, and liquidity risk management is no exception.

The board of directors of a financial services institution has the ultimate authority and responsibility for approving, overseeing, and monitoring its overall risk appetite and various individual components of its risk profile including liquidity risk. This overall risk appetite and profile, including the liquidity risk component, should be approved by the board to ensure alignment with the broader business strategy of the enterprise, and supported by relevant policies, procedures, roles, and responsibilities. As a practical matter, the board often delegates its authority for establishing liquidity risk appetite to company management in the form of committees, officers, and departments including the asset-liability committee (ALCO), enterprise risk management committee, corporate treasurer, and Chief Risk Officer (CRO).

Leading institutions are expanding board oversight of liquidity risk management to ensure the board has both a broad understanding of liquidity risk management concepts as well as sufficient knowledge of underlying technical details. Further, board reporting has improved to show greater depth and frequency of liquidity risk information and integration between business performance, financial, and other risk metrics to give boards greater clarity and integrated view into the changing business and risk profiles of their institutions.

Leverage the Three Lines of Defense to Align and Integrate Management of Liquidity Risk The three lines of defense depict the institution's internal risk management posture. Each line—the business, the independent risk management function, and the internal audit function—has specific responsibilities with respect to the end-to-end liquidity risk management process, from overall governance, strategic planning, risk appetite setting, risk identification, assessment, and management, through reporting, as well as internal controls.

In the context of liquidity risk management, corporate treasury, and/or ALCO typically serve as the first line and establish the firm's liquidity risk appetite with input and approval from the CRO and the independent risk oversight function. The CRO's independent risk oversight team provides the second-line defense, informing the setting of liquidity risk appetite and monitoring the institution's risk profile with a holistic view across different types of risk (e.g., credit, market, operational, liquidity) under changing market conditions. The third-line function, carried out by internal audit, is responsible for providing an independent, periodic assessment of the firm's internal control systems, including risk management, to the board.

While the corporate treasury function and ALCO bring both a business orientation and a risk management mind-set to their respective roles, it is important for an institution that follows an organization model comprising three lines of defense to empower its second-line risk managers to perform their own independent liquidity risk monitoring, review the assumptions and processes for decision making used by the first line, and challenge those views held by the first line that may prove vulnerable under evolving market conditions and thereby subject the firm to unintended risks. It is critical that institutions overcome legacy organizational silos to ensure that each line of defense effectively carries out its respective role with appropriate oversight and also achieves effective coordination and communication across the organization. A key ingredient to ensuring the effectiveness of second-line oversight is investing in the appropriate staff resources and training on new developments on supervisory guidance and industry practices to ensure continuous and well-informed effective challenge rather than periodic "check the box" reviews.

Overall Risk Culture

Lead and Inspire by having the Right Tone at the Top Effective risk management increasingly depends on the corporate culture to motivate, promote, and support prudent risk taking along with appropriate risk management policies and procedures. While risk policies and procedures might be in place, organizational leaders who do not lead by example jeopardize gaining the buy-in and confidence from their teams.

In setting and reinforcing the institution's risk culture, leaders must instill the risk management mind-set into employees. Leading institutions use rewards and consequences to demonstrate that risk management is everyone's responsibility. These firms maintain a rigorous recruiting process that embeds desired risk culture characteristics into hiring requirements and puts mechanisms in place to encourage escalation, rapid response, investigation, and attention by all employees. In instances where risk management raises concerns and objections to the actions or exposures taken by the business, executive management will need to review the relevant information and make decisions in accordance with the institution's risk strategy and appetite.

See the Independent Risk Function as a True Advisor and Partner to the Business Risks can be more effectively managed when they are controlled at the point of initiation—typically, by the business unit. Despite an increase in board-level support driven by a heightened regulatory environment, there remain additional opportunities for collaboration between the corporate risk and front office functions. Incentives, objectives, and level of influence are often mismatched, straining the corporate risk and front office relationship and making collaboration and actual risk management more challenging.

At leading institutions, there has been a fundamental shift in the firm's overall risk culture, with independent risk groups moving toward acting as risk advisors and business partners. Such institutions have strong risk cultures and improved collaboration in the organization by ensuring the risk management function has a seat and voice at the table. In this respect, institutions have implemented organizational and communication changes that support stronger partnership and collaboration between the independent risk function and business units by defining how risk groups are involved in key business decisions up front, and assigning key risk-related business decisions to those groups and individuals best equipped for execution.

MEASURING AND MANAGING LIQUIDITY RISK

Liquidity Stress Testing (LST)

Align Liquidity, Capital, Risk, Financial, and Performance Approaches and Methodologies Historically, the implementation of liquidity, capital, risk, and financial performance frameworks and tools have typically followed different time frames and paths, leading to variations and fragmentation in an institution's approaches, processes, and infrastructure/support systems.

Leading institutions are taking a more integrated approach to the management of liquidity risk by recognizing the complex interplay of liquidity risk with market, credit, operational, and other risks. Operationally, firms are focused on addressing both business-driven and regulatory change imperatives by taking a more holistic approach to the design, development, and implementation of the overall risk management framework and its components. They actively seek to further align such risk management operating models, processes, and platforms over time to address the changing scope and scale of its business activities and leverage emerging technologies to meet evolving regulatory requirements. The results have helped improve business and financial performance management (e.g., risk-adjusted performance analysis, and product pricing), forecasting analytics (e.g., stress testing capabilities to evaluate joint potential capital and liquidity impact under severe adverse scenarios), data quality and reporting, and cost efficiencies stemming from increased system automation.

Apply Rigorous and Effective Challenge in Development of Models and Assumptions The importance of forecasting and risk models and associated model management practices has risen significantly over the past several years, particularly given their prominence in regulatory guidance pertaining to enhanced liquidity and capital stress testing requirements. In addition to the overall modeling framework and methodologies, there is significant emphasis on both the numeric values produced by models and the governance processes overseeing those values that are derived and/or determined by expert judgment.

In validating these model assumptions, leading institutions not only leverage existing model validation groups, but also follow a formalized governance structure in applying effective challenge to the models by involving senior stakeholders from senior management, business, finance, risk, and other support groups. Assumptions are scrutinized and challenged to evaluate their robustness. The focus on both the quantitative results and qualitative controls, including supporting documentation in the form of technical model descriptions, validation reports, and effective challenge session minutes, illustrates the high bar needed to effectively demonstrate sound risk modeling practices.

Design a Strong LST Framework, Starting with Key Elements, and Enhance Continuously The scope and complexity of significantly enhancing or building new LST frameworks and tools can be daunting, particularly given the heightened expectations of regulators and the many challenges that come with such an effort. Few institutions are immune to the various constraints of limited time frames, data quality challenges, scarcity of available resources, and cost containment pressures. Adding to those potential obstacles are the complexities associated with intertwining and aligning different liquidity risk and capital-related methodologies for stress testing, business continuity planning, recovery and resolution planning, and overall enterprise risk management.

Leading institutions are developing a more strategic view of these enhancements and continuing to enhance their liquidity risk management capabilities, focusing on "core" or key enhancements needed to address immediate issues and/or pending regulatory mandates. They are implementing changes in a modular or phased manner that enables "quick wins" and allows them to maintain momentum by demonstrating success to internal and external stakeholders. Project plans include short-term goals and demonstrate long-term vision; planning horizons capture additional improvement opportunities with approved budgets for forecasted financial and staff resources needed to support the long-run efforts. Leaders in these institutions also take a more strategic and long-term view of liquidity risk management enhancement initiatives, seeing them as part of the institution's continuous improvement efforts rather than "one-off" regulatory compliance projects.

Intraday Liquidity—Risk Measurement, Management, and Monitoring Tools for Financial Institutions

Prioritize System Enhancements to Communicate Unanticipated Intraday Liquidity Events
The batch processing approach used by many institutions captures the liquidity impact only from activities with more predictable cash flows, including loan events, investment banking activity, and securities that settle at known dates in the future. Other events, such as client cash and securities withdrawals, same-day settlement transactions, collateral calls, and clearinghouse payments, may result in unanticipated liquidity impacts that pose challenges for a batch process. To address these issues and improve the institutional awareness of the intraday liquidity position, firms are improving the flow of communication among the treasury, operations, and cash management functions. Before, these communications tended to be manual in nature, by email or phone, as the systems used by these groups traditionally did not communicate directly with each other during the business day to reflect client or firm activity that could unexpectedly impact liquidity.

By developing linkages between the daily monitoring systems used by treasury, operations, and cash management personnel to account for unexpected activities, leading institutions are now able to have these groups work more efficiently while reducing the potential for intraday liquidity surprises. Firms should continue prioritizing system enhancements for businesses that generate most of the unanticipated liquidity activity, such as prime brokerage, securities clearance, and trading (e.g., fixed-income, exchange traded funds, and commodities). By focusing efforts on these businesses, an institution will capture much of its intraday liquidity pressure points rather than needing to undertake a very costly, extremely time-consuming, large-scale overhaul of its entire transaction processing and risk technology infrastructure.

Establish Linkages between Intraday Credit and Liquidity Monitoring In the years since the crisis, banks have enhanced their intraday credit risk monitoring to better understand risk concentrations across multiple asset classes, particularly with respect to trading counterparties. These efforts have resulted in the formation of specialized groups that monitor counterparty credit quality throughout the day and alert the businesses to declines in credit worthiness.

Cross-pollinating information between liquidity, operations, and cash management personnel with these credit risk–monitoring functions allows firms to better understand how credit problems can affect projected liquidity and expected cash flows. The credit risk team can alert liquidity managers of a decline in credit worthiness of a counterparty that is expected to settle transactions or make payments previously forecasted as part of the bank's liquidity pool, thereby allowing those managers to respond effectively by altering the liquidity composition and timing of payments of the bank to account for such potential losses. Credit considerations become particularly acute with respect to foreign currency exposure, as late or failed settlements from one counterparty may impact a firm's ability to obtain a currency that it must deliver to another counterparty.

Incorporate Intraday Exposure Analysis to Size the Working Capital Reserve A common approach to estimating working capital begins with projecting the daily liquidity sources and uses for business operations and then augmenting these projections with stress analysis of historical end-of-day exposures. The analysis includes stressing the liquidity reserve to account for potential disruptions in projected cash flows from events such as the failure of an agent bank or financial market utility, tightening of credit provided to the firm, or an increase in failed trades and delayed settlements.

While this approach highlights scenarios of potential liquidity disruptions during periods of market stress, it may not appropriately estimate the magnitude of these events. A firm's intraday liquidity needs could be significantly higher than its historical end-of-day exposure may indicate. Leading firms have now started to estimate their working capital needs using intraday exposures to account for these large spikes in business activity and the resulting liquidity needs throughout the business day that may not otherwise be reflected in end-of-day metrics.

The Convergence of Collateral and Liquidity

Invest in Collateral Management Infrastructure to Gain Cost and Operational Efficiencies and also to Extract Liquidity Risk Management Benefits   The business case for upgrading collateral management capabilities is bolstered by placing liquidity risk management considerations squarely alongside the imperatives for improved credit risk management, processing efficiency, and cost savings. Collectively, such considerations are starting to drive implementation of unified target operating models, rationalized technology platforms, and greater automation within the world of collateral management.

While focusing on just the credit risk–mitigating aspects of collateral narrows the field of vision considerably, the broader reality is that heightened volatility in fast-moving capital markets activities can trigger unexpected collateral calls which, in turn, can increase an institution's exposure to firm-wide liquidity risk. In such instances, the ability to identify and mobilize eligible collateral effectively, to both meet margin calls and increase access to secured financing, can become the key to economic survival.

Integrate Collateral Management more Closely with Front Office and Treasury Functions   Structural market reforms under the Dodd-Frank Act in the U.S. and the European Market Infrastructure Regulation are giving rise to greater pre- and post-trade transparency. At the same time, such reforms are also making market participation more expensive and operationally complex by requiring increasing quantities of high-quality collateral to be posted for both centrally-cleared and non-cleared swap portfolios. More stringent capital and liquidity regulations under Basel III require banks to hold greater quantities of the same high-grade collateral. The nexus of these different pressure points around collateral increases the business imperative to take a wide-angled lens view of how best to invest in cost-effective technology platforms and capabilities that can meet multiple business and regulatory requirements.

As exchange-traded execution platforms begin covering an ever-broadening swath of the derivatives marketplace, clearinghouse cross-product margining will continue to grow. There will be renewed focus on reaching beyond the cheapest to deliver in order to fully exploit the collateral eligibility of each available asset with greater differentiation. Achieving effective integration and management of both collateral and liquidity requires moving the collateral management function away from being purely a back office function focused on credit risk toward a domain requiring closer collaboration between front office and treasury functions to better facilitate sound trade placement decisions and leverage collateral to its fullest liquidity potential.

Optimizing Collateral Management Helps to Optimize Liquidity Risk Management
Driven by the desire to source, fund, and allocate collateral efficiently, firms are focusing on achieving collateral optimization by putting in place cross-functional teams, rationalized operating models, common technology platforms, and proper collateral management processes. With optimization, leading market participants are starting to realize improved yield from each asset, minimize the cost of financing that asset, reduce capital charges associated with regulatory capital requirements, reduce liquidity risk, and eliminate over-collateralization. This represents the clear prize to be gained from combining capital and liquidity costs while simultaneously viewing collateral and liquidity as two sides of the same coin.

Early Warning Indicators

Select Internal Early Warning Indicators that Complement Market-Derived Measures Internally-focused early warning indicators (EWIs) provide a perspective on the liquidity profile and health of the institution. These measures are critical in understanding how the firm's liquidity position could be changing over time and what types of vulnerabilities may emerge as a result of business and strategic decisions.

Leading institutions supplement their use of external EWIs with a suite of internally focused indicators. These internal measures should capture trends in specific markets and businesses in which the firm participates as well as those that serve as funding sources. Internal EWIs should be selected in concert with external EWIs to identify emerging risks and evaluate if the nature of these risks is idiosyncratic, systemic, or some combination of the two. Many institutions select broad stock or bond market indices as indicators of overall economic health; however, leading firms will focus on indicators that are specific to their business and funding profile, such as loan portfolio performance, operational loss metrics, or industry-specific bond and swap spreads. Specific indicators may alert management to market trends and warrant further investigation.

Link the EWI Dashboard to a Strong Escalation Process Leading institutions select and calibrate EWIs and related thresholds to transmit meaningful signals to management about the need for corrective action in light of changes in the broader business environment or impending potential firm-specific distress. Once a EWI registers a change in status, a robust and well-established escalation process will help ensure that management (and potentially the board) reviews the trends to better understand the cause, identify the potential impacts of evolving business dynamics, and take appropriate actions. The firm's selection of EWIs and their calibration should be reviewed to reflect any changes to business mix and activities and the changing nature of the macroeconomic and market environments.

EWIs should be forward-looking, selected so as to provide a mix of business-as-usual (BAU) and stressed environment information, and assessed against limits at predetermined intervals (e.g., daily, weekly, monthly). Continued deterioration in a single or combined set of EWIs should trigger the firm's emergency response tools, such as the contingency funding plan.

Contingency Funding Planning

Bring Contingency Planning to the Forefront and Align to Business and Risk Strategy Development
The contingency funding planning (CFP) should serve as a critical component of the organization's liquidity risk management framework by ensuring that risk measurement and monitoring systems, such as liquidity stress testing, early warning indicators, limits, operating metrics, and regulatory ratios, are operationalized and drive timely management action in times of stress. The goal is accomplished most effectively by fully integrating the firm's risk identification and assessment, scenario development, stress testing, and limit structure into a robust CFP escalation process.

In designing and updating CFPs, institutions typically look to their existing business and risk profiles, risk monitoring capabilities, and external market conditions. While this helps establish a strong CFP at a particular point in time, the relevance and effectiveness of the CFP will likely change given the evolving nature of the institution and changing market conditions; therefore, ensuring the relevance and alignment of the CFP to the institution's business and risk profile and evolving external market conditions is key.

In addition to the periodic updates to the CFP, leading institutions are taking a more proactive stance on the development of the CFP by incorporating it as part of, or in parallel with, their strategic planning exercises, thereby positioning the CFP to be more forward-looking and flexible. As a result, the CFP's key features such as escalation triggers, EWIs, contingent actions, and strategies are more attuned to the institution's current activities as well as its projected areas of growth including new businesses, products, client segments, and geographies.

Further, the collaboration among relevant stakeholders from management, businesses, finance, risk, operations, and other supporting functions enables an improved forum for effective challenge discussions of key business forecasting assumptions and their associated impact on liquidity risk and operational strategies—particularly with respect to crisis response, alternative crisis funding arrangements, and relevant market dynamics—during potential periods of severe stress periods and market disruptions.

Align and Integrate CFP to Business and Risk Continuity Strategies While the CFP serves as a critical component of the liquidity risk management framework, it should be considered not as a stand-alone instrument but rather as a tool within the suite of capabilities and resources for managing the institution through a liquidity crisis.

For leading institutions, the alignment and integration of related capabilities, such as their business continuity planning (BCP) and recovery and resolution planning (RRP) strategies with the CFP, helps to standardize and streamline governance models, operating processes, and reporting tools and infrastructure, and further enhance management's decision-making capabilities, particularly during critical periods of severe market disruptions. This alignment requires common data taxonomies for defining/classifying the business and functional group segments and associated activities to ensure consistency across the enterprise. Additionally, institutions will need to define a comprehensive list of liquidity risk management applications and related systems, including front office activities, analytics, and reporting support, to ensure continuity of critical services under BAU and stressed operating environments.

Planning, Preparing, and Practicing for the Unexpected In a liquidity crisis, the importance and robustness of the CFP's design needs to be matched by the institution's ability to execute the playbook. Its people need to understand their roles and responsibilities under the streamlined command structure and its communication protocols so they can implement the steps needed to prepare for and manage the liquidity crisis.

The effectiveness in executing the CFP is further enhanced through periodic testing. While not all components/strategies of the CFP may be tested, leading institutions that perform frequent exercises which best simulate the potential liquidity crisis environment will improve the CFP's operational effectiveness and response times—aspects that are critical during a crisis. Further, the test simulations may also identify potential gaps and/or improvement opportunities that would otherwise be undetected if the CFP were left collecting dust on the bookshelf.

Liquidity Risk Management Information Systems

Enhance Ownership and Accountability of Liquidity Risk Data As regulatory reporting requirements have increased over the past several years, institutions have been challenged to keep pace with the ever-growing regulatory requirements for additional and more granular information. In stretching to meet pending regulatory deadlines while simultaneously juggling the needs to manage the ever-increasing portfolio of systems and applications, institutions have had little time to develop and implement a holistic approach to the management of liquidity data. Consequently, this has resulted in data quality challenges, including incomplete or duplicated data, variations in reported results due to the use of multiple data sources, and increased manual and time-consuming efforts in reconciling and enriching information needed for reporting across the different parts of the enterprise.

Recognizing such challenges, leading institutions have often designated risk data "czars" to lead and coordinate data management practices across the enterprise, and spanning the risk data management lifecycle—including data capture, enrichment, quality maintenance, analytics, reporting, and archiving.

Manage Liquidity Data Comprehensively: From End-to-End and Top-to-Bottom
Institutions leading the charge to improve their liquidity risk management capabilities have invested significantly in developing a comprehensive view of liquidity information, improved data quality, and "data lineage" as information is captured, enriched, analyzed, and reported.

Leading institutions have undertaken a spectrum of initiatives along the following focus areas:

i. Integration of risk, asset liability management, funds transfer pricing, transaction processing, and forecasting systems to enable more comprehensive data sets and shared common analytic engines/modules (e.g., trade capture systems, collateral management systems, G/L and financial systems)

ii. Standardization of liquidity data definitions and attributes through improved reference and position data collection (e.g., detailed features of product and asset class characteristics, contractual maturities of existing positions, overlay of behavioral assumptions), regulatory reporting classifications, and other segmentations (e.g., holding company, lines of business, legal entities/jurisdictions)

iii. Development of integrated analytics and reporting suites for multiple purposes (e.g., CFP dashboard metrics and thresholds, resolution planning, strategic planning and forecasting)

Develop a Vision and Continue to Build on a Scalable and Flexible Liquidity Risk Architecture As institutions continue to enhance their liquidity risk architecture and platform(s), they should remain mindful of the interconnections between liquidity risk systems and applications, ensuring that IT initiatives at the enterprise level and at other parts of the organization properly consider potential implications and considerations for liquidity risk as part of their planning and scoping exercises.

In this context, leading institutions demonstrate strong capabilities in several areas. First, they have a strong understanding of the information technology, systems, and data "blueprint"—both the current and the future state design, along with detailed phased implementation and change management strategies and plans. Second, there is an executive owner, such as the chief information officer or a risk data czar, who provides oversight and drives coordination, ensuring a comprehensive view of liquidity risk data and how such information is used across the enterprise. Finally, there is a strong business case and well-defined requirements for IT investments, coupled with the support and buy-in from senior management.

Recovery and Resolution Planning

Embed Liquidity Needs for Resolution Planning into BAU Liquidity Reserves Resolution planning requires firms to identify and measure the liquidity necessary to resolve the firm in an orderly manner. Leading institutions use the liquidity estimates at the firm-wide and legal entity levels that are produced for resolution planning to assess the size of the liquidity reserves they will maintain to support liquidity risk strategies, both over the course of BAU activities as well as in recovery and resolution circumstances.

These firms model liquidity needs for their resolution strategies on a daily basis and adjust the size of their BAU liquidity base to ensure sufficient liquidity resources needed under recovery and/or resolution. They also set limits by using their resolution liquidity estimates and develop associated response actions, bringing them to the forefront of integrating resolution planning considerations into their liquidity risk management architecture.

Integrate LST and Contingency Funding Planning into the Resolution Plan
In developing a resolution plan and addressing the resulting liquidity impact, institutions should make assumptions concerning sources and uses of funding, including deposit runoffs, drawdowns on outstanding lines of commitment, and additional collateral demands. As part of this exercise, many institutions leverage the assumptions in their liquidity stress testing and/or contingency funding plans to forecast the aggregate amount of net liquidity needed to support their resolution strategies. Leveraging existing liquidity risk management and forecasting tools in this manner is similar to the approach originally prescribed by the regulators of estimating required liquidity under the Liquidity Coverage Ratio (LCR).

Leading institutions are taking additional steps to further embed their own internal liquidity risk management tools into resolution planning by forecasting liquidity at set intervals (e.g., daily, weekly, monthly, and quarterly) throughout the resolution planning horizon. These projections better identify potential liquidity and funding mismatches that might not be readily apparent when strictly analyzing point-in-time, aggregate liquidity requirements.

Understand Liquidity Traps and Frictions to Cash Transfer U.S. regulators require covered institutions to identify potential liquidity traps in their resolution plans. Traditionally, most firms have provided only commentary with respect to legal entities and national jurisdictions in which liquidity could be trapped but have not fully factored these impacts into their liquidity models and forecasts.

Leading institutions have advanced this analysis by estimating the potential amount of trapped liquidity, along with other potential frictions to the transfer of liquidity among entities, and included this impact in their resolution plan liquidity forecasts. They have also developed liquidity risk triggers and response actions to ensure that entities with national or jurisdictional liquidity requirements will have adequate funding under different stress scenarios and environments.

OPTIMIZING BUSINESS PRACTICES

Strategic and Tactical Implications of the New Requirements

Align and incorporate the institution's strategic and business imperatives into regulatory initiatives. The post–financial crisis regulatory environment has forced financial firms, particularly banks, to operate with significant excess liquidity, higher regulatory capital, greater capital buffers, and far less leverage, all of which now prevail against the backdrop of structural market reforms that have eliminated or severely curtailed previously permissible, seemingly profitable businesses.

In this brave new world, the leaders will need to separate themselves from the laggards by employing more astute financial analysis and discipline over appropriately calibrated investment horizons, rather than the financial engineering and short-termism that characterized banking industry returns over the decade preceding the financial crisis. Banks seeking to be "end-game players" will need to structure optimal asset mixes that enable them to achieve higher returns while meeting minimum regulatory liquidity and capital requirements. Strategies being considered with respect to products and services, industry concentrations, regional focus, customer segments, distribution channels, and pricing should be driven first and foremost by mission appropriateness, sound management practices, competitive positioning, and institutional capabilities that leverage technology and human capital. Leading institutions are starting to address regulatory requirements up front during strategy formulation rather than merely downstream as an afterthought or with just a compliance mind-set, allowing them to better leverage the platforms and architecture that they are building for both business and regulatory objectives.

Bigger may not Necessarily be Better—and the Answer is Different for each Institution Present day rules and regulations facing banks in relation to liquidity and capital, and the supervision thereof, clearly establish explicit and implicit higher thresholds for larger firms, particularly those deemed to be systemically important. Larger firms are held back from becoming even larger and further exacerbating the risk of being "too big to fail." Smaller firms may feel the need to bulk up, as a result of market opportunities, out of competitive necessity, or because of the need to acquire additional scale to increase the productivity of higher liquidity and capital levels.

While institution size will continue to remain important, across-the-board scale for its sake alone may not necessarily be the correct answer either. Rather, combining selective scale with operational excellence is the right approach to take. Achieving the optimum asset mix referred to earlier will require continual refinement due to differences in business models, competitive positioning, barriers to entry, customer needs and preferences, institutional capabilities, legacy factors, and jurisdictional regulatory requirements. What will work for one institution is far from guaranteed to be the right answer for another, and firms will need to take a candid view of their competitive positioning and the general business environment.

The liquidity rules under the LCR and the Net Stable Funding Ratio are considered more advantageous for banks that rely on retail deposits and long-term funding than those with heavy reliance on short-term or wholesale funding or with concentrations of certain customer segments. The increased stress testing and regulatory capital requirements favor those banks with portfolios that show less deterioration under market downturn scenarios. The leverage ratio constraints would suggest that banks work harder to optimize the relative levels of their risk-weighted assets (used for regulatory capital calculations) and actual assets, a relationship known as RWA density. And the upcoming requirement to hold a minimum amount of Total Loss Absorbency Capacity (TLAC) for systemically important institutions adds even more complexity to determining the right mix of a firm's capital stack.

Over the last few years, many firms have focused on their competitors' actions in relation to the new financial services rules and regulations, so they could develop their own approaches in a similar manner that did not stray from the mainstream. Leading institutions, in contrast, met the challenge of these new regulatory requirements, sometimes even as first movers, by proceeding forward with internally generated conviction, ingenuity, and resolve. They have been quick to understand and incorporate the impact of these new regulations into refining and redefining their business strategies. It is these attributes, rather than the "me too" mind-set, that will be required to establish the right strategic direction for each institution as well as identify the tactical steps for superior execution.

Regulations may vary Across Jurisdictions, but Strong Risk Management is Fundamental and Good Business Practice For much of the 1990s and into the mid-2000s, financial services rules and regulations grew out of, and often codified, the advances in risk management that were being innovated and implemented by the industry itself. However, the financial crisis of 2007–08 exposed the gap between risk management theory and the actual practice of implementing and embedding risk management techniques and discipline into the actual running of businesses. The ensuing raft of regulations issued by various national agencies after the financial crisis attempted to strengthen the safety and soundness of the banking sectors in individual countries by pushing firms to close the gap between theory and practice; however, it can be debated that some of these requirements have added costs to banks without conferring appropriately commensurate benefits.

The resulting fragmentation of rules has posed compliance challenges for global firms that must meet these requirements in multiple jurisdictions, even as some areas remain open for interpretation and further clarification. At the same time, banks also have often taken a piecemeal approach to meeting the requirements of various rules and regulations. This has proved to be less cost-effective and efficient than would be the case if they were to take a holistic view of regulatory requirements and business imperatives in advance of upgrading fundamental risk management practices. Most supervisory agencies will acknowledge their intent is to encourage firms to constantly improve risk management capabilities that will justify their costs by allowing business units to continue to perform prudent, value-added risk intermediation to earn an appropriate return. Firms that effectively leverage sound risk management capabilities will be better positioned to achieve business objectives, all while meeting different and changing regulatory requirements, rather than by merely seeking conformity to the average and minimum compliance with the rules.

Funds Transfer Pricing (FTP) and the Basel III Liquidity Framework

Charge Business Units for Liquidity Costs—Liquidity can no Longer be Treated as a "Costless" Risk—and let Them Figure Out how to Generate Appropriate Returns With the increased amounts of liquidity that banks and other financial institutions are now required to hold, liquidity will rightfully take its place alongside capital in the continuing debate about how far into the organization these costs should be allocated. The greater the amount of liquidity (and capital) costs that are stranded at the corporate center of a firm, the more its business units will be disincentivized to innovate products and services, pricing, and delivery mechanisms that reflect an accurate, fully loaded view of profitability, leading to a sub-optimal asset mix and continued or increasing investment into less profitable business.

The central treasury function should include both normal and stressed liquidity costs within the enhanced FTP framework that is applied to the measurement of business unit performance. Corporate center managers alone cannot be held responsible for developing ways to improve enterprise profitability and overcome the drag of liquidity risk costs. They must coopt the ingenuity of their business unit partners in targeting strategies, products, services, and customer propositions that will generate appropriate returns that reflect the increased cost of liquidity risk. The financial institutions that began traveling down this path earlier have gained an advantage over competitors.

Leverage and Integrate Basel III and Liquidity Stress Testing   The core construct of the Basel III liquidity framework—that sizing of the liquidity buffer should be driven by measurement of stressed cash outflows—is a useful concept for FTP design and should be well integrated. While traditional FTP approaches addressed cash volatility implicitly and indirectly through core and volatile splits and term liquidity premium assignments, the Basel framework (as well as internal stress testing) enables explicit linkage of product-level attributes to the sizing of the liquidity buffer. Leading banks are capturing these attributes (e.g., mix of operational and non-operational deposits) directly into their FTP models, with the ultimate goal of fully charging out the buffer to volatile and contingent liabilities.

More Granular is Better, but Directional Accuracy is Preferable to Pinpoint Precision   The days of easy money and quick profits in the financial services industry are over, at least for the foreseeable future. FTP frameworks will need to reflect granularity and differentiation with respect to which business lines, products, customer segments, and even individual clients are users or contributors of liquidity. The inherent tension that exists between business units and corporate centers will always impede the attainment of finely tuned FTP frameworks that capture the costs of liquidity risk with pinpoint precision. However, the blunt and imperfect nature of most existing FTP frameworks still allows most institutions considerable room for improvement by incorporating additional details of liquidity costs to create better performance metrics. Given that future improvements in the profitability of banks and other financial institutions are likely to occur in marginal steps rather than quantum leaps, real success will come from adopting and applying the discipline of these enhanced, albeit still imperfect, FTP frameworks.

FURTHER CONSIDERATIONS FOR THE PATH FORWARD

While we recognize that each institution is different, we believe the prior discussion on leading practices provides the practitioner with a preliminary set of important ideas and insights into the different dimensions of liquidity risk management governance, framework components, processes, and information technology infrastructure. As institutions continue to build out and enhance their liquidity risk management practices, we offer the following thoughts for the path forward:

Focus on strategic purpose and leverage capabilities to drive competitive advantage. Regulatory deadlines can increase the pressure to show progress by rushing investments and directing focus on short-term results. Institutions should shift away from viewing regulatory requirements as compliance-only efforts, but rather look for opportunities to leverage the improved liquidity risk management capabilities to drive strategy execution and enhance competitive positioning in a crowded and increasingly complex marketplace.

See the big picture and be mindful of interplay/interconnections. Liquidity risk management, even more so than other risk types, cannot be viewed in a silo and must be examined for its interplay with other risks faced by the institution. While institutions tend to focus on credit, market, and operational risks, each of these risks can quickly ignite a liquidity event that may result in significantly more damage to the institution's stability and long-term prospects. As such, it is critical for institutions to understand these linkages so that they may effectively design monitoring, assessment, and response programs that are properly tuned to identify and mitigate such risks and the potential for adverse cascading events.

Operate as a partner with the other parts of the organization. Large budgets and significant spending will provide little success, yield weak results, and ultimately go to waste if the organization fails to involve and empower the appropriate stakeholders. Liquidity risk management touches stakeholders throughout the institution and therefore requires buy-in from all corners of the firm, including the board, management, business leads, finance, risk, treasury, operations, and other support functions. Their knowledge, insights, involvement, and support are necessary in effectively designing and implementing the spectrum of capabilities to address liquidity strategy and risk appetite setting, risk culture and organization, stress testing frameworks, liquidity risk measures and early warning indicators, analytics, contingency funding plans, risk reporting, and information technology infrastructure.

CHAPTER 3

Liquidity Stress Testing

Stephen Baird[1]

The global liquidity crisis, which lasted from approximately August 2007 to the end of 2008, ushered in the broader financial crisis and highlighted the importance of prudent management of liquidity risk. Prior to the crisis, liquidity was readily available at low cost, and many banks, though apparently well capitalized, did not have an adequate framework for ensuring ample liquidity to see them through a prolonged dislocation in the financial markets. Believing that the funding of contingent obligations and the inability to roll over existing contractual obligations were highly unlikely, these institutions did not conduct stress tests that adequately reflected the severity and duration of the liquidity crisis that actually occurred during this period.

The liquidity stress test provides the critical underpinning to a bank's liquidity risk management framework by determining the amount of liquidity that must be held in order to ensure the institution can meet financial obligations under stressed conditions. A robust liquidity stress test is based on a projection of cash flows arising from assets, liabilities, and other off-balance sheet items under a variety of systemic and idiosyncratic scenarios that can occur over varying time horizons. The results of the liquidity stress test provide the foundation for setting the bank's liquidity risk appetite, establishing appropriate limits and targets, and developing an effective contingency funding plan.

In this chapter we will define what is meant by "contingent liquidity" within the context of liquidity risk management and the liquidity stress test in particular. We will review the key components of a liquidity stress test, including (a) the appropriate scope and structure of the liquidity stress test across the enterprise, (b) scenario development, and (c) the development of key assumptions. We will also discuss the broader governance context of the liquidity stress test, including the governance around the liquidity stress testing process, how outputs support the liquidity risk management regime of the organization, and the controls required within and around the

---

[1]Stephen Baird is a director in PwC's Chicago office.

process. Intraday liquidity considerations, however, are separately discussed in Chapter 4.

While the industry has made significant strides in enhancing liquidity stress testing capabilities since the dark days of 2007–08, banks and their regulators will be working hard to meet a number of challenges over the next several years in order to realize the goal of establishing a fully robust liquidity stress testing program. In this chapter we will focus on two of these emerging trends. First, the industry should improve the level of integration and consistency between the liquidity stress test, the capital stress test, and, more broadly, risk measurement and monitoring, performance measurement, and regulatory reporting. Second, banks should invest in achieving a sustainable technology infrastructure that ensures liquidity stress testing is performed in an efficient and controlled manner.

As was seen during the financial crisis, the perception of a liquidity problem that may arise through an insufficient liquidity risk management framework can be just as problematic for a financial institution as an actual inability to meet financial obligations. The fall of Washington Mutual Bank (WaMu) provides an instructive example.

IMAGE IS EVERYTHING: THE COLLAPSE OF WASHINGTON MUTUAL

Ignited by a sudden $17 billion run on bank deposits lasting approximately nine days, WaMu, the thrift division of Washington Mutual, Inc., was seized by the Office of Thrift Supervision on September 25, 2008—to date, the largest such seizure in U.S. history. Once considered the banking industry's version of Walmart, WaMu filed for bankruptcy protection under Chapter 11 one day after the Office of Thrift Supervision placed its thrift operations into FDIC receivership, thus becoming the second largest such bankruptcy filing in U.S. history—surpassed only by that of Lehman Brothers a week earlier. In a deal brokered chiefly by the FDIC, JP Morgan Chase & Co. purchased WaMu, preventing a potentially devastating insurance payout to WaMu's depositors.

The root of the deluge of retail deposits flowing out of WaMu's branches can be traced to market perceptions of the bank's solvency. Two of WaMu's major sources of unsecured funding—commercial paper and federal funds purchased—dried up almost completely. This was interpreted by the rest of the bank's lenders to mean the bank was no longer a viable counterparty and led to the bank's collapse. Yet, representatives of WaMu were quick to note that its operations did not depend on the availability of short-term financing. In fact, this position was likely correct. At the time of its demise, WaMu still had one of the country's largest retail branch networks, and only a few months before had received an investment from a private-equity firm, increased its liquidity reserves to $50 billion, and shuttered underperforming business units. In short, although the bank held a significant sub-prime exposure, it was well positioned to fund operations through a competitive buyout process and possibly achieve long-term recovery albeit with a smaller scale thrift division. Nonetheless, the crushing blow to WaMu's reputation resulting from dismal outlook reports left the bank with a widespread public perception of illiquidity and scant options outside of bankruptcy.

References:

"WaMu Is Seized, Sold Off to J.P. Morgan, In Largest Failure in U.S. Banking History" Robin Sidel, David Enrich, Dan Fitzpatrick. *The Wall Street Journal*; published September 26, 2008

"Saying Yes, WaMu Built Empire on Shaky Loans" Peter S. Goodman and Gretchen Morgenson. *The New York Times*; published December 28, 2008

"WaMu Slumps as Gimme Credit Cites Liquidity Concern" Ari Levy. *Bloomberg Financial News*; published July 24, 2008

"WaMu: We have $50 billion in liquidity" Aaron Smith. CNN Money.com; published July 25, 2008.

MEASURING CONTINGENT LIQUIDITY REQUIREMENTS

The objective of the liquidity stress test is to measure the amount of liquidity the institution must maintain in order to ensure continuing ability to meet financial obligations under stressed conditions. In order to construct an effective liquidity stress testing framework, it is important to clearly define what is meant by "liquidity" for liquidity stress testing purposes. Within this context, liquidity refers to *funding* liquidity risk—the risk that the institution will not have adequate capacity to fund its obligations without incurring unacceptable economic losses. Assessing *asset* liquidity—the risk of incurring losses due to difficulty converting assets into cash—while not the objective of the liquidity stress test, must also be carefully considered in the liquidity stress test since it can also impact the amount of funding that can be made available from the sale of assets.

As a source of funding liquidity, businesses, including financial institutions, utilize liquidity for four purposes: operational, restricted, contingent, and strategic.

Operational liquidity represents the cash that is needed to fund the business on a daily basis, and it is required to ensure orderly clearing of payment transactions. Depending on the nature of the institution's business, operating cash needs might be quite volatile and, as a result, a cushion is added to account for the unpredictability of daily settlements and the excessive system and management effort that would be required to manage cash to its theoretical minimum. Operational liquidity must be maintained to ensure the institution's operations and is therefore unavailable to meet financial obligations under a liquidity stress test.

Restricted liquidity represents liquid assets that are available to be used only for specifically defined purposes. For example, a bank may be required to collateralize certain wholesale borrowings. Restricted liquidity is unavailable to meet general financial obligations under a liquidity stress test, but should be applied to any assumed outflows which they support.

Contingent liquidity represents the liquidity that is available to meet general financial obligations under a stress scenario. This liquidity is available in the form of the institution's liquid asset buffer, which comprises access to financial assets that are of very high quality and can be easily converted into cash without any real loss of market value. Measuring required contingent liquidity to cover stressed cash outflows is the principal objective of the liquidity stress test.

Strategic liquidity represents the cash that is held by the institution to meet future business needs that may arise outside the course of normal operations, but it is not primarily aimed at supporting the bank during times of stress. For example, strategic liquidity may be held to fund future acquisitions or capital expenditure programs. Strategic liquidity may be redirected to meet contingent liquidity requirement needs. As a pragmatic matter, this will likely be feasible only if such liquidity is present via holdings of highly liquid assets.

This liquidity taxonomy is illustrated in Figure 3.1:

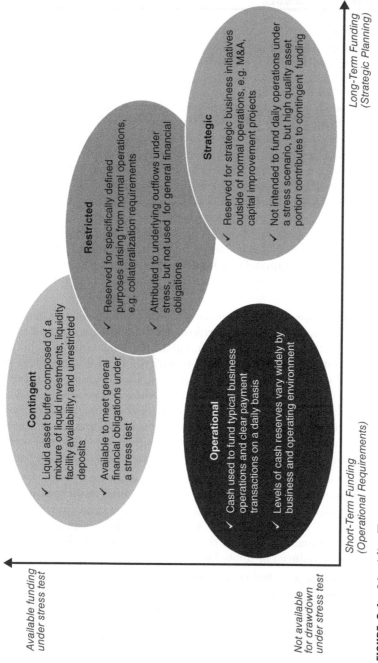

Contingent

✓ Liquid asset buffer composed of a mixture of liquid investments, liquidity facility availability, and unrestricted deposits

✓ Available to meet general financial obligations under a stress test

Restricted

✓ Reserved for specifically defined purposes arising from normal operations, e.g. collateralization requirements

✓ Attributed to underlying outflows under stress, but not used for general financial obligations

Strategic

✓ Reserved for strategic business initiatives outside of normal operations, e.g. M&A, capital improvement projects

✓ Not intended to fund daily operations under a stress scenario, but high quality asset portion contributes to contingent funding

Operational

✓ Cash used to fund typical business operations and clear payment transactions on a daily basis

✓ Levels of cash reserves vary widely by business and operating environment

Available funding under stress test

Not available for drawdown under stress test

Short-Term Funding (Operational Requirements)

Long-Term Funding (Strategic Planning)

FIGURE 3.1 Liquidity Taxonomy

31

OVERVIEW OF THE MODEL

If the objective of the liquidity stress test is to measure the amount of required contingent liquidity, then the institution must construct a cash flow model that accurately and precisely measures the following components:

Liquid asset buffer. The liquid asset buffer represents the contingent liquidity that is currently in place. The liquidity stress test framework must clearly define the market and operational characteristics that securities must meet in order to qualify for inclusion in the liquid asset buffer. In general, requirements should ensure that the liquidity-generating capacity of securities included in the liquid asset buffer remains intact even in periods of severe idiosyncratic and market stress. The fundamental characteristics of liquid asset buffer securities should include low credit and market risk, ease and certainty of valuation, trading in an active and sizable market, and low concentration of buyers and sellers. The liquid asset buffer should also meet operational requirements that ensure the liquidity is under the control of the central treasury area of the entity undergoing the stress test.

Stressed outflows. Stressed outflows are those assumed to occur under stress scenarios. Stressed outflows may result from the need to prematurely settle non-contractual maturity obligations as well as the inability to refund contractual maturity obligations that under normal circumstances could be rolled over. The institution's framework should clearly define the types of outflows to be modeled, which typically fall into the categories of retail deposit outflows, unsecured wholesale funding outflows, secured funding runoff, derivative transaction funding, loss of funding on asset-backed issuances, and drawdown of credit and liquidity facilities.

Stressed inflows. Stressed inflows are assumed to partially offset the stressed outflows. Inflows may include secured funding transaction maturities, loan repayments from customers, and drawdowns on liquidity facilities available to the institution. Depending on the assumptions used in a particular stress scenario, the level of inflows may be reduced or limited by market conditions.

Stressed liquid asset buffer. The liquid asset buffer, net of stress outflows and stress inflows, indicates the adequacy of the current liquid asset buffer given the stress scenario assumptions.

The components of the liquidity stress test model are depicted in Figure 3.2.

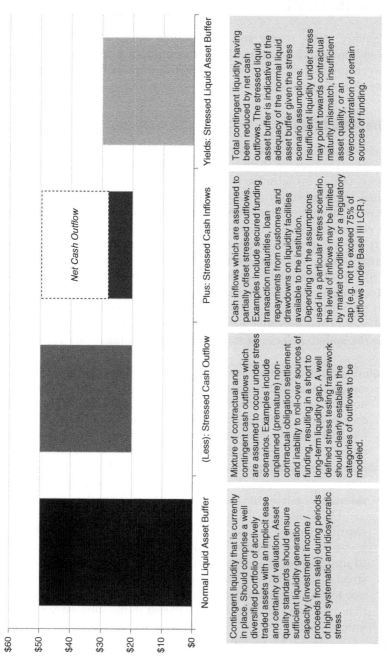

Normal Liquid Asset Buffer	(Less): Stressed Cash Outflow	Plus: Stressed Cash Inflows	Yields: Stressed Liquid Asset Buffer
Contingent liquidity that is currently in place. Should comprise a well diversified portfolio of actively traded assets with an implicit ease and certainty of valuation. Asset quality standards should ensure sufficient liquidity generation capacity (investment income / proceeds from sale) during periods of high systematic and idiosyncratic stress.	Mixture of contractual and contingent cash outflows which are assumed to occur under stress scenarios. Examples include unplanned (premature) non-contractual obligation settlement and inability to roll-over sources of funding, resulting in a short to long-term liquidity gap. A well defined stress testing framework should clearly establish the categories of outflows to be modeled.	Cash inflows which are assumed to partially offset stressed outflows. Examples include secured funding transaction maturities, loan repayments from customers and drawdowns on liquidity facilities available to the institution. Depending on the assumptions used in a particular stress scenario, the level of inflows may be limited by market conditions or a regulatory cap (e.g. not to exceed 75% of outflows under Basel III LCR.)	Total contingent liquidity having been reduced by net cash outflows. The stressed liquid asset buffer is indicative of the adequacy of the normal liquid asset buffer given the stress scenario assumptions. Insufficient liquidity under stress may point towards contractual maturity mismatch, insufficient asset quality, or an overconcentration of certain sources of funding.

FIGURE 3.2 Components of the Liquidity Stress Testing Model

DESIGN OF THE MODEL

The liquidity stress testing model forms an integral component of an end-to-end process that begins with risk identification and event analysis in order to ensure that the roster of scenarios appropriately captures material liquidity risks (Figure 3.3).

Organizational Scope

The consolidated stress test should be the lynchpin of any liquidity risk framework. However, an institution may determine there is a need to conduct stress testing on subsidiary entities within the organization. The organizational levels at which a bank may stress liquidity include the parent, subsidiary legal entities, lines of business, service business units, and shared service centers. Each of these cases may be addressed through a separate liquidity stress test, where necessary. For less material entities or those entities where risk is assessed to be manageable, less complex entity-level liquidity risk reporting might be sufficient. As a general rule, the institution should consider the organizational level at which (a) liquidity is commingled, and (b) liquidity oversight has management accountability. Combinations of legal entities and operating units having both of these characteristics will provide the building blocks of the enterprise-level liquidity stress test:

> **Liquidity transfer restrictions.** Liquidity may be trapped in certain legal entities, potentially creating a distorted view of the consolidated liquidity position of the institution. For example, foreign exchange controls may inhibit the conversion of foreign currency in off-shore legal entities. The bank should assess the impact of such restrictions on enterprise-level liquidity, considering not only a normal operating environment but stressed conditions as well. Bank holding companies, for example, should assume little or no access to banking subsidiary cash during a crisis due to capital adequacy requirements.
>
> The existence of liquidity transfer restrictions does not necessarily give rise to the need for an additional stress test where it can be demonstrated that a subsidiary would not be required to upstream cash to the parent. For example, an institution may stress the consolidated entity and the holding company but choose not to test individual banking subsidiaries under the assumption that movement of cash from the parent to the subsidiary would be unrestricted.
>
> **Currency.** While the liquidity stress test should be performed in the currency of the entity being tested (the home country for the

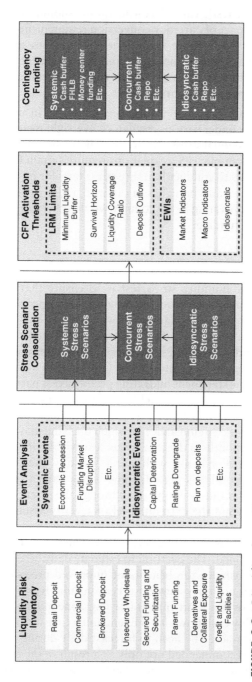

FIGURE 3.3 Liquidity Stress Testing Design Components

consolidated test), careful consideration should be taken for the liquidity impact of currency conversion requirements. For example, less established offshore subsidiaries or branches sometimes carry a significant currency mismatch, and the settlement time frame for the home country parent to swap fund an unanticipated outflow may prove problematic in a crisis.

Regulatory jurisdiction. For institutions operating in multiple foreign jurisdictions under various regulatory oversight regimes, the need to conduct individual stress tests for foreign subsidiaries or groups may arise. For example, U.S. regulations require certain foreign banking organizations to conduct liquidity stress tests for intermediate holding companies and branches in order to address concerns that foreign banks operating in the country would otherwise be over-reliant on offshore funding.

Planning Horizon

The objective of the liquidity stress test is to ensure that the institution can maintain adequate contingency funding through a period of prolonged stress. To meet this goal, the planning horizon of the liquidity stress test should be at least twelve months. The bank may choose to project cash flows beyond twelve months; however, longer-term projections may be subject to significant forecast error depending on the time horizon of the baseline balance sheet and income statement budgeting performed as part of the strategic planning process. Moreover, the likelihood of the bank continuing operations indefinitely under stress without a recovery or resolution process taking place is unrealistic. One circumstance in which the bank may choose to forecast beyond twelve months is the case where a survival horizon is calculated under the stress test. For banks with ample liquidity, the survival horizon may extend well beyond this period; some banks have a survival horizon that may extend as far out as two years, although the extent of the modeled stress will abate beyond the extreme level of severity assumed in the very short term.

The frequency of cash flow measurement within the overall time horizon must also be determined. The decision to estimate daily, weekly, or monthly cash flows should balance the benefits of improved precision against the reduced forecasting accuracy beyond a certain time frame. Stress models that forecast daily over a short time frame (e.g., one month) and transition to weekly or monthly cash flows for the remaining time horizon are likely to provide the best balance. The need to forecast daily during the initial stage of the stress test is recommended not only as a result of the relatively higher predictability of these cash flows, but also because, as was seen during the financial crisis, the most critical period of stress for the institution may in fact occur during those first few days.

TESTING TECHNIQUES

There are three general approaches to performing a liquidity stress test— historical statistical techniques, deterministic models, and Monte Carlo simulation:

Historical statistical techniques, such as cash flow at risk (CFaR), model a historical pro forma cash flow based on the observed cash flow volatility of the institution.

Deterministic models, such as the development of hypothetical liquidity stress scenarios, model the liquidity impact of a forward-looking or historical-based scenario that has been developed by the institution.

Monte Carlo simulation is a statistical technique that relies on simulation modeling and can be used to assess liquidity risk by stress testing specified variables over a future time frame.

Stochastic techniques that rely on observations of historical volatility of cash flow variables, whether using historical statistical models such as CFaR or Monte Carlo simulation techniques that rely on historical observations of volatility, are viewed less favorably in the wake of the financial crisis. By its nature, liquidity stress is an extreme "tail event," and deterministic scenarios, despite their reliance on many assumptions that are derived through expert judgment, are viewed by regulators and most financial institutions as the most effective tool for assessing liquidity risk. An additional challenge of stochastic approaches is their limited ability to accurately predict the management countermeasures that would occur during a liquidity crisis event. The remainder of this chapter will focus on the development of a deterministic liquidity stress test framework.

BASELINE SCENARIO

The starting point for building the liquidity stress test is the baseline balance sheet funding and liquidity plan. As a banking organization builds out its liquidity stress test framework, it is sometimes necessary to enhance the structure of the baseline plan as well to ensure that the base case is consistently structured and at the same level of detail as the stress scenarios. It is also advisable to house the baseline analysis in the same reporting and analysis platform as the liquidity stress test. The objective is to ensure that the institution can gauge the severity of each stress scenario by making a valid comparison to the baseline forecast.

SCENARIO DEVELOPMENT

By its very nature, liquidity failure is a high-impact, low-frequency event. Fortunately, only a handful of large financial institutions have collapsed due to insufficient liquidity. Unfortunately for this very reason, there is little data upon which to build reliable, predictive models that can accurately estimate the minimum level of liquidity an institution can expect to maintain within a confidence interval. Even in the recent financial crisis, a combination of government intervention, monetary stimulus, and customer delevering led to a liquidity buildup that quickly stuffed the cash coffers of all but the shakiest banks.

As a result of these limitations and the highly complex, interconnected nature of liquidity behavior, the industry approach to performing a liquidity stress test is to develop a set of discrete, deterministic scenarios. While the menu of liquidity stress test scenarios has become somewhat standardized across the banking industry since the financial crisis, it is important that each financial institution carefully consider its unique or idiosyncratic material risks when building out its scenario framework.

There are two general types of liquidity stress scenarios—historical scenarios and forward-looking (hypothetical) scenarios.

Historical Scenarios

Historical scenarios are based on actual liquidity failures and attempt to translate those events to the financial institution performing the stress test. The failures of WaMu and Northern Rock in 2008 are common reference events. The advantage of historical scenarios is that they are empirically based. The disadvantage of this approach is that few such failures have actually occurred; and for the ones that have taken place, very limited data are available. Additionally, future business conditions may cause new and unanticipated liquidity events, creating a potential blind spot for management.

Hypothetical Scenarios

Hypothetical scenarios are based on a forward-looking view in which the financial institution experiences severe liquidity stress. Banks typically develop multiple scenarios. Liquidity stress scenarios should exhibit the following characteristics:

Distinguish between systemic and idiosyncratic risk. Some liquidity stress impacts are the result of systemic stress, such as a reduction in the market liquidity of securities, while other impacts are the result of bank-only stress, such as a deposit run. See Figure 3.3 for a detailed description of these impacts. Banks should develop at least one scenario for each of the cases of systemic, idiosyncratic, and combined idiosyncratic and systemic in order to capture these varying impacts.

Distinguish between levels of severity. Assuming graduating levels of severity, for example, by developing adverse and severely adverse variations of the idiosyncratic scenario, enables the institution to broaden its view of liquidity risk and applicable limits.

Clearly define the scenarios. The bank must establish a specific, detailed description of the business and market events associated with each scenario in order to provide the foundation for assumption development as well as linking stress testing to early warning indicators in contingency funding plans. In developing and documenting each stress scenario, the bank should ensure the level of detail is sufficient to provide a comprehensive view into the specific conditions the institution is experiencing. Scenario descriptions typically include, at a minimum:

- The general level of stress (e.g., high) of market, economic, and credit conditions
- Conditions of wholesale secured and unsecured funding markets
- Changes in counterparty haircut requirements by collateral type
- Liquidity impacts on securities in the liquidity buffer and other assets in the event of sale
- Details of credit grade downgrades
- Deposit runoff assumptions by product and customer type, and with consideration to other factors such as insurance coverage
- Description of impacts on specific counterparty relationships
- Rating trigger impacts on derivative margin and collateral calls
- Impact of regulatory actions or limit breaches in foreign jurisdictions
- Assumed drawdowns on unfunded credit and liquidity facilities
- Assumed debt calls and buybacks

Consider more holistic approaches to scenario development. Standard industry liquidity stress test scenarios, including those required by regulators under the Basel III liquidity coverage ratio (LCR), are highly prescriptive. This philosophy is in sharp contrast to the approach taken for capital stress testing, where a set of high-level macroeconomic developments are assumed and then carefully assessed to link their impacts to the bank's financial performance and capital position. In addition to the liquidity-specific scenarios described here, the institution should also consider scenarios based on broader economic and business impacts. Doing so will ensure the bank is considering systemic, interdependent risk behavior rather than simply developing isolated liquidity assumptions.

In addition to assumption-based hypothetical scenarios, the bank may also perform a reverse liquidity stress test. The objective of a reverse liquidity stress test is to determine which conditions would need to exist, given the bank's current liquidity level, to cause its current business plan to become unviable. To construct such a scenario will require determination of which factors will have the most significant impact on liquidity and stressing these assumptions to the institution's destruction. Developing such a reverse stress test scenario, while simple in theory, presents a number of problems as there are a large number of factors which could combine to destroy the institution. It can also be difficult to develop a destruction scenario if the bank is highly liquid without making fantastic, apocalyptic assumptions. As a result, reverse stress testing is not a universally performed exercise among financial institutions; however, the FRB's SR Letter 12-7 does provide guidance on reverse stress testing, which is applicable to institutions above $10 billion in consolidated assets. In this context, the failure considerations (which most banks qualify as a liquidity driven event) under recovery and resolution planning might be viewed as constituting a reverse stress test. Nevertheless, it is advisable to at least think through a reverse stress test in developing traditional stress test scenarios as a way of facilitating an understanding of the priority risks the institution should be testing (Table 3.1).

DEVELOPMENT OF ASSUMPTIONS

Liquidity stress testing is built on hypothetical and historical scenarios, and as a result is highly dependent on the validity of assumptions in generating meaningful results. For many key assumptions there is limited historical or market data to draw upon in building a fact base. Nevertheless, applying segmentation frameworks that enable differentiation of assumptions across varying levels of cash flow risk enhances the rigor of the liquidity stress test.

TABLE 3.1 Key Liquidity Stress Impact Factors

Category	Key Liquidity Stress Impacts
Deposit runoff	Depositors accelerate demand deposit withdrawals
Deposit runoff	Term depositors exercise early withdrawal rights
Loss of wholesale funding	Inability to roll over short-term, maturing unsecured wholesale funding
Loss of wholesale funding	Early termination of unsecured wholesale funding credit lines and/or early redemption of wholesale fundings
Loss of secured funding	Loss of willing counterparties for secured funding
Loss of secured funding	Limitation of security types available for secured funding and/or increased collateral haircuts
Loss of secured funding	Loss of access to asset-backed funding facilities due to lack of funding, embedded options, or lack of eligible assets
Reduced investment portfolio liquidity	Increased liquidity haircuts and/or reduced valuations of liquidity portfolio securities
Derivative cash flows	Increased derivative margin/collateral calls due to increased market volatility of underlying position
Derivative cash flows	Increased collateral calls due to reduction in collateral value
Ratings downgrades	Collateral or other liquidity impacts due to ratings triggers
Credit/liquidity facilities	Accelerated drawdown of credit and liquidity facilities by customers/counterparties

In addition to developing internal views of stressed liquidity behavior, the institution should reference the Basel III (including as implemented in local jurisdictions) liquidity coverage ratio cash flow rates.

Generally, in developing liquidity stress testing assumptions the institution should do the following:

1. Qualitatively assess the expected liquidity behavior for each type of cash flow to determine where there is significant liquidity risk.
2. Determine the appropriate level of segmentation for each type of risk based on an assessment of behavioral differences, bearing in mind any limitations in ongoing data availability.
3. Qualitatively assess and order by rank varying levels of liquidity risk for each segmentation factor, potentially utilizing a scoring system.
4. Develop quantitative modeling assumptions based on any historical data available, such as experiences during the financial crisis, or available from other sources such as peer benchmarking.

5. Develop matrices of relative modeling assumptions based on scored risk levels and baseline historical data.
6. Adjust assumption matrices as appropriate for each stress scenario, for example, reflecting differences in relative overall severity or assumptions concerning idiosyncratic or systemic risk.

The following assumptions can have an outsized impact on the results of the stress test, and should be considered carefully in developing the model:

Investment portfolio haircuts. The ability to obtain liquidity through pledging, funding through a repo transaction, or outright sale of investment portfolio securities will have a critical impact on available liquidity under stress. For systemic stress scenarios, it is assumed that haircuts will widen on securities as was observed during the crisis. The model should include varying haircut assumptions for each security type where liquidity characteristics differ, for example, differentiating between agency mortgage-backed securities and non-agency mortgage-backed securities. The model should also include expected haircut differences between secured financing channels used by the institution, for example, Federal Home Loan Bank funding, and repo facilities.

Developing a scoring system that orders by rank the relative liquidity along these various segmentation dimensions can be a useful framework for this purpose. The institution can then assign specific haircuts to each type of security and funding channel based on the assessed liquidity risk. The starting point for developing liquidity haircuts is a review of current market conditions (assuming such conditions are normal), and comparing these advance rates to what the bank experienced during the financial crisis. If the bank does not have such data available, it will need to be obtained through peer comparisons where possible.

Deposit outflows. Deposit runoff is, for most institutions, the most significant threat to liquidity and the most important behavioral dynamic to model. For the typical, heavily deposit-funded bank, liquidity stress test models built on simplistic assumptions concerning deposit behavior will most likely yield meaningless results, even if other aspects of the model have been calibrated rigorously.

Unfortunately, there is a scarcity of historical data to rely upon in developing deposit runoff assumptions. While the runs that occurred during the crisis, particularly those at WaMu and Northern Rock, provide useful reference points, the institution should build a set of detailed deposit runoff assumptions based on

TABLE 3.2 Deposit Behavioral Characteristics

Typical behavioral assessment factors

Consumer	Small Business	Commercial and Institutional
▪ Relationship tenure ▪ Checking product usage ▪ ATM usage frequency ▪ Rate paid ▪ Internet usage ▪ FDIC coverage ▪ Direct control vs. escrow	▪ Relationship tenure ▪ Value-added product usage ▪ Credit usage ▪ Branch usage frequency ▪ FDIC coverage ▪ Rate paid	▪ Relationship tenure ▪ Credit usage ▪ Treasury and trade usage ▪ Balance level ▪ Net borrowing position ▪ Industry segment ▪ Company size ▪ Rate paid

a behavioral segmentation framework that captures differences in stressed deposit behavior.

Table 3.2 summarizes behavioral differences typically observed in deposit portfolios. The institution should carefully analyze the historical behavior of its deposit portfolio—preferably at the account rather than portfolio level—to develop an appropriate internal segmentation framework. Empirical analysis is unlikely to yield a perfect experiment indicative of behavior during a hypothetical crisis. However, such an analysis is suggestive of customer "stickiness" and provides a more rigorous foundation than high-level, qualitative assumptions.

Unsecured wholesale funding. Availability of unsecured wholesale funding is generally assumed to be heavily reduced in a stress scenario, particularly under idiosyncratic stress. The bank should review each funding channel to differentiate by key liquidity factors, most significantly overnight versus term funding. There is likely to be little historical data available assuming the institution has not experienced a significant stress event. Banks typically apply highly conservative assumptions when reflecting on the drastic impact that a stress event is likely to have on wholesale funding availability, particularly term funding.

Collateral requirements. Collateral requirements should be expected to increase during a stress scenario as a result of both valuation impacts on existing collateral as well as increased collateral levels required as a result of changes in derivative positions. How the institution develops assumptions for collateral call levels (as opposed to collateral valuation impacts, which should align to unsecured wholesale funding models) will depend on the level of detail required. The institution may choose to review its historical collateral call levels, particularly during times of stress, and select the most significant liquidity requirement experienced during a historical period. A more detailed approach would be to model each position independently.

Other contingent liabilities. The model should address each material source of contingent liquidity outflow, including drawdowns of customer credit lines, liquidity facilities, letters of credit, trade financing arrangements, securitization facility runoff, and other contractual arrangements. Where possible, the institution should review the behavior of such contingent liabilities during the financial crisis. If historical data is not available, conservative assumptions are appropriate.

Non-contractual commitments must also be incorporated into the model. Particularly for lower stress scenarios, the institution will still seek to maintain reputational strength and avoid damage to business franchise value. Achieving these objectives may require voluntary financing transactions such as completion of underwriting pipeline deals and repurchase of securities issued in order to protect counterparties from mark-to-market losses. Quantitative assumptions for these requirements can be developed using the projected level of activity as appropriate.

Business dial back. The liquidity stress test should incorporate a set of realistic assumptions concerning the institution's ability to reduce liquidity-draining business activities such as new loan origination. These assumptions should be developed through discussions with business unit management, who will have a view into the level of reduced funding activity that can occur without causing significant reputational problems.

OUTPUTS OF THE MODEL

The outcome of liquidity stress testing, along with the other components of the institution's liquidity risk measurement framework, provide the foundation for assessing tactical and structural liquidity relative to internally established limits and regulatory expectations. In particular, the liquidity stress test forms an integral part of an institution's liquidity risk escalation process. The bank's liquidity limit structure, and in particular the contingency funding plan, should be tied directly to the results of the liquidity stress test. These linkages may exist through, for example, survival horizon metric minimums, minimum available liquidity limits, and stressed liquidity metric limits.

The liquidity stress test should enable the production of a regular reporting package that contains the following for each of the entities being tested:

Stress testing assumptions. Key assumptions include (1) overall stress level represented by the scenario; (2) indication of whether the scenario is systemic, idiosyncratic, or both systemic and idiosyncratic; (3) documentation of the overall macroeconomic, market, and company-specific events leading to the stress scenario; and (4) description of the cash flow impacts of the scenario.

Liquidity position metrics. The principal measurement outcome of the liquidity stress test is the level of available liquidity relative to net cash outflows under each scenario. The exact form of this metric varies across institutions but may be expressed as a percentage of net outflows or as a dollar value relative to a policy minimum. Some institutions distinguish between tactical and structural liquidity in measuring the results of the liquidity stress test. The Basel III LCR, for example, provides a thirty day view into available liquidity under stress. To measure the longer-term or structural liquidity position, the institution may calculate a survival horizon relative to a limit. For example, the bank's policy may be to maintain available liquidity to support twelve months of net outflow under a specific stress scenario.

Prospective liquidity position metrics. In addition to measuring the current liquidity position, the bank should measure the prospective liquidity profile of the bank over the stress horizon. Key indicators of liquidity risk include prospective available liquidity, ratios indicative of wholesale funding dependence (e.g., net non-core funding dependence), and metrics indicative of potential overconcentration in specific funding channels (e.g., percentage of funding from brokered deposits). When monitoring prospective liquidity, it is important to highlight any specific stress points along the horizon where survival would require potentially problematic debt issuances, intercompany funding transactions, or capital actions. The institution may choose to establish limits for prospective liquidity in addition to current liquidity, for example, maintaining a certain survival horizon throughout the stress test.

Capital and performance metrics. In addition to capturing the liquidity impact of the stress test, it is also important to measure the balance sheet more holistically. For example, assessing the economic impact of the investment portfolio by measuring yield net of a regulatory or economic capital charge enables the institution to assess the trade-off between low-yielding, low-haircut instruments and higher performance, less liquid ones. Monitoring key capital metrics for each entity ensures that the model captures the impact of any capital actions required to support liquidity during the stress period.

The frequency with which the liquidity stress test is performed will vary and typically depends upon the cadence of management oversight and operational and technological capabilities of the institution. At a minimum, the liquidity stress test should be performed quarterly in order to support review by the asset liability management committee. More advanced banking organizations have made significant investments in building the ability to perform liquidity stress tests more frequently, in some cases even daily.

GOVERNANCE AND CONTROLS

As an integral part of the institution's liquidity risk governance framework, the liquidity stress test should be the subject of, while at the same time supporting, effective oversight in order to help ensure the liquidity risk profile is aligned to the bank's risk appetite and capacity. The specific roles should consist of the following:

Asset-liability committee (ALCO). The ALCO, consistent with its board, management risk committee, and executive management delegated oversight of managing liquidity risk, typically has overall responsibility for the liquidity stress testing framework. Specifically, the ALCO should be responsible for the following:

- Ensuring the establishment, review, and approval of a liquidity stress testing policy. The liquidity stress testing policy should detail the scenarios to be run, key assumptions, roles and responsibilities, reporting requirements, and limits. The specific structure of liquidity stress testing documentation may be tailored to the policy structure of the bank. Many institutions include this policy as an appendix or supporting standard to the overall liquidity risk management policy or as a component of the contingency funding plan. The liquidity stress testing policy should be renewed at least annually.
- Suggesting and approving liquidity risk scenarios, including major changes to liquidity scenarios and/or assumptions.

- Setting liquidity risk policy limits dependent on stress test outcomes and escalating exceptions. For certain limit tiers, escalation may be required to the board of directors.

Treasury. The treasury unit, as the first line of defense, typically has ownership of the liquidity stress test modeling process. Treasury should be responsible for the following:

- Maintenance of liquidity stress testing procedures.
- Recommending stress test scenarios.
- Reviewing and monitoring the liquidity characteristics of the institution's assets and liabilities and making recommendations to the ALCO concerning stress testing assumptions. Treasury should work with other functions within the organization, in particular business line management, in developing assumptions for customer assets and liabilities. A formal requirement should be established in the liquidity stress testing policy that management reviews the key analytical assumptions of the liquidity stress test at least quarterly.
- Producing stress test-based liquidity risk reporting.

It is recommended that the liquidity stress test baseline balance sheet data (i.e., the current positions and contractual maturities) be fed from, or at least reconciled to, reporting prepared by a group independent of treasury, such as financial control, independent risk management, or middle office.

Within large, complex banking organizations, it is expected that multiple treasury units will perform liquidity stress tests for their respective entities. In such cases the corporate treasury group should ensure that the global liquidity stress testing policy establishes a consistent framework of scenarios, assumptions, and model design across the enterprise.

Risk management. The independent risk management function, as the second line of defense, is responsible for providing independent oversight of liquidity stress testing along with the other components of the liquidity risk management program. Specifically, risk management is responsible for the following:

- Administering the liquidity risk stress testing policy
- Reviewing and providing effective challenge of the scenario design and assumptions
- Ensuring the institution's approach to liquidity stress testing is in line with acceptable industry practices and regulatory rules and guidance
- Reviewing and approving the liquidity stress test–based limits

- Monitoring of liquidity stress test–based limits
- Ensuring the institution's ALCO, executive management, and board are kept well-informed of the bank's liquidity risk profile as indicated by the stress testing results

    Where multiple risk units within the institution are overseeing liquidity stress testing, the independent risk management function should be responsible for coordinating globally with regional and business unit risk management teams to ensure enterprise-wide consistency.

Internal audit. Internal audit, as the third line of defense, should periodically review the liquidity stress testing framework, procedures, and controls to ensure compliance with policy, regulatory, and control requirements.

Model risk management: Model risk management is responsible for providing independent validation and changing management governance of the liquidity stress testing model in line with the institution's model risk management policy. Practices vary among institutions in defining and evaluating models for oversight. It is assumed, however, that the liquidity stress testing model will be assessed as highly critical given its foundational role in monitoring the bank's risk profile.

LIQUIDITY OPTIMIZATION

The primary goal of the liquidity stress test is to determine the appropriate size of the liquidity buffer. However, the liquidity stress test should also be referenced in developing the composition of the buffer, with the objective of maximizing the efficiency of the liquidity portfolio. Given a target level of contingent liquidity required to support risk limits and regulatory requirements, Treasury will be able to choose between portfolio alternatives that vary in terms of both yield and capital requirements. This choice gives rise to an optimization opportunity:

Liquidity versus yield: Typically, higher yielding instruments will have less favorable liquidity characteristics and/or add duration to the investment portfolio. Maximizing the yield and/or duration of the portfolio (even under the usual strict investment policy constraints) is likely to be suboptimal for the institution's return on asset performance as a whole. This yield maximizing portfolio will be inefficient due to the additional balance level required to offset stress test haircuts and the mismatch between the portfolio's inflows and the stress test outflows. For example, taking the simplified stress testing example represented by the Basel III LCR, maximizing the size of the Level 2A portfolio (e.g., by investing in agency mortgage-backed securities) that require a 15% haircut, may reduce overall return on assets relative to investing slightly lower yielding treasury securities that require no haircut.

Conversely, maximizing the liquidity profile of the portfolio at the expense of yield may be equally inefficient. Armed with a robust liquidity stress testing model, treasury should avoid constructing a needlessly conservative liquidity portfolio when the pattern of stressed net outflows demonstrates that the institution can comfortably stretch the duration and risk profile of its investments.

Liquidity vs. capital. Depending upon the institution's economic and regulatory capital framework, a similar trade-off exists for incorporating the capital impact of various portfolio alternatives. Continuing with the example of Level 2A agency mortgage-backed securities, maximizing the investment allocation of these instruments may be suboptimal given the additional regulatory and potentially economic capital requirements associated with these instruments. For banks whose capital position is such that any additional asset amount gives rise to an additional equity capital requirement under leverage ratio limits, the additional haircut required for higher-risk instruments will also be problematic.

FUNDING OPTIMIZATION

An important insight provided by the liquidity stress test model is the impact of varying funding sources with differing liquidity characteristics. In fact, a key objective of the focus on enhancing liquidity stress testing since the financial crisis has been to create an incentive for financial institutions to favor "sticky" funding sources such as retail branch deposits at the expense of "hot" money sourced from wholesale channels. By explicitly modeling the liquidity impact of these funding alternatives, treasury can and should develop a target funding profile that balances liquidity and cost. For example, the superior liquidity profile of commercial deposits linked to treasury management services should serve to bolster the business case for investing in target industry segments with more intensive working capital requirements. Building this linkage requires a funds transfer pricing (FTP) framework that accurately incorporates the stressed liquidity profile of various business segments across the enterprise.

ESTABLISHING A SUSTAINABLE INFRASTRUCTURE

The strongest liquidity stress testing analytical framework will have little value without a data management infrastructure to support it. In order to support efficient and controlled ongoing stress testing and reporting, the institution should maintain an information technology infrastructure that performs automated data collection, aggregation, capturing of market data, report generation, and analytics. The challenge for many large, complex financial institutions has been that developing such an infrastructure for liquidity stress data has required significant modifications to existing data warehouse capabilities built largely on general ledger and transactional customer data. In building an infrastructure that supports liquidity stress testing, the institution should ensure that several critical requirements are met. These include:

> **Position data collection and aggregation.** A data management model must be established to ensure that required liquidity position data are captured in an automated fashion. The specific architecture employed by an institution will vary, but could include the use of standardized templates or data hub structures. Required liquidity attributes may need to be associated to each position to enable automated development of model inputs. The position data will also need to conform to the required organizational granularity. For large, internationally active banking organizations, this is likely to require data across numerous legal entity, business line, and jurisdictional dimensions. In addition to capture current positions, the institution should retain historic data in the data hub for historical analysis–based model calibration. The objective is to ensure that liquidity data is housed in a single location and forms a single source of truth.

> **Regulatory report generation.** Building on this automated position capture should be the ability to generate regulatory reports (e.g., the Basel III LCR) with a minimum of manual intervention. Solutions may include functional replicas of official regulatory reports—or customized proprietary versions if official templates are not available—that are populated with associated validations and regulatory adjustments, requiring minimal user manipulation. Such solutions may be developed as proprietary applications or included within the reporting functionality of third party treasury platforms.

Analytics. The liquidity stress test model should contain the features and functions that management would expect in any robust analysis tool. These would include, for example, the ability to perform sensitivity analysis on stress test assumptions, the ability to save scenarios, and the ability to easily generate various legal entity views. In addition to such flexible forecasting functionality, leading practice is to include analytic functionality that, for example, assesses the economic capital impact of various liquidity portfolio allocations.

Liquidity dashboard. Key risk indicators and performance drivers should be tracked on a predefined basis and distributed to risk managers. Liquidity stress test results may be included in an existing risk dashboard or circulated separately.

INTEGRATION OF LIQUIDITY STRESS TESTING WITH RELATED RISK MODELS

Liquidity stress testing should not be performed in a silo without consideration of other related risk frameworks, such as asset liability management (for interest rate risk), capital stress testing, and recovery and resolution planning. These models may employ related assumptions concerning the balance sheet behavior of certain accounts, and developing these assumptions independently is likely to lead to an inconsistent overall risk management framework. More importantly, it is imperative that a banking organization consider the correlations between risk types that are likely to surface in a systemic or idiosyncratic stress scenario. For example, in a capital-stressed environment, an institution may be required to take a capital action requiring the raising of liquidity at the holding company level. If raising such liquidity requires incurring losses on investment portfolio liquidation (all the more likely in a stressed environment), additional capital pressures may occur.

In theory, the institution should maintain a holistic risk model that assesses the impact on liquidity, capital, and balance sheet structure under a common set of scenarios. In practice, such an approach can be problematic due not only to the modeling complexity involved, but also as a result of the need to develop unique stress scenarios for each risk type. For example, a bank may stress capital based on a recessionary scenario that adversely affects credit performance but is also associated with falling interest rates (as expected during a recession) and a less severe impact on liquidity than what would be typically assumed under an idiosyncratic "run on the bank" liquidity stress test scenario. Nevertheless, the bank should carefully consider the interdependencies and connection points between the liquidity stress model and other risk models:

Liquidity stress testing and capital stress testing. Linking capital and liquidity stress testing requires, first, ensuring that the liquidity stress test incorporates any required capital infusions of subsidiary entities. For each liquidity stress test scenario, capital impact assumptions must be developed based on the overall market and idiosyncratic conditions assumed to occur under the scenario. The level of detail in developing these assumptions may vary from a high-level capital infusion assumption for affected subsidiaries to detailed credit loss and pre-provision net revenue modeling.

Second, the capital stress testing framework should include a liquidity stress evaluation to assess the impact of any required liquidity impacts on capital adequacy. In conjunction with performing the capital stress test, the institution should perform a liquidity impact analysis to determine whether additional capital impacts may occur through investment portfolio and required funding actions that would cause further deterioration in capital adequacy.

Liquidity stress testing and asset liability management. Interest rate risk models are designed to assess the interest expense and economic value of equity impacts of severe movements in interest rates. Such a stress event could have a significant impact on capital but is less likely to have a direct impact on the bank's short-term liquidity profile. As a result, a liquidity impact analysis is typically not run concurrently with interest rate risk stress testing analogous to what must be performed for capital stress testing. Nevertheless, a consistent behavioral framework should be applied to both the interest rate and liquidity stress testing models. For example, if the liquidity stress test model assumes that certain operational deposits do not run off in a stress event, the interest rate risk model should segment these deposits and assume that they would have duration at least as long as non-operational deposits.

When it comes to the liquidity stress model, however, it is important to consider interest rate impacts. In particular, the liquidity stress test scenario framework, liquidity risk dashboards, and liquidity risk early warning indicators should not neglect to include the possibility of an interest rate shock and the potential impact such an event would have on indeterminate liabilities. For example, in an environment where rates are historically low and there is significant risk of a yield curve steepening (i.e., the current environment), the institution must carefully consider the impact of deposit disintermediation due to interest rate increases. A significant yield curve steepening could present significant liquidity risk to the institution, even in the absence of any safety and soundness concerns, as depositors seek the higher yields available in longer-duration investments.

Liquidity stress testing and funds transfer pricing. The FTP framework, while not a risk model, is a strategically important tool for driving business decision making. One of the key objectives of any FTP framework is proper pricing of liquidity, whether provided by the treasury center for lending purposes or credited to liability-generating activities. The FTP framework should leverage and be consistent with the contingent liquidity requirement for assets and liabilities measured by the liquidity stress test model. For example, if it is determined that a 25% cash buffer is required to support a wholesale operational deposit (to borrow a Basel III LCR assumption), the cost of carrying this buffer should be passed through within the FTP framework.

CONCLUSION

The liquidity stress test is a core component of the bank's liquidity risk framework, and following the financial crisis has become an increased area of scrutiny and expectation among regulators and other stakeholders. While nearly all financial institutions of significant size have a basic liquidity stress testing process in place, there are typically a number of areas of potential improvement. As banks continue to refine and improve their liquidity stress capabilities, they should focus on four areas:

- **Ensuring the appropriate scope and structure of the liquidity stress test.** While stress testing the consolidated entity is a common practice, it is important to carefully review jurisdiction, legal entity, charter, and foreign exchange liquidity restrictions to ensure testing is performed with each appropriate view.
- **Building the model on robust assumptions.** While there is unlikely to be a perfect historical experiment upon which to base stress scenario assumptions, the bank should nevertheless make a diligent attempt to build the most robust set of assumptions possible. Increasing the level of granularity—such as by enhancing the level of segmentation for deposit behavioural analysis—typically yields beneficial results.
- **Improving integration with related risk and performance models.** Longer term, the industry will continue to evolve toward unifying

what is currently a set of relatively isolated frameworks in addressing liquidity risk, capital, asset liability management, and performance measurement. Developing better linkage between stress testing and performance management and across risk categories will create the necessity to holistically assess risk-based performance results in business and treasury banking activities.

- **Automating the process.** Creating a sustainable liquidity risk infrastructure is a necessary foundation for improved analytics and more frequent monitoring. For most institutions, this will require establishing and maintaining a tailored data hub, an automated data model, and robust analytics and reporting capabilities.

CHAPTER 4

Intraday Liquidity Risk Management

Barry Barretta and Stephen Baird[1]

INTRODUCTION

The banking industry's interest in intraday liquidity risk in the United States can be traced back to the early 1980s. This was an era of extremely high interest rates and tight money, engineered by Paul Volcker, who was appointed chairman of the Board of Governors of the Federal Reserve System (Federal Reserve) in August of 1979. Chairman Volcker is widely credited with ending the "stagflation" crisis in the United States by dramatically raising the Federal Funds rate upon taking office (from an average of 11.2% in 1979 to a peak of 20% in June of 1981), and ushering in an extended period of high real interest rates. Regulators and major industry players became aware of the large overdrafts that were endemic in the banking systems in the middle of the business day during this period, as the disincentives for banks to leave idle cash reserves at the Federal Reserve and correspondent banks began to grow.

With the opportunity cost of cash so high, major banks employed aggressive cash management techniques to minimize their cash balances on deposit. At the time, the Federal Reserve did not pay interest on bank deposits and correspondent banks could not pay interest on operating balances in demand deposit accounts (both of which are now permitted). As a result, banks actively managed their balances down to the minimums called for by: (a) reserve requirement regulations (at their Federal Reserve accounts); and (b) compensation arrangements for services provided by correspondent banks. This often meant their accounts were in a negative position during the day (hence the terms intraday daylight and overdraft).

---

[1] Barry Barretta was formerly a director in PwC's Chicago office, and Stephen Baird is a director in PwC's Chicago office.

Against this backdrop, the Federal Reserve released a policy in 1985 that began the process of containing, and eventually shrinking, daylight overdrafts in the banking system.

There were two reasons why central banks were concerned about daylight overdrafts. First, central banks wished to avoid inadvertently extending credit to their member banks. If one of the banks were to fail during the day when its account was in a large deficit position, the central bank (and potentially the taxpayers) would be on the hook for any losses. Second, when viewed across the whole system, intraday overdrafts were significantly expanding the effective money supply, causing central bankers to worry that their policy actions could be blunted or accentuated by this "shadow" money supply. Table 4.1 compares the annual average peak intraday overdraft (calculated system-wide) and the M1 money supply in five-year snapshots beginning in 1986, when the Federal Reserve began measurements. As Table 4.1 indicates, peak overdrafts routinely approached 10% or more of the money supply in those early years. Conversely, in today's environment, which is characterized by low interest rates and accommodative monetary policy, intraday overdrafts are much smaller, both in nominal terms and in proportion to the M1 money supply.

The trend in aggregate intraday overdrafts illustrated in Table 4.1 demonstrates the success of the Federal Reserve's efforts to more effectively manage payment systems risk. As mentioned earlier, in 1985, the Federal Reserve issued its first policy addressing intraday credit, which focused on daylight overdrafts incurred as a result of Fedwire funds transactions. This policy sought to limit intraday overdrafts by requiring all institutions that incurred intraday overdrafts in their Federal Reserve Bank accounts to establish a maximum limit, called a net debit cap, which was determined by

TABLE 4.1 Relationship of U.S. Banks' Average Peak Intraday Overdrafts to M1 Money Supply

	1986	1991	1996	2001	2006	2011	2013
Peak Intraday Overdraft ($billions)	62.9	106.2	67.4	99.4	140.0	29.4	16.6
M1 Money Supply ($billions)	666.3	859.0	1106.9	1140.2	1374.8	2009.6	2511.3
OD as % of M1	9.4%	12.4%	6.1%	8.7%	10.2%	1.5%	0.7%

Data Source: Federal Reserve Board of Governors website (www.federalreserve.gov), money supply data

a self-assessment process, and required approval by the institution's board of directors. Since then, the Board of Governors has continued to expand and modify its payment systems risk policies by introducing new tools and refining existing ones to reduce the aggregate level of intraday overdrafts. Subsequent significant revisions include:

- Extension of payment types beyond wire transfers to include Automated Clearing House (ACH), Fedwire Securities Service transfers, and offshore dollar clearing (1985–1992).
- Assessment of a 24 basis point fee for intraday overdrafts in excess of a deductible equal to 10% of the institution's risk based capital (1994).
- Increase in the fee for intraday overdrafts to 36 basis points (1995).
- Expansion and enhancement of the Federal Reserve's Net Settlement Services for private clearing and settlement systems, provided initially to Clearing House Interbank Payments System (CHIPS) in 1981 (1999).
- Acceptance of collateral to secure intraday overdrafts for a select few institutions, enabling them to exceed their net debit caps (the so-called "max cap") (2001).
- Increase in the fee for unsecured intraday overdrafts to 50 basis points, along with the introduction of a zero fee for fully collateralized overdrafts. The Federal Reserve also adjusted net debit cap multiples, eliminated the deductible amount, and increased the penalty fee to 150 basis points for institutions that do not have discount window access (e.g., a government sponsored entity or Banker's Bank) and incur a daylight overdraft (2008).

International interest in intraday liquidity risk began to accelerate during the mid-1980s as well. In 1980, the central banks of the Group of Ten (G10) countries established a working group called the Group of Experts on Payment Systems, which in 1990 became the Committee on Payment and Settlement Systems (CPSS) and is now the Committee on Payments and Market Infrastructures (CPMI), a committee of the Bank for International Settlements (BIS). The Group of Experts on Payments Systems began compiling data on payments systems in the G10 countries, which was first published by the BIS in 1985, and has continued as a series that has become known as "red books." In 1989, the Group of Experts on Payments Systems published the *Report on Netting Schemes*, which focused on the efficiency of financial markets and payment systems, and the effects of netting on counterparty credit and liquidity risks.[2] It is in this early work that the Group of

---

[2] Group of Experts on Payment Systems of the Central Banks of the Group of Ten Countries. February 1989. http://www.bis.org/cpmi/publ/d02.pdf.

Experts on Payments Systems identified reduction of daylight overdrafts as an objective and driver of netting arrangements.

Most recently, the CPMI (which now consists of representation from twenty-five central banks) has been focused on developing, promulgating, and monitoring implementation of its *Principles for Financial Market Infrastructure*, a set of standards and policies designed to guide credit, liquidity, and systemic risk management at payments, clearing, and settlement systems.[3] Reflecting the influence of CPMI, the central banks of most developed countries around the world are striving to align their regulations with the risk management principles espoused by CPMI (formerly CPSS). In the United States, this first began in 2004, when the Federal Reserve modified its Payment System Risk (PSR) policy to adopt the CPSS-published *Core Principles for Systemically Important Payment Systems* (the Core Principles),[4] and the *Recommendations for Securities Settlement Systems* (RSSS),[5] as the minimum standards for systemically important payment and securities settlement systems, respectively. To this day, the Federal Reserve, Commodity Futures Trading Commission (CFTC), and the Securities and Exchange Commission (SEC) continue to incorporate the work of CPSS into their rulemaking and regulatory guidance.

CPMI has worked in conjunction with the Basel Committee on Banking Supervision (BCBS), another committee of central bank experts that is part of BIS. BCBS began publishing guidance on managing liquidity risk in banking organizations in 1992 and has been updating it periodically since. In response to the 2007-08 financial crisis, BCBS significantly expanded its work in liquidity risk and began incorporating intraday liquidity risk into its framework. In April 2013, BCBS published *Monitoring Tools for Intraday Liquidity Management*, a paper designed to help regulators and banks track intraday risk more empirically.[6] The reader is encouraged to reference the various papers on liquidity risk management available on the BIS website. This continuum of work demonstrates how the industry focus has evolved from identifying and understanding intraday liquidity risk to measuring and managing it.

---

[3]CPSS. "Principles for Financial Market Infrastructures." April 2012. http://www.bis.org/cpmi/publ/d101a.pdf.

[4]CPSS. "Core Principles for Systemically Important Payment Systems." January 2001. http://www.bis.org/cpmi/publ/d43.pdf.

[5]CPSS. "Recommendations for Securities Settlement Systems." November 2001. http://www.bis.org/cpmi/publ/d46.pdf.

[6]BCBS. "Monitoring Tools for Intraday Liquidity Management." April 2013. http://www.bis.org/publ/bcbs248.pdf.

USES AND SOURCES OF INTRADAY LIQUIDITY

This section provides an overview of the challenges faced by a bank treasurer in managing intraday liquidity risk and enumerates the sources and uses of intraday funds for a typical large bank.

To understand how to better manage intraday liquidity risk, it is useful to start with an analysis of how daylight overdrafts are created in the first place. The U.S. banking system starts and ends the day with plenty of cash on deposit at the Federal Reserve (nearly $1.5 trillion as of December 31, 2012, per the Federal Reserve's balance sheet). In fact, some level of deposits at the Federal Reserve is mandated by reserve requirement regulations. So, why do banks face a shortage of liquidity during the day? The answer is twofold.

First, certain market conventions and behaviors that have been engrained over decades serve to institutionalize intraday overdrafts. For instance, a bank can borrow fed funds in the interbank market any time during the business day with delivery of funds occurring almost immediately, but the return of borrowed funds typically takes place as a first order item the following morning. Even though the transaction is priced as a one-day loan, in reality, the borrower has use of the funds for less than twenty-four hours. The typical pattern is to borrow to cover funding shortfalls in the afternoon, and return the funds at opening of business the next day. Thus, a bank that is a net borrower of fed funds may overdraft its Federal Reserve account during the middle of the day after returning borrowed funds from the previous day.

Another example is the settlement of positions at financial market utilities (FMUs). Many (but not all) FMUs have one settlement window, typically at the end of day, during which bank participants settle their accounts with the clearinghouse by transferring (or receiving) funds to (from) the clearinghouse accounts, which may be held at another bank or the central bank. Let's assume that a bank participant is expecting a large credit in its account from a clearinghouse at end of day in conjunction with having sold a large block of securities. The bank likely would not be able to sell off or invest those funds upon receipt at end of day. Rather than maintain a large, un-invested balance overnight, it will prefer to have its account in a deficit position until the credit is received from the clearinghouse.

The second type of behavior that generates daylight overdrafts is the provision of intraday credit to clients. Many banks allow their corporate and institutional clients to deploy cash intraday without sufficient funds in their accounts. For instance, a commercial client may expect a large wire transfer to be received in the afternoon but still wish to fund its payroll in the morning. In another example, a bank that provides securities-related custody services may extend intraday credit by allowing its client to purchase an asset prior to receiving credit for a maturing asset or selling an investment later in the day. Banks establish daylight overdraft lines of credit to help facilitate these transactions for their clients and typically do not receive direct compensation for doing so.

With all of this occurring, the funds management group of a large bank's treasury has a difficult task in managing intraday liquidity. A bank's cash position is impacted by literally thousands of transactions per hour, both client- and bank-related activity, much of it not known in advance by the treasury group. Additionally, most banks do not have all of their cash positioning data in one system. They can monitor their central bank accounts real-time (and often correspondent accounts) through online account reporting tools, while other data resides in systems managed by lines of business and operations. Table 4.2 contains the common uses of intraday liquidity. The list that follows provides further explanation:

Outgoing wire transfers. Outgoing wire payments, on behalf of clients or the bank's own account, are typically the largest use of intraday liquidity. Payment activity runs the entire length of the business day and typically follows a fairly predictable pattern. Some large banks have to carefully manage the volume of outgoing payments when their daylight overdraft approaches the level of their debit cap. This is accomplished by "throttling" outgoing payments and closely monitoring incoming credits to ensure the cap is not exceeded. Most large value payment systems (LVPSs) and some other payment, clearing, and settlement systems (PCSs) have hard controls that prevent participants from exceeding their intraday credit limits.

Settlements at PCS systems. Most PCS systems have one settlement per day, with many occurring in the late afternoon timeframe. This may serve as either a source or use of funds depending on the net position of a participant on any given day.

Funding of nostro accounts. Banks manage the cash they place in correspondent bank accounts to a target average monthly balance as part of the compensation provided to the correspondent for its banking services. On any given day, the account funding position may act as a source or use of funds to the bank's overall liquidity profile, depending on the net position of the activity flowing through the account that day. Nostro account balances are replenished or drawn down on a daily basis.

TABLE 4.2 Uses of Intraday Credit

Funding Requirement	Description	Impacted by Client Activity	Impacted by Bank Activity	Ability to Forecast
Outgoing Wire Transfers	Payments on LVPS such as Fedwire and CHIPS	Yes, clients provide bank instructions	Yes, Bank Treasury and lines of business have payment needs	Bank activity can usually be forecasted with 1 to 2 days' notice; client payment activity is more difficult to predict
Settlements at Payment, Clearing and Settlement (PCS) Systems	Net cash settlements at payments systems, clearinghouses	Not directly initiated by clients, but includes client activity	Yes, position monitored by operations groups	Can be forecast for securities that have multi-day settlements (e.g., T+3); more difficult for same day settlement activity
Funding of Nostro Accounts	Cash transfer to a correspondent bank for services provided	Not directly initiated by clients, but includes client activity	Yes, position monitored by operations groups	Securities settlements are generally predictable; client payment activity flowing through correspondents is less predictable
Collateral Pledging	Obtaining and earmarking of collateral required by an outside beneficiary	Yes, some clients require collateral to cover bank trading liabilities or deposits	Yes, banks are required to post collateral for margin at FMUs or other trading counter-Parties	Dependent on trading volumes and asset price changes, generally known one day in advance
Asset Purchases/ Funding	Exchange of bank cash for another asset such as a client loan	Yes, clients can draw down on lines of credit or letters of credit	Yes, assets may be securities for the bank's investment portfolio or fixed assets	Bank fixed asset activity should be known in advance; securities purchases may be same day settlement; client loans are more difficult to predict

Collateral pledging. Some banking activities, such as over-the-counter capital markets trading and deposits of certain public funds, require a bank to earmark and set aside collateral. Acquiring additional collateral to support an increasing liability (or as a result of a mark-to-market induced margin call) is a frequent use of intraday funding. Collateral positions are adjusted on a daily basis.

Asset purchases/funding. Funding other balance sheet assets, such as securities purchases for the investment portfolio, client loans, and fixed asset purchases, is another common use of intraday liquidity.

Fortunately for the bank treasurer, there are multiple sources of intraday funding available. Each source varies in its contribution to overall funding from day-to-day, but each is critical to the overall funding landscape. Table 4.3 lists the common sources of intraday liquidity. The list that follows provides further explanation:

Cash balances. The most obvious source of intraday liquidity is the starting cash held on the bank's balance sheet at the beginning of the day. This includes deposits at the central bank and at a correspondent bank's accounts.

Incoming funds flow. Incoming flows from payments and FMU settlements are the largest source of intraday funding in periods of normal market function. Some inflows, including LVPS payments, are real-time. Other credits are batch-oriented, such as net settlements with clearinghouses, retail payments systems, etc.

Intraday credit: Central banks serve as a large source of intraday credit for the banking system and their borrowing terms vary across jurisdictions. The Federal Reserve provides an unsecured committed line of credit (in the form of its Net Debit Cap program) and charges interest for tapping the line. The Bank of England requires intraday overdrafts to be collateralized by the highest quality government securities, but does not charge interest.

FMUs and other banks may also provide intraday credit. Interbank daylight overdraft lines of credit are generally uncommitted and free, but there are some signs of change, especially in Europe. FMUs extend daylight credit by allowing a participant to enter trades or transactions during the day while potentially accumulating a large settlement position that must be met at end of day. The final section of this chapter discusses multiple risk management tools used by FMUs to mitigate these exposures.

Liquid assets. Banks typically carry a buffer of highly liquid, near-cash investments that can be liquidated for cash within short order. This pool of assets includes money market instruments, time deposits, banker's acceptances, and high-quality, short-term government debt.

Overnight borrowings. Fed funds, London Interbank Offered Rate (LIBOR), and Eurodollar deposits are examples of overnight borrowings that can provide quick, intraday liquidity for a bank. These types of borrowings are not repaid on the same day, so they will remain on the borrower's balance sheet overnight. When determining whether or how much to borrow overnight, the bank treasury must weigh the potential cost of having excess liquidity at the end of the day against the risk of not being able to complete the current day's business (or facing reputational risk exposure from delayed transactions) due to breaching a daylight overdraft limit.

Other term funding. Similar to overnight borrowing, a bank can tap into other funding sources (e.g., Federal Home Loan Banks (FHLB) borrowings, term repos) further out on the maturity curve if the lenders are able to provide funding at a time of day that meets the bank's intraday funding needs. Again, the bank would only do this if it has the appetite for longer-term funding (one week, one month, etc.). This type of borrowing is generally viewed as an incremental factor to include in a given day's liquidity positioning ledger rather than a consistent source of intraday funding.

The bank treasurer's challenge is to manage the cacophony generated by high volumes of incoming and outgoing cash transactions (originated at multiple sources all over the bank) in a way that ensures the bank remains within the limits of its daylight credit resources, and ends the day with the appropriate target balances in its accounts. This challenge is exacerbated by several factors.

The first factor is the variability of cash flow patterns. While many activities generate consistent patterns of inflows and outflows over time, there can be high levels of volatility day-to-day with little advance notice of large cash requirements or sources.

The second factor is the impact of market forces. Daily volatility in asset prices can result in unanticipated margin calls that require additional cash funding. In addition, central bank money desks that implement monetary policy directly may influence available liquidity in the marketplace, impacting a bank's ability to source or deploy intraday funds.

The final factor is the lack of real-time data. Most bank treasurers today do not have a comprehensive, single source for real-time balances and expected transaction flows, which complicates the task of determining and forecasting cash throughout the day.

TABLE 4.3 Sources of Intraday Credit

Funding Requirement	Description	Client Activity	Bank Activity	Ability to Forecast
Cash Balances	Deposits at the central bank and at correspondent bank nostro accounts	No, clients do not directly impact closing/start of day cash balances	Yes, Bank Treasury determines level of closing/start of day cash balances	Bank activity can usually be forecasted with 1 to 2 days' notice; client payment activity is more difficult to predict
Incoming Funds Flow	Incoming cash payments and cash credits from FMU	Yes, incoming client payments are credited to the bank's accounts at the central bank and correspondents	Yes, activities conducted for the bank's business can impact cash balances	Bank activity can usually be forecasted with 1 to 2 days' notice; client payment activity is more difficult to predict. FMU credit can be forecast for securities that have multi-day settlements (e.g., T+3); more difficult for same day settlement activity
Intraday Credit	Credit line or overdraft permitted during business hours and covered by close of business. Lines are often uncommitted and provided without interest charges.	No, client activity does not directly impact the amount of intraday credit extended to a bank	Yes, counterparties will often adjust intraday credit extensions to reflect business activity from other areas of the bank (e.g., OTC trading)	Some intraday credit facilities are disclosed and well known to a bank (e.g., FRB net debit cap). Others are not disclosed but can often be inferred from historical data

Liquid Assets	Cash, money market deposits, and short-term government debt (e.g., T-Bills) which can be quickly converted to cash	Yes, client may be sources of liquidity in converting liquid assets to cash (e.g., repo transaction)	Yes, bank trading and investment portfolio activity can impact the amount of liquid assets available.	Liquid assets held in the investment portfolio and in other money market investments tend to have low volatility and as a result are predictable
Overnight Borrowings	Fed Funds, Eurodollar borrowing, overnight deposits	Yes, clients may be direct sources of liquidity for overnight borrowing (e.g., overnight deposit)	No, other Bank lines of business do not regularly supply overnight funding	Client supply of overnight borrowing tends to be fairly predictable, but with moderate volatility
Other Term Funding	Other term deposits, repos from FHLB, money market funds, etc.	Yes, clients may be direct sources of liquidity for term funding	No, other Bank lines of business do not regularly supply term funding	Client supply of term funding tends to be fairly predictable, with low volatility

RISK MANAGEMENT, MEASUREMENT AND MONITORING TOOLS FOR FINANCIAL INSTITUTIONS

This section provides an overview of the leading practices for managing intraday liquidity risk at large banks.

Governance of Intraday LRM

All risk management frameworks start with a governance structure that defines the roles and responsibilities of various bank employees and committees in overseeing risk-related activities. The following list provides characteristics of an effective governance structure for overseeing intraday liquidity risk:

> **Active risk management.** In many institutions, intraday liquidity risk is accepted as a cost of doing business and is not as actively managed with the same level of rigor as other types of enterprise risk or even other liquidity risks. The leading banks with large volumes of PCS activities recognize the criticality of understanding and working to reduce their intraday liquidity risks. These institutions classify settlement and systemic risks as components of their risk taxonomy, and critically, incorporate them into the firm's risk appetite framework.
>
> **Integration with risk governance.** Oversight of intraday liquidity risk management is integrated into the bank's overall risk oversight structure. This ensures that:
>
> - The intraday liquidity risk management framework follows the industry's three lines of defense model, with particular emphasis on expertise in the second line of defense to coordinate across the institution.
> - Roles and responsibilities for all aspects of intraday liquidity risk management in all lines of defense are clearly defined.
>   - Treasury is the first line of defense, actively managing the intraday and end-of-day funding positions of the bank as well as the risk management programs related to funding activities.
>   - Corporate Risk Management is the second line of defense, responsible for overseeing funding-related policy and procedures: advising in the development of risk management programs, monitoring the ongoing risk-taking activities across all of a bank's funding desks, aggregating reporting across the bank, and providing an independent view of the effectiveness

of the bank's overall intraday liquidity risk management programs.

■ Internal Audit is the third line of defense, responsible for independently assessing the bank's adherence to its intraday risk policies and procedures.

■ Key decisions are made and reviewed by the appropriate level of management.

■ Oversight committees have the appropriate representation from the critical areas (e.g., treasury, operations, IT, lines of business).

Risk assessment. At leading institutions, intraday liquidity risk is incorporated into the risk taxonomy and is a component of risk self-assessments. Through this analysis, settlement risks related to existing and potential new products and operational processes are identified, measured, and evaluated. The line of business and risk management review the effectiveness of controls in mitigating settlement risk.

Risk measurement and monitoring. There are two perspectives from which leading institutions monitor their intraday liquidity risk: (1) the amount of intraday credit the institution is extending to clients, and (2) the amount of intraday credit the institution utilizes. For the first perspective, systemically important financial institutions (SIFIs) with large transaction banking and/or capital markets businesses have made significant investments in recent years to upgrade their ability to compile and monitor their clients' real-time cash positions. This has historically been a significant challenge due to the wide array of client activities that can impact cash accounts and the batch-orientation of DDA and other feeder systems. Banks with these capabilities are well positioned to pass on the intraday overdraft charges they receive from central banks onto clients, if the industry moves in that direction.

The second measurement perspective should provide a holistic and comprehensive view of all intraday credit used by an institution. This is more challenging for several reasons:

■ **Availability of data for its cash accounts.** While many FMUs can provide useful statistics on intraday credit usage, not all of them can provide real-time account position data, especially in a way that can be captured and stored. Data on intraday credit usage from correspondent banks is also spotty.

■ **Data aggregation.** Consolidating data into a single repository that enables comprehensive analysis and monitoring poses significant institutional challenges. Few banks have made the investments required in technology infrastructure to provide full, real-time position monitoring across all of their PCS activities, in all markets, and in all of their lines of business and subsidiaries.

Measurement of Intraday Liquidity

This subsection describes commonly used measures that are useful for under-standing and tracking bank intraday liquidity risk. Many of these items were highlighted in the BCBS' "Monitoring Tools for Intraday Liquidity Manage-ment."[7] The first set of measures is helpful for understanding the profile of the institution's intraday flows. The second set of measures provides ratios for monitoring risk levels. Institutions may wish to set risk limits/thresholds, and perform ongoing monitoring against these measures.

Measures for Understanding Intraday Flows

Total payments. A bank and its intraday risk management teams should maintain statistics concerning the amount of payments it makes on all electronic payments systems in which it participates. For every payment, a bank would store in a data warehouse the critical information needed for analysis, such as payment amount, time received or originated, times for each processing step in the payment workflow, routing information, payer and payee, payment system used, any suspensions of the payment, and so on. Compiling this information would allow a risk manager to summarize the data for a variety of purposes, including, for example, the following:

- Total payments sent and received for non-financial institution clients
- Total payments sent and received for financial institution clients
- Total payments sent and received for bank activity
- Net position in the settlement account at any time of day in aggregate
- Net position in the settlement account at any time of day, filtered by payment type
- Trend in payments volumes over time, for correlation analysis

Other cash transactions. A bank should also track its intraday and end-of-day settlement positions at all financial market utilities in which it participates. The bank should try to maximize the amount of transaction-level detail captured and stored for further analysis. Securities settlements networks (SSN), particularly those utilizing a

---

[7]BCBS. "Monitoring Tools for Intraday Liquidity Management." April 2013. http://www.bis.org/publ/bcbs248.pdf.

central counterparty (CCP) model, often manage their intraday and overnight risk exposures through collateralization (discussed in more detail in the next section). A bank participating in an SSN should strive to capture snapshots of its account and collateral positions throughout the trading day. For example, the Federal Reserve uses one minute intervals for tracking collateral positions.

Settlement positions. If complete data to reconstruct account positions at any time of day is not available, at a minimum a bank should maintain data on its settlement positions with all its FMUs. These critical, deadline specific payments, often with large transaction amounts, are critical to managing intraday liquidity and systemic risk. A bank should monitor patterns in settlement positions and correlate them with external market factors to improve its ability to predict upcoming liquidity requirements earlier in the day.

Time sensitive obligations. Similar to settlement positions, these transactions require completion at a specific time during the day. Examples include transactions concerning market activities (such as the return of borrowings), margin payments, and other payments critical to a bank's business or reputation (e.g., client closing on a corporate acquisition). Failure to settle certain time sensitive obligations could result in a financial penalty or other negative consequences. A bank should monitor the volume and settlement patterns of these time specific obligations by recording the amounts and deadline times.

Total intraday credit lines to clients and counterparties. A bank risk manager looking after the bank's own intraday liquidity risk needs to understand the potential and actual amounts of intraday credit the bank is extending to clients and counterparties. In some cases, these intraday credit lines could be committed and disclosed to the client, but most are uncommitted and undisclosed. In addition to the credit lines, the bank should have data regarding average and peak usage, and the ability to model activity at the client and portfolio levels.

Total bank intraday credit lines available and usage. As demonstrated through the requirements for preparing resolution plans, regulators increasingly expect financial institutions to understand and manage the amount of systemic risk they pose to the overall financial system (in addition to the risk posed to taxpayers and industry-funded insurance plans). A key component of that analysis is the amount of intraday credit that a bank relies on in business-as-usual conditions and the maximum amount of intraday borrowing it can draw down. This data captures the amount of committed and uncommitted intraday credit (and usage thereof) the bank has at its disposal, ideally across all of its cash and settlement accounts.

Measures for Quantifying and Monitoring Risk Levels

Daily maximum intraday liquidity usage. This is a measure of the bank's usage of an intraday credit extension. While many cash accounts can facilitate real-time reporting, this calculation does not require real-time monitoring of an account (provided the bank has the ability to recreate all of a day's positions *ex-post*) to capture all of the negative positions. The measure is the ratio of the day's largest net negative balance relative to the size of the committed or uncommitted credit line. Typically, the peak and average of this metric is tracked over a period of time (e.g., monthly).

At a minimum, this measure should be tracked for every cash account held at the central bank, FMUs, and correspondent banks. Ideally, a bank should also monitor its consolidated position across all accounts between which liquidity can be readily transferred intraday without restrictions in order to get a true picture of its intraday liquidity usage. This is logically done for accounts denominated in the same currency and connected to a common payment system but can be done for multiple currencies and in different jurisdictions if cash and collateral can be freely transferred between the jurisdictions intraday.

Intraday credit relative to tier 1 capital. This measure is a broad representation of the intraday settlement risk posed by a bank. The measure should be tracked for total intraday credit and *unsecured* intraday credit, available and used, under the theory that posting high-quality collateral mitigates intraday settlement risk. Available, unsecured intraday credit relative to an institution's tier 1 capital is a rough measure of the inadvertent systemic risk that the institution poses to the financial system. Such measures, when viewed as a time series, as well as horizontally in comparisons to other institutions, provide bank risk managers with an understanding of the relative systemic risk of their business model as well as changes in their risk profile over time.

Client intraday credit usage. This measure is derived by comparing a client's peak daily intraday overdraft to the established (committed or uncommitted) credit line. Tracking aggregate intraday credit exposures provides a bank with an indicator of required liquidity needed to support its clients' business activities. Monitoring the averages, volatility, and correlation of these measures to other money market indicators provides useful insights for understanding how client activity impacts the bank's ability to manage its own intraday liquidity.

Tracking client usage of intraday credit lines at the individual client level enables risk managers to pinpoint clients that run frequent overdrafts and determine if these clients need to change their practices or if the bank needs to increase its charges for this credit extension. Monitoring these measures over time can provide indicators of the success of any initiatives undertaken to modify client behavior in order to reduce reliance on intraday credit. Finally, bank risk managers can use this data to inform policies regarding the provision and size of intraday credit lines relative to industry cohorts and client risk levels.

Payment throughput. These measures track the percentage of outgoing payment activity relative to time of day. For banks that are direct participants in FMUs, it is useful to actively measure and monitor the flow of outgoing payment transactions relative to total payments or time markers for several reasons: (1) to track its volume patterns and help ensure that all of the day's payments are processed in time; (2) in some cases, to meet FMU requirements for submitting a target percentage of payments by a deadline; and (3) to help the bank identify and monitor its peak periods over time and the correlation of this activity with its intraday liquidity on hand and intraday credit usage.

In addition, a bank can track its peak intraday credit usage relative to total volumes with an FMU to provide an indicator of the efficiency of the FMU's usage of daylight credit. FMUs employ different system rules and operating models resulting in variations in how efficiently they use intraday liquidity. Understanding these differences can enable a bank to redirect payment flows as a tool to manage intraday liquidity needs, assuming it has the requisite operational capabilities.

Role of Stress Testing

The previous indicators are important in understanding and monitoring a bank's need for and use of intraday credit under business-as-usual conditions. However, intraday liquidity requirements and usage patterns can change substantially during periods of market stress. As a result, a bank that regularly relies on intraday credit should have the ability to model the impact of different events on its requirements and the availability of intraday liquidity (i.e., modeling the impact of different scenarios on the indicators mentioned). While the banking industry has historically developed effective stress tests of overall liquidity management that have been instrumental in developing liquidity contingency plans, the industry as a whole needs to extend these capabilities to intraday position modeling. Regulators may push the industry to develop these capabilities as the focus on intraday liquidity risk increases over time.

The process of stress testing of intraday liquidity risk management can yield multiple benefits for a bank. As is typical in stress testing exercises, the benefits are not just the empirical results but, more importantly, the interactions and discussions, brainstorming, and other critical thinking that senior management engages in when working through the scenarios. Bringing together the right set of people with subject matter expertise in liquidity, risk management, client management, correspondent banking, operations, and technology to think through the scenarios can be beneficial in yielding new insights and ideas.

Understanding how a proposed stress event might impact a bank's positions and the behavior of other market participants helps it to identify key vulnerabilities and their sensitivity to external factors. Developing and modeling potential responses to a stress event helps in formulating contingency plans and playbooks for how a bank might respond to an event. Finally, developing the technology infrastructure to support robust modeling provides the institution with an extremely useful capability for working through an actual crisis. This implies the need for a data aggregation capability (either a data warehouse or tools that can assimilate and transform data "on the fly") with data updated frequently, ideally daily. In addition, the bank would need tools that enable it to pull historical data, modify the data with different sets of assumptions, and simulate a processing day under those assumptions.

Banks should continuously build and expand the types of scenarios they can model in stress testing. In its April 2013 guidance, the BCBS suggests that a bank have at least the following four scenarios:[8]

- **Own financial stress.** A bank suffers, or is perceived to be suffering from, a stress event.
- **Counterparty stress.** A major financial institution counterparty suffers an intraday stress event which prevents it from making payments.
- **Customer stress.** The customer bank of a correspondent bank suffers a stress event.
- **Market-wide credit or liquidity stress.**

These four items can be thought of as stress categories as within each one of these, a bank could develop multiple scenarios with different characteristics. For example, in the "own financial stress" category, there could be different scenarios for a deteriorating credit portfolio and an idiosyncratic operational risk event that results in a large loss. Counterparty stress could involve a trading partner, an FMU, or a correspondent bank through

---

[8] BCBS. "Monitoring Tools for Intraday Liquidity Management." April 2013. http://www.bis.org/publ/bcbs248.pdf.

which the bank routes payment and/or securities transactions. Finally, a market-wide category could, for instance, have scenarios for extremely tight money market conditions, multiple bank failures, widespread decrease in the market value of securities held as collateral, a very large corporate action, or operational failures.

BCBS guidance also encourages banks to develop reverse stress testing capabilities, and testing other scenarios such as the impact of natural disasters, currency crises, and so on.

RISK MANAGEMENT, MEASUREMENT, MONITORING TOOLS FOR FMUS

This subsection provides a high level overview of risk management practices at FMUs. FMUs comprise payments systems, securities settlement networks, exchanges, and central securities depositories. There are a number of characteristics that render each entity unique, including: clearing and settlement services provided, ownership structure, membership and operating rules, degree and nature of central bank involvement and support, and risk management practices. As a result of this diversity, a comprehensive discussion of FMU risk management practices is beyond the scope of this book. However, a discussion of intraday liquidity would be incomplete without a discussion of FMUs due to their importance in intraday funds management. This subsection will provide a brief overview of FMU risk management, and focus on selective risk practices observed in the industry that are relevant to the discussion of intraday liquidity risk.

Overview of FMU Risk Management

FMUs have long focused on how they would handle the failure of one of their participants to complete its settlement obligations. FMUs have evolved to have several lines of defense in managing participant risk.

The first line of defense is membership criteria. FMUs often have size and creditworthiness criteria that constrain the profiles of direct members. In addition, some FMUs permit indirect members which do not participate in the interbank payment system itself, but rely on direct or "corresponding" members to send their payments to the clearing system. In those cases, the direct members are underwriting the risk of the indirect participants.

While this approach allows FMUs to more easily apply credit risk analysis to their counterparties, membership "tiering" potentially introduces intraday settlement risks to the system. This risk is particularly acute because of exposures between first- and second-tier banks and the concentration of all payment activity at a smaller number of settlement banks. The particular risks of tiering are: (1) the failure of a direct member affecting the indirect members that are relying on it to handle their payments; (2) other members may be hesitant to send payments to the member clearing bank of a large, failing institution; and (3) increased operational interdependence.

Recognizing these concerns, some FMUs have tried to reduce their tiering. In 2010, the Bank of England made the reduction of tiering in the Clearing House Automated Payment System (CHAPS) one of its key risk reduction objectives. At the time, CHAPS had only eighteen banks as direct members of the payment system. By comparison, Target2 had 866 direct members, Fedwire had more than 7,000 direct members, and direct membership of the Hong Kong interbank payment system is compulsory for all licensed banks in the territory. Since then, CHAPS has taken steps to encourage more members to join as direct members by waiving new member fees and replacing its proprietary messaging system with Swift, as most banks already have a Swift connection.

Monitoring the risks of their participants is the second line of defense used by most FMUs. This can take several forms, depending on the FMU and the risk level. Most FMUs have periodic (annually or quarterly) reviews of their participants' financial statements to ensure maintenance of minimum capital levels and other financial guidelines that are stipulated in the membership rules. Some FMUs require submission of monthly financial statements for the direct member legal entity (e.g., the broker-dealer sub of a large bank).

In addition to the financial conditions of the participants, FMUs also monitor their participants' settlement positions and margin collateral. Securities settlement networks have monitoring programs that, during their overnight cycle (some are more frequently), recalculate the risk potential and the collateral values of each participant's account to ensure the bank has sufficient margin posted.

When an FMU is concerned about the default risk of one of its members, there are several risk mitigation actions it may consider to reduce intraday settlement risk. For example:

- Securities settlement networks that run risk margining may decide to run cycles several times per day for higher risk participants. This means the FMU may make an intraday margin call, requiring additional collateral from the participant pursuant to changes in its risk and collateral positions.
- A payment system may reduce a member's net debit cap (which is essentially an intraday credit line), or require a participant to pre-fund its account and not permit it to run intraday overdrafts.

- An FMU may require a participant to post additional collateral, or post a letter of credit or performance bond from a third party institution to backstop its credit risk.

The third line of defense for many FMUs is a mechanism to facilitate settlement in the event of a participant failure. This is accomplished by mutualizing the default risk, thereby dispersing credit risk and potential losses across a broad number of entities. FMUs commonly build risk mutualization provisions into their operating rules to ensure than any realized losses do not result in an interruption of service. The operating rules are intended to establish a process by which a failed participant's positions can be quickly covered and settled so that the FMU can re-open for normal activity.

Risk mutualization can take several forms. Many FMUs (particularly those employing a CCP model) utilize a "guarantee" fund (also commonly referred to as a default or settlement fund). Guarantee funds are prefunded pools of cash and highly liquid assets reserved for the potential failure of one or more participants. This typically requires participants to contribute cash to an asset pool, with the amounts based on their volumes or risk levels. If a participant fails with a debit that cannot be fully covered by its margin collateral, then the FMU would draw on the guarantee fund to settle the failed participant's positions and then allocate the losses back to the remaining participants. Each participant would then need to replenish its contribution to the guarantee in order to resume a normal level of trading the next day.

Similarly, the involvement of a central bank in underwriting PCS activities could be considered risk mutualization due to the central bank's ability to pass on losses to governments and ultimately taxpayers. This model is frequently observed with LVPSs that are operated by the central bank. In order to achieve immediate finality of payment (meaning the payment is final when the amount is credited to the participant's account), many central banks underwrite all of the participant credit risk on their national LVPS. This is the model used by the Federal Reserve for Fedwire.

FMU Tools to Manage Intraday Settlement Risk

As mentioned above, the second line of defense for an FMU is monitoring the risk exposures of its participants. For its highest risk exposures, an FMU typically monitors the participant's settlement requirements on a real-time, intraday basis. FMUs use several tools to monitor and manage these intraday exposures and to assist their participants with their own intraday liquidity risk management.

Net debit caps. Many FMUs utilize a net debit cap to limit their risk exposure to a single participant. A net debit cap constrains the size of a negative position in a cash account, typically suspending further transactions until additional liquidity is added to the account. Net debit caps are standard at large value payment systems, and used at other types of FMUs as well. In managing a deteriorating credit risk situation, an FMU may reduce or even eliminate a participant's net debit cap, requiring the participant to provide more liquidity to settle its positions.

Collateral. Cash or securities collateral is a key component for FMU risk management. As with net debit caps, in a deteriorating credit situation, an FMU may begin to monitor a participant's risk position and its initial and variation margin collateral values in real-time to ensure sufficient coverage. Depending on a number of factors, the FMU may require a participant to adjust its collateral position by modifying the acceptable composition of collateral, advance rates on certain securities, and concentration limits.

Liquidity savings mechanism. FMUs have to balance their risk management considerations with their business objectives of minimizing cost and maximizing value to participants. Many FMUs have developed innovative ways to clear and settle transactions that reduce the overall operating liquidity required by the system (i.e., liquidity savings mechanism). These tactics essentially increase transaction throughput for a given amount of liquidity. This achieves both objectives by reducing the size of settlement positions (and settlement risk) and minimizing the cost of idle liquidity for a participant. Examples of liquidity savings mechanisms include transaction netting (bilateral and multilateral), net credit caps (which may suspend transactions to a participant until they provide more outgoing liquidity), transaction throughput requirements (e.g., requiring a certain percentage of outgoing transactions to be submitted by a mid-day deadline), transaction prioritization capabilities, and intra-system lending (e.g., securities lending).

Settlement windows. Some FMUs have established settlement deadlines in a way that reduces intraday liquidity risk. Instead of having one consolidated settlement position, typically at end of day, some FMUs have staggered multiple settlement windows throughout the day. This can be achieved by having individual settlement times for specific asset classes or currencies.

Contingent liquidity. FMUs maintain backup credit lines from both commercial banks and central banks to be able to provide liquidity in a crisis situation. These lines are not used under business-as-usual conditions and are only maintained for emergencies.

CONCLUSION

While initial management efforts concerning intraday liquidity risk date back to the 1980s, the 2007-08 financial crisis highlighted a number of deficiencies in industry practices and led to more rigorous research efforts and industry focus on this area. It is fair to say that, across the financial services industry, understanding intraday liquidity risk and developing tools to manage it remain works in progress. While some banks and FMUs exhibit leading-edge capabilities, in general, industry participants need to make significant investments to enhance their risk management frameworks, systems, and data management to truly understand their intraday liquidity risk profile and be able to manage that risk during periods of market stress. With the implementation of Basel III, regulators are increasingly focused on liquidity risk in general and have signaled their intent to ensure that banks include intraday liquidity risk in their liquidity risk programs. As a result, this will be an exciting area of banking to watch over the next few years.

Glossary

This section provides definitions for key terms that are frequently used in discussions of intraday liquidity risk management.

D

Daylight Overdraft (DOD):

Daylight overdraft, also referred to as intraday overdraft (IOD), refers to a cash account with a negative cash position during the business day. This results when the cumulative amount of debit transactions posted to the account exceeds the sum of the opening balance plus posted credit transactions

F

Financial Market Utility

An organization whose purpose is to process and settle payments and securities transactions; these entities are also referred to as Financial Market Infrastructure (FMI) or Value Transfer Networks (VTNs). This includes:

- Wholesale payments systems, such as wire transfer networks, also referred to as Large Value Payment Systems (LVPSs)

- Retail payment systems, typically low value transfer networks settling large numbers of transactions such as automated clearinghouses and credit card networks

- Trade execution facilities, such as exchanges
- Securities settlement networks (SSNs), including clearing and settlement networks
- Central securities depositories (CSDs) that hold book-entry issued assets

Some FMUs are referred to as central counterparties (CCP). In this model, which is used frequently for securities settlements, an FMU inserts itself as a legal intermediary in the transaction, centralizing the counterparty credit exposure of settling transactions in a single entity. CCPs net and clear exchange and OTC-based trading securities transactions, often handing off to a CSD for final settlement.

I

Intraday Liquidity

Cash funding which can be accessed at any point during the business day to enable banks to continue processing transactions; this can include the interbank funds markets, wholesale money markets, and intraday credit lines provided by central banks or FMUs.

Intraday Liquidity Risk

The risk that a bank or FMU is unable to meet a payment or settlement obligation at the expected time due to inadequate liquid funds (cash); also known as settlement risk

N

Net Debit Cap

A risk management tool utilized by providers of intraday liquidity to limit their risk exposure; a debit cap constrains the size of a negative position in a cash account, typically suspending further transactions until additional liquidity is added to the account.

Netting/Net Settlement

The process of offsetting obligations between two or more banks, which reduces the size of final settlements and intraday liquidity risk; "bilateral" netting occurs between two banks; "multilateral" netting occurs on a payments or securities settlement system.

Nostro Account

A cash account maintained by a bank outside of its home market at another correspondent bank to support payments and/or securities transactions in that market.

P

Payment Finality

Refers to the point at which the value (payment) received by a beneficiary becomes final and cannot be reversed for any reason. This is the point at which the beneficiary has full, irrevocable ownership of the value transferred.

Payments, Clearing, and Settlement Services (PCSs)

PCS is used to describe a broad range of services that support funds transfers, securities transfers, foreign exchange transactions, trade execution, and derivative transactions.

S

Systemically Important Financial Institutions (SIFIs)

Financial institutions of significant size that provide market-critical services are generally defined as systemically important. In general, the label implies that the failure of a SIFI has the potential to spread loss and market distress to other institutions by nature of the SIFI's size and interconnectedness.

Systemic Risk

The risk of simultaneous failure of multiple participants in a financial system or market; systemic risk generally refers to a "contagion effect" in which the failure of a single entity has a cascading effect, causing multiple subsequent failures because of the amounts owed by the first failed entity to other participants. Exposures to the failed entity can be either deliberate credit extensions made in the ordinary course of business (such as loans, trading activity, balances related to correspondent banking) or inadvertent or unforeseen credit exposures.

Inadvertent exposures could arise, for example, as a result of the allocation to a solvent bank of credit losses pursuant to the loss sharing arrangement of an FMU. In fact, one could argue that all intraday settlement risk exposures are inadvertent in the sense that they are viewed as a cost of doing business and not a risk exposure for which a bank is being directly compensated. One of the objectives of managing intraday liquidity risk is to minimize or eliminate inadvertent credit exposures.

T

Time Critical Payment

A payment obligation that is due at a specific time during the day such as a clearinghouse settlement deadline or a client payment required to close on a financial transaction (e.g., a mortgage loan or an acquisition of a company).

CHAPTER 5

The Convergence of Collateral and Liquidity

Thomas Ciulla, Bala Annadorai, and Gaurav Joshi[1]

A WORD ON COLLATERAL AND COLLATERAL MANAGEMENT

Broadly speaking, there are three uses of collateral: meeting margin calls, funding on a secured basis (using repo, securities lending, and central bank programs), and complying with regulatory liquidity ratios. When meeting margin calls, collateral, whether in the form of cash or securities, is a counterparty credit risk mitigant. Specifically, collateral can be particularly useful in the event of counterparty default. When a transaction is forward settling or has payment obligations that occur over time, collateral helps to ensure the security of each party. A classic, simple example is the collateralization of a bilateral interest rate swap. Two parties enter into an agreement for a five-year swap. One party will make quarterly fixed payments based on a certain rate (perhaps LIBOR) while the other party will make floating payments on the same schedule. The trade is valued fairly at the market at initial execution, and as rates move through the life of the swap, payments vary with one party being in the money while the other is not. This can change over the life of the swap, especially with much longer-dated contracts. Each party assumes that these payments will be made and has likely entered into other obligations with still other counterparties, assuming they will receive regular payments, as per the terms of the swap.

But what if one of the parties defaults before the expiration of the contract? What if interest rates swing against one of the parties (leaving it out of the money) and it defaults on the obligation or simply decides to abandon a losing deal? Or, what if the counterparties have several swaps between them

---

[1]Thomas Ciulla is a principal in PwC's New York office; Bala Annadorai is a director in PwC's New York office; and Gaurav Joshi is a manager in PwC's New York office.

and one of the parties decides to accept payment on those in the money while defaulting on those that are not (e.g., cherry picking)? If that were to happen, then the in-the-money counterparty is left exposed without payments that were expected. If that counterparty maintained a matched-booked, its trading book would no longer be in balance and it would incur risk (and perhaps default). In the extreme, under conditions of acute market volatility and stress, it can cause contagion, where parties default to one another in a chain reaction.

If the trade referenced in the example was collateralized, the impact of default would be reduced and perhaps even eliminated. As the value of the trade shifted after execution (T+1), each party to the trade would perform a mark-to-market calculation (preferably daily). The out-of-the-money counterparty would transfer or pledge collateral to the in-the-money counterparty (i.e., the secured party) for the change in value since execution. The secured party would hold this collateral and in the event of default, would liquidate that collateral, and, if desired, replace the trade (leaving aside the concept of independent amount, to assist with trade replacement costs). The concept of central clearing, which is a cornerstone of new global legislation, largely works in a similar fashion; it is predicated on proper collateralization to guard against default and allows for orderly trade/collateral liquidation and replacement (portability). Collateralization does not replace best-practice risk management nor should it be used to offset the risk of trading with high-risk counterparties. Correspondingly, counterparty due diligence (even in a cleared environment when considering clearing brokers and central counterparties) is always the best and first step in determining with whom to trade.

Transacting with collateral means that it should be managed, which is by no means a passive endeavor. While a detailed explanation of the tenets and methods of collateral management are outside the purview of this chapter, it is possible to lose money even when a trade is collateralized. Strictly from a risk perspective, and ignoring the liquidity management aspects of the problem, managing collateral entails identifying, assessing, and mitigating these risks. Participants who choose to exchange collateral should have proper documentation. These documents should be negotiated, operationalized, and legally enforceable in multiple jurisdictions, which may have differing bankruptcy codes. Many collateralized counterparties have become general unsecured creditors of a defaulting counterparty's estate because the documentation was not adequate to support the collateral claim, or collateral was domiciled in a remote location that did not recognize swap trades as different from other types of obligations (e.g., safe harbor provisions).

Furthermore, there are a host of operational processes that should be considered to support collateralization. This includes management and storage of the aforementioned documents, which can be modified and require renegotiation. Counterparties are likely to perform valuations of both trades (some of which are difficult to value) as well as the underlying collateral (also not always liquid and price transparent). Ideally, counterparties in over-the-counter (OTC) trades should value their positions and collateral daily while central counterparties should perform these tasks on an intraday basis. In addition to operational risk, participants who exchange collateral incur settlement risk. As many organizations use multiple custodians in various locations, the risks and tasks of ensuring settlement are significant. Invariably, with bilateral swap trades, participants will disagree on margin calls. These differences may arise due to valuation disagreements, trade timing, or for predatory reasons. Reconciling disputes and determining, as well as settling, collateral quickly is a difficult and time-consuming process (further compounded by the issue that one of the parties is exposed during the dispute period).

When parties choose to exchange collateral, they will likely develop a framework to manage the collateral with the dual purpose of minimizing risk and maximizing liquidity. In meeting these two objectives there are many issues to consider when exchanging collateral, particularly with respect to optimizing collateral that is held to maximize liquidity and/or to satisfy regulatory requirements. Collateral optimization is discussed in detail later in this chapter.

CAPITAL MARKETS BEFORE 2008

There was a time when forward settling financial transactions were often left uncollateralized. Funding was plentiful and inexpensive. Regulation canted toward the unobtrusive, bank-friendly capitalization levels prevailed, and market participants traded freely, ultimately creating wealth. In this time, large banks and broker-dealers built massive operations to support ever-greater volumes and product ranges. These operations were often conducted in silos, focusing on a specific asset type and usually had little interaction with other internal and related functions. These concerns were paid little attention because revenues were great and inefficiencies could be readily absorbed. The clients of large banks were seemingly well served and there was abundant liquidity across a vast array of products. Moreover, banks were willing to develop innovative, custom products designed to fill any need, no matter how esoteric. Many of these trades were unsecured (not required to be secured with collateral), generating even greater volume and wealth. When collateral was required, the capital and liquidity necessary to finance this collateral were of greater concern than risk mitigation. Margin calls were generally not required on a daily basis and often only initiated after exposures became large. When forced to post, highly rated and/or regulated participants could opt to hold pledged collateral remotely from the secured party. When collateral was physically exchanged it was often reused for other obligations, greatly increasing its efficiency and velocity as well as creating additional layers of operational and logistical complexity.

During this time, there were other participants who played vital roles in facilitating financial market transactions. Custody banks helped settle and safeguard assets and facilitated securities lending; but their potential was still unrealized, as they would soon come to assume a much greater role. Exchanges, often with proprietary trade clearing arms, provided trade liquidity and guaranteed performance, but many trades were still executed OTC and brokered by phone. Market utilities conducted mundane but critical functions such as trade confirmation, yet many trades were still confirmed manually, well after the time of execution, or worse, not confirmed at all. This was true of collateral transfers, which were often risky free-delivers, and very often left unconfirmed. True, this introduced both inefficiency and risk; but these were tolerated, as unwanted events were infrequent and, more importantly, contained.

Inefficiency was costly, irrespective of revenue, and banks underestimated the risk to which they were exposed. At times, a severe disruption would warn the market that change could perhaps be beneficial. When this happened, sometimes with the default of a counterparty deeply entwined in the market fabric, the industry would respond. Often times nudged by subsequent regulation, markets and processes evolved. Risks, such as those presented by counterparty default, were addressed through mechanisms such as netting, robust trade documentation, and greater collateralization. With risk management foundations established, there was a greater focus on obtaining collateral, which, while still relatively ubiquitous and inexpensive, eventually would catalyze the movement toward greater operational efficiency in the pursuit of improved liquidity.

What was a natural progression toward better risk management and operational efficiency was greatly influenced, and ultimately accelerated, by the global financial events that occurred during 2007–08. Financial stalwarts that were previously thought to be impervious to market disruption approached and/or proceeded into default. Market interconnectedness was exposed as other organizations defaulted, unable to secure funding lines. Many who did not default assumed a safety crouch and withdrew from financial markets, stanching liquidity and exacerbating the crisis. Critically, previously free-flowing wholesale funding markets faltered. The insidious pro-cyclical nature of credit-triggered margin calls, coupled with a glutted collateral liquidation market and the rapid downgrade of many different types of collateral assets, put global capital markets at the mercy of central banks, which ultimately interceded to prevent market collapse.

CAPITAL MARKETS POST-2008

The events of 2007–08 ushered improved, if not new, methods of risk and liquidity management. A deluge of global regulation that followed the crisis ensured that wholesale financial markets would function much differently, with regulators blatantly stating their intent to make markets transparent, resilient, and ultimately less reliant on central bank (i.e., public) funding in times of stress. The practice of collateral management, which touches both credit and liquidity risks simultaneously, transformed with a greater focus being applied to the latter. Correspondingly, the business case for embarking on collateral management transformation efforts strengthened. Banks, for example, previously explored enterprise collateral management solutions due to their inherent operational efficiency benefits. These benefits were achieved by breaking regional product silos and replacing them with unified target operating models that transcended region and collateralized trading products, such as OTC swaps, derivatives, repurchase transactions, and securities lending. These new target-operating models were supported with a common technology platform, decommissioning best-of-breed point solutions. With this approach, banks were not only able to achieve greater efficiency through reduced systems, greater automation, and redeployed staff, but were also better able to understand holistic counterparty risk. At the same time, buy-side participants moved from manual, spreadsheet solutions, to vendor packages and/or outsourced solutions (often provided by custody banks).

Now, over a half-decade removed from the latest financial crisis, as market participants struggle to cope with the weight of new global regulation, collateral management solutions are explored not only in pursuit of efficiency but also liquidity. The Dodd-Frank Act, European Market Infrastructure Regulation (EMIR), and Basel III intend to manage risk, while also introducing greater pre- and post-trade transparency (the capital demands of Solvency II for the insurance industry may also be considered). The by-product, in part, is that market participation will become more expensive and operationally complex. As a result, market participants will no longer be able to ignore the inextricable link between collateral, trade clearing, and liquidity. The risk mutualization and netting benefits manifest with trade clearing, and the risk mitigation benefits inherent in increased capital buffers, will be realized only through a significant application of collateral, in addition to costly enhancements to operating models, systems, and trade documentation.

Another factor joining collateral and liquidity is that collateral presents significant liquidity risk. This risk can be realized when internal future exposure models move against the organization. When this occurs, perhaps in times of market volatility, very large collateral demands can arise quickly and unexpectedly. Retail and commercial banks, much larger in absolute size than their capital markets counterparties, experience cash flows that are generally much more predictable and immune to the effects of market volatility. As such, capital markets liquidity managers are likely to be more concerned about unexpected large collateral calls than other liquidity risks. When liquidity drains occur, treasury (liquidity) managers will endeavor to source new cash from all available sources. This is most often performed in repurchase transaction (repo) markets where collateral will be pledged against the cash borrowed. When this occurs, the ability to identify and mobilize eligible collateral quickly and effectively will be the key to survival. To ensure that high-quality assets are available in an emergency, Basel III liquidity regulations require banks to hold a buffer of high-quality liquid assets sufficient to cover thirty days of net cash outflow under stressed conditions. There is a further convergence of collateral and liquidity when coupled with additional capital requirements.

The convergence is driven by the demands of increased margin calls (ever more frequently real-time, intraday), organizational funding requirements (e.g., repo trading), and regulatory capital mandates (e.g., the liquidity asset buffer under Basel III). Innovative collateral management solutions will focus on how to identify and utilize collateral in the pursuit of providing liquidity while also realizing the traditional goals of operational efficiency and counterparty default risk mitigation. In short, there is a new industry perspective that lies beyond the frontier that is enterprise collateral management. Convergence is the *basso continuo* of this new perspective. Convergence of collateral and liquidity is driving tactical and strategic efforts that allow continued, profitable participation in a highly collateralized, capital constrained environment. Convergence of functions, technology, and collateral pools are each part of the scheme. Convergence affects participants that are loosely termed sell- or buy-side as well as the collateral service providers and market utilities that provide critical infrastructure. The new reality dictates that market utilities will assume greater prominence. Custody banks and depositories will be well positioned to provide more extensive solutions, such as middle-office outsourcing, liquidity services, and collateral mobilization while at the same time, shadow banking activities will be assumed by nontraditional market participants who are not yet saddled with banking capital regulations. Like blacksmithing at the advent of the automobile, it is irrelevant how, or how well, the function is performed today because it is changing in fundamental ways.

THE CASE FOR ACTION

Collateral management is moving beyond the back office, migrating toward and integrating with the front office and treasury functions since the costs of funding enterprise obligations (e.g., margin calls, maintaining proper regulatory capital) are best performed holistically and will affect how trade profitability is measured. The legal and credit functions, historically involved with the collateral management process, are ever more closely aligned. This functional convergence is primarily driven by two types of regulation that, when combined, exert increased pressure on the collateral and liquidity process. First, margin requirements for both cleared and OTC swap portfolios will likely result in market participants requiring and posting greater quantities of high-grade collateral. Second, regulations that set minimum capital requirements will likely force directly affected market participants to hold greater quantities of the same high-grade collateral. The costs of these regulations will likely be passed to users of bank financial products; therefore, no participant is immune to the cost of regulation.

Regulation exacerbates the situation further by providing market participants with an opportunity to safeguard pledged collateral by either allowing or requiring collateral to be segregated, thus preventing re-hypothecation, limiting collateral velocity, and shortening collateral chains. Further still, all collateral is not created equally. Specifically, some transactions can only be collateralized with highly rated liquid assets, such as sovereign debt and cash, while other obligations can be satisfied with lower grade collateral—thus, prompting the desire for collateral optimization as discussed later in this chapter.

Finally, there are rafts of other related regulations (or pending regulations) that will likely result in the need for more collateral. In addition to the new costs associated with the OTC swaps market, the repo market will be affected by proposed mandatory haircuts on repo collateral, the Basel III Liquidity Coverage Ratio, looming mandatory clearing of repo transactions, and U.S.-based tri-party repo reform. The latter will virtually eliminate the practice of clearing banks providing intraday credit to borrowers (generally broker-dealers). Coupled with money market reform and risk-weighted asset regulations, the repo market is likely to shrink even further from its pre-crisis peak volume, adversely impacting collateral velocity at a moment when the need is likely most acute. Securities lending markets could see the introduction of mandatory central clearing while new collateral requirements for forward settling mortgage-backed securities will put further strains on collateral and liquidity.

At the same time, operational costs can be reduced to offset declining earnings. There are the direct costs of bearing the inefficiencies of redundant functions; these costs are generally most pronounced at sell-side and large buy-side institutions. These include the costs to support the aforementioned product silos where redundant people, processes, and technology drain organization resources. In addition, there are lost opportunity costs, affecting both sell- and buy-side institutions, which will be difficult to tolerate in a capital constrained environment. Lost opportunities manifest in many ways such as using suboptimal collateral to collateralize a trade or not recognizing collateral call and substitution opportunities. When organizations, particularly banks and broker-dealers, were able to realize significantly greater profits, these superfluous excesses could be tolerated. However, in an environment that demands rigorous management of operational and opportunity costs, radical reductions will continue to be enacted.

THE SELL-SIDE

As a result of capital-related regulations, such as Basel III, banks will likely limit what will now be costly unsecured funding. If that goal is to be realized, then new, comprehensive operating models, with robust support technologies, will likely be employed so that shared organizational assets (e.g., collateral) can be best identified and allocated.

Years removed from the latest financial crisis, sell-side organizations, especially large, global banks, and broker-dealers are often organizationally fragmented (generally by region). These organizations often have separate balance sheets for distinct geographies with each region using technologies and operating models that are different from their adjacent organizational brethren. Further, within these regions, there are often product silos that may have unique operating models and supporting technologies that create little synergy with related in-house functions. While some organizations have migrated to an enterprise collateral management system and operating model, there are still silo-based organizations employing best-of-breed solutions that can either be propriety in-house builds or sourced from vendors. Irrespective of origin, it is an expensive, inefficient model that is not viable in a cost-constrained environment. Additionally, the model has proved problematic for several reasons prior to cost becoming a primary consideration.

First, as the collateral, clearing, and treasury functions converged, disparate, best-of-breed solutions were unable to respond as they often lacked the functionality to support more than one specific product (e.g., bilateral OTC swaps, repo, futures, options, etc.). Organizations that presciently embarked on enterprise collateral management solutions often struggled to integrate diverse collateralized trading functions across geographies and various legal entities. When those challenges were successfully addressed, these same organizations encountered limitations with the solutions' ability to link to the front office, while also meeting organizational treasury needs.

Multiple systems also led to inconsistent collateral analytics, and therefore inconsistent and incomplete answers to senior management and regulator questions regarding counterparty exposure and organizational risk. Users of different collateral, clearing, and treasury systems did not have consistent and/or timely data needed to make decisions that ultimately affected them collectively. Often, the use of inadequate or inconsistent data produced inaccurate liquidity forecasting, suboptimal funded margin calls, and lost opportunities through inventoried collateral left idle.

The replacement of LIBOR by overnight index swap (OIS) discounting for OTC derivatives also brought a front office perspective to what was previously a back office-oriented business. The front office traders at a select few firms questioned the theoretical correctness of the discount curve used to calculate the present value of future cash flows. At the same time, they initiated a thorough review of legal and collateral terms embedded in International Swaps and Derivatives Association's Credit Support Annexes (CSAs). Seeking to exploit collateral optionality embedded in most CSAs regarding types of cash currency and securities eligible to secure trades, collateral optimization in the pursuit of greater liquidity benefits was born and inextricably linked the front and back office.

Second, these best-of-breed solutions were not only expensive to maintain—as a result of licensing fees, add-ons to meet the inevitable functionality gaps, organization-specific enhancements, and the relatively large number of support staff—they often lacked automation, especially across silos and geographies. This lack of automation resulted in manual processes, which led to an increase in staff, and raised support costs even further. Beyond those direct costs however, were the less obvious, and therefore more insidious, costs of manual processing. As automation breaks occurred, processes would often be moved to spreadsheets. While that migration was costly in itself, it also produced errors while at the same time moving the organization further from one version of the truth. The manual processes also prevented organizations from reaping the benefits of straight-through processing (STP). STP processes are generally less expensive to execute, as they require no manual processing and are less error prone. They also have the benefit of providing data where it is needed and in the fastest, most efficient manner. A simple example of accurate, timely data benefiting the entire enterprise can be divined from the bilateral OTC margin call process. When the data to issue margin calls prior to the agreement deadline is available, collateral can settle same day, which yields a counterparty credit risk benefit. At the same time, if Treasury and/or the collateral trading desk are aware the collateral is available, funding and liquidity benefits arise that can provide a significant competitive advantage.

Convergence mandates close functional alignment. Funding costs and decisions are made centrally. In this model, cross-product collateral functions move beyond enterprise collateral management and become aligned to the front office, and funded through a merged treasury and repo function. Ideally, convergence is realized through an integrated, cross-organizational operating model that is supported by a common technology platform (which is often vendor-based but could certainly be a proprietary build) where collateral management, sourcing, and optimization are performed cohesively. Funding decisions are no longer made within functional silos but instead consider enterprise imperatives. As a result, the silo (i.e., the business or trading desk) is likely to sacrifice what is best for its profit and loss (P&L) in order to better service the enterprise. This is a key concept, as doing what is best for the bank is imperative if the organization is to remain competitive in a liquidity-challenged environment.

THE BUY-SIDE

Whether directly impacted by regulation or indirectly through increased costs passed on by dealers, buy-side users of all stripes are being forced to change their operating models. To group the wide range of buy-side participants into one category would be to deemphasize their unique collateral and liquidity needs. An asset manager, insurance company, hedge fund, pension fund, and a regulatory exempt corporate end-user will each face the market differently. Each participant is a natural holder of various collateral types, and will therefore have different collateral and liquidity requirements. Still, they share the same broad challenges with respect to collateral and liquidity. Each will find collateralized trading more expensive in the face of aforementioned regulations; each should enable technology to participate efficiently; and each should balance the need to protect collateral assets (i.e., asset segregation) against the desire to generate returns (i.e., participation in repo and securities lending markets).

State Street Bank conducted a buy-side focused study[2] in an attempt to quantify the impact of derivatives clearing regulatory reform. A common theme amongst the data is that hedge funds are seeking to strengthen, or in some cases create, links to treasury functions to support the monitoring of

---

[2]State Street Corporation. 2012. "Charting New Territory: Buy-Side Readiness for Swaps Reforms." VisionFocus, State Street.

funds for collateral. The point is revealing for two reasons. First, it is certainly understandable that similar to their sell-side counterparties, buy-side participants (hedge funds in this case) would want links to the treasury function for improved liquidity management. However, the second point underscores a broader buy-side challenge: In many cases buy-side participants lack the infrastructure to address the more complex collateral and liquidity functions demanded in this new environment. There has been significant progress by the segment on the whole since 2008. The largest participants have sophisticated functions that in some cases rival bank infrastructures. Mid-size and smaller participants have generally moved the bulk of their processes off spreadsheets and have either implemented vendor-based solutions or outsourced their collateral management and, in some cases, their entire middle-office needs to providers such as custody banks.

Buy-side market participants have often had to prioritize tasks as demands continued to grow. Organizational resources were applied to selecting clearing brokers and central counterparties (CCPs); developing clearing mechanics; addressing registration, documentation, and reporting requirements; and preparing for change while wishing to avoid becoming first adopters in an uncertain environment. As a result, efforts to build treasury functions and corresponding links to the collateral function may have been delayed by some firms. Finadium Consulting conducted a survey of OTC derivative[3] end users who clear trades and otherwise participate in the collateralized trading markets. The survey found that only roughly half of those in the population had considered collateral optimization, citing lack of resources as a challenge.

This will rapidly change as buy-side participants confront the economic realities of efficient collateral sourcing, driven in part by the desire to reduce initial margins and independent amounts while at the same time maximizing returns. These firms will look to address inefficient operating models and better leverage technology in order to be more successful market participants. Efficient collateral (and therefore liquidity) sourcing will require connections to clearing brokers, central clearing parties, custodians, repositories, and other market participants (e.g., portfolio reconciliation services and documentation management providers) to understand both obligations and the disposition of assets. It will also likely necessitate tracking collateral, irrespective of location, and understanding attributes such as settlement status, link to obligation, rating change, and pending corporate action. Asset managers will likely need to understand their accounts and subaccounts to

---

[3]Galper, J. 2013. "Large OTC Derivatives End-Users on Clearing and Collateral: A Finadium Survey." Finadium LLC.

determine how assets can be most efficiently utilized. Similarly, buy-side participants of all stripes will want the ability to cross product margin whenever possible, freeing liquidity for other purposes.

Northern Trust published a survey and analysis[4] of U.S. pension funds that were subject to the September 2013 Dodd-Frank mandatory OTC swap clearing deadline. Encouragingly, the survey revealed that, contrary to some hyperbolic predictions, there is little concern of a shortfall in the high-grade collateral needed for swap trade clearing. The study notes that the sector as a whole is prepared to meet increased initial margin requirements with collateral inventory on-hand. This analysis, however, in no way undermines the buy-side case for action to better manage collateral in the pursuit of increased liquidity.

Variation margin calls (for the pension funds addressed in this study as well as other participants with long maturity trades), funded exclusively with cash, will pose sourcing issues. Coupled with other liquidity pressures, such as onerous bilateral margining rules, buy-side participants will likely need to manage collateral more carefully. Buy-side participants will require functions that include various degrees of collateral optimization, cross product margining, pre-trade optimization, and effective, proactive collateral reallocation and substitution; however, the manner in which they achieve the ability to perform those functions will vary.

While some insurance firms, pension funds, and smaller buy-side participants lack the strong derivative culture and supporting infrastructure of their sell-side counterparts, many other buy-side participants do have the necessary fundamentals to build the functionality likely needed to thrive in a capital constrained environment. While many of the enterprise vendor collateral and liquidity solutions are more prevalent on the sell-side, there are buy-side participants who use the same leading practices as the sell-side. While very few build custom solutions, enterprise vendor packages are emerging as viable responses to specific buy-side need. The merits of building, buying, and/or outsourcing functions are discussed later in this chapter. Those details aside, however, it is fair to say that enterprise vendor packages will likely need to be modified for purpose along with a strategy to address functionality gaps (as no package will fulfill all business requirements). In any case, enterprise vendor solutions, and even best-of-breed solutions, will likely need to focus on middleware. Transmitting data to other participants, venues, and utilities will be vital. Electronic messaging will be the preferred method of communication. As electronic messaging is still

[4]Koszewski, C. 2013. "Capital Requirements for Pension Funds in the Wake of Dodd-Frank." Line of Sight, NorthernTrust.

more prevalent on the sell-side, buy-side users will likely need to adopt the technology more uniformly. Buy-side firms will also want to master CCP pricing and fully understand the pricing models to avoid disputes and improve liquidity regardless of whether they address their collateral management needs internally or through outsourcing.

Any conversation regarding the buy-side's readiness for change should include the role of collateral service providers, specifically custody banks. There is competing evidence as to whether these participants will seek outsourcing as an option for their middle office (including collateral management) and liquidity needs. The Finadium study[5] suggests that large end users feel their operations are too complex to be outsourced. Anecdotal evidence certainly supports that contention as nontraditional buy-side participants (e.g., supranationals) approach the markets, and trade differently from a typical hedge fund, for example.

On the other hand, the State Street Bank study[6] indicates the opposite view. This study, also supported by substantial anecdotal evidence, suggests segment outsourcing is on the rise. Many buy-side firm middle office functions are performed manually and will be unable to fulfill future state needs. The costs of developing the technology and operations needed to support new operating models is debatable; some feel outsourcing economics are supported while others feel the costs are excessive and that the function can be performed more effectively and less expensively in-house. What is undisputable, however, is that the time frame for compliance is short and may leave no option but to pursue outsourcing, as it is unlikely the required infrastructure can be built in time to meet rapidly approaching deadlines.

Perhaps the most relevant metric when gauging buy-side appetite for outsourced solutions is the readiness of custody banks. Since the financial crisis, the major custody banks have invested heavily to support this segment. Each has continued to enjoy increased market share with some large, marquee participants outsourcing their entire middle office functions. Almost each of the major providers has an end-to-end, full trade lifecycle management solution to address the needs of buy-side participants. Clearing, valuation, collateral management, reconciliation, and settlement can be taken as a complete service suite or in modules, as needed. Some of these providers act as a central security depository (CSD) and others have formed alliances with global repositories to move and settle collateral efficiently, freeing up

---

[5]Galper, J. 2013. "Large OTC Derivatives End-Users on Clearing and Collateral: A Finadium Survey." Finadium LLC.
[6]State Street Corporation. 2012. "Charting New Territory: Buy-Side Readiness for Swaps Reforms." VisionFocus, State Street.

liquidity. These same providers also offer collateral transformation, segregation, optimization, documentation, and automation solutions. Subsequently, many participants see outsourcing to a highly rated, non-conflicted custody bank as the natural strategy to rapidly meet their collateral and liquidity needs.

BNY Mellon, as a provider of full service middle office services, has explicitly organized around collateral and liquidity with the launch of its Global Collateral Services function in 2011. Its alignment mirrors the shape and likely need of the segment and industry as a whole: Where collateral management and liquidity were once handled separately, they are now best served with a seamless function. The decision of buy-side market participants to fulfill these needs through outsourcing or by building in-house capabilities will be influenced by a variety of factors. Many will likely combine some elements of both approaches.

Posting initial and variation margin has already proved to be problematic for some participants. New collateralized trading rules, such as those for mortgage-backed securities, will only complicate the problem. Still, these are relatively rudimentary issues and successful participation in capital markets calls for these tasks to be performed efficiently. Specifically, efficiency equates to automation that is enabled by STP and electronic messaging and provides one view of organizational truth. Careful use of collateral assets is also necessary and is best achieved with a tight alignment of the functions that use collateral.

ON COLLATERAL OPTIMIZATION

Market participants seek to realize the greatest possible yield from each asset, minimize the cost of borrowing, and eliminate over-collateralization, all while never leaving collateral (potential liquidity) idle. To that end, collateral optimization solutions have become increasingly more sophisticated. At the time of this writing, and still largely a sell-side issue, both proprietary and vendor optimization solutions have continued to mature.

Optimization is not binary and varies in both form and degree. One day, an organization might choose to post high-grade collateral at a CCP and on another day, perhaps during market crisis, it might choose to hold that same collateral for funding (i.e., Federal Reserve eligible collateral). However, before endeavoring to describe the tenets and challenges of collateral optimization (the focus of this chapter), there are other optimizations that should be briefly mentioned.

The leading theories concerning collateral, liquidity, and clearing state that market participants, broadly speaking, should be concerned with seven optimizations. These include the optimization of collateral, cross product margining, funding, financing/funds-transfer-pricing, liquidity, portfolio, and balance sheet. There are arguably others as well. Optimizing trade placement processes, for both cleared and bilateral trades, for example, will limit the need for collateral by identifying optimal netting opportunities (while simultaneously considering eligible collateral, haircuts, and concentration risk). Ultimately, the exact number and distinction is irrelevant as success will be determined by how well these are managed and mastered collectively.

While collateral optimization is the focus of this chapter, cross product margining demands attention as well. Cross product margining is common in prime brokerage arrangements and is one of the advantages of using and consolidating vendor arrangements to a limited number of providers (excepting concentration risk). For some time, bilateral OTC swap participants have performed cross product margining within asset classes (e.g., rates and credit swaps with a common counterparty) but have often been less successful in margining across products (bilateral repos and OTC swaps). While much of the bilateral market will migrate to clearing, the desire to effectively cross product margin in search of greater capital efficiency and risk mitigation will grow. Buy-side market participants will often employ clearing brokers (generally Futures Commission Merchants in the United States). These entities function like prime brokers in many respects, and their clients will look to maximize cross-margin opportunities while balancing concentration, credit, and collateral protection (segregation) issues. Whether these clearing entities act as an agent (U.S. client clearing model) or a principal (UK client clearing model) in centrally cleared transactions, all trades are ultimately sent to a clearinghouse (unlike the prime brokerage model), increasing the desire for the aforementioned pre-trade clearing optimization prior to selecting collateral to post against these trades.

Clearinghouse cross product margining continues to grow, complicating trade placement decisions. For example, as of this writing, clearinghouse cross margining of futures contracts with corresponding OTC rates instruments is nascent, with users unable to tap the full intended benefit. However, as the risk and margining models become more sophisticated, trade volumes increase, and both the clearinghouses and their users gain more comfort with the underlying processes (e.g., initial and variation margining, default fund contributions, and default distribution protocols), the process of determining where to place futures and OTC trades will likely need to be performed collectively. Optimal trade placement and facilitating optimal cross product margining, affects both the buy- and sell-side. For each, cross product margining will become more complex as other products move to clearing environments. The same clearinghouses that clear futures and swaps will more frequently clear repo and even securities lending trades. Clearinghouse interoperability is fraught with legal and risk challenges and, therefore, not considered a near-term solution. As a result, market participants will continue to identify cross-margining opportunities.

Ultimately, collateral optimization is an extension and by-product of the other optimizations, and the most challenging. Collateral optimization has many definitions and corresponding approaches for implementation. In rudimentary form, optimization allows for the delivery of the least expensive asset against an obligation; provision of transparency into the enterprise asset inventory; and, taken to the extreme, facilitation of collateral trading desks tasked with managing the supply and demand of the enterprise's collateral needs. Larger organizations will implement cross-function, collateral-centric operating models that are enabled by sophisticated, targeted, and module-based proprietary or vendor solutions. Others will outsource the function, often to agent custody banks, which then often use the same vendor solutions (interestingly, as do many of the clearinghouses). Coupled with greater exposure to stringent capital rules, the largest participants on both the buy- and sell-side of the market understand that collateral optimization is a cornerstone of their efficient collateralized trading.

Collateral optimization is driven by the desire to source, fund, and allocate collateral efficiently. When applied to margin calls, it focuses on finding the cheapest to deliver asset to meet each obligation. While cash is still used most prevalently to meet margin calls, it is not always the best asset to post to a counterparty. In a survival situation, a bank that is borrowing cash from a central bank might not want to use its cash to pledge against margin calls (conversely, if a bank is cash rich, then optimization might not be as important). In considering funding rates and costs, collateral optimization entails minimizing funding costs. This includes increasing liquidity (e.g., raising cash) often by borrowing cash inexpensively through repo markets while at the same time holding the best quality bonds. Finally, collateral optimization reduces the costs of maintaining a capital liquidity buffer for regulatory purposes (where applicable).

The ability to view collateral across all asset classes, business lines, and depots, along with attributes such as disposition of collateral, open positions, location of pledged assets, and pending corporate action, is critical to achieving collateral optimization. Analytics are an important component of collateral optimization and include performing "what-if" scenario analysis across portfolios and by asset class, counterparty, and business line to understand potential funding and credit implications. Well-honed analytics will facilitate the identification of potential/anticipated margin requirements, on both the trade and portfolio level, to determine the potential cost/benefit and placement of each trade (e.g., bilateral, cleared or exchange traded derivatives). Collateral optimization analytics can enhance intraday capabilities to monitor credit and market events for counterparties and asset classes. Ultimately, advanced collateral optimization solutions will provide enterprise transparency to achieve the most efficient use of inventory while still effectively managing counterparty credit risk.

Reaching beyond cheapest to deliver in order to really exploit each asset in an effort to minimize borrowing costs requires reaching across the organization. To accomplish this, optimization processes could be run at the start of the business day with results being sent to all invested parties. With this information, holistic decisions can be made on how obligations and funding requirements are to be met. While many participants still use spreadsheets or have limited optimization tools that are silo-based, implementing an enterprise collateral optimization solution will force new communication and inter-organization working models. Stakeholders will likely need to learn to use the cash or bonds that the optimizer suggests. This is a change from many current models, where the stakeholders make decisions on asset use based on their silo's needs. Still, the in/outbound workflow for the optimization process should consider the expected as well as the unexpected. Optimization results produced in the morning could change rapidly if, for example, a margin call is higher than expected, requiring more collateral that might need to be sourced from either a bond trader or treasury. In any case, cross-organization operating models and communication are as much a part of the optimization process as the rules engine and optimization algorithm.

Larger inventories and enterprise-wide view of those assets are more conducive to efficient collateral optimization. Mid- to large-size organizations on both sides of the market will likely need to integrate the front office, treasury, risk management, legal, and operation functions. In an effort to generate alpha, the front office will want to gain greater control of collateral selection for its trades. This selection will be facilitated by data provided by a rules-based engine that considers collateral costs, opportunity costs, as well as various restrictions concerning legal jurisdictions, credit mitigation, and operational concerns. Treasury's view of effective collateral use will center on adhering to economic and regulatory capital requirements for collateral and liquidity. Risk management will focus on protecting the enterprise and will require access to the same data (or version of the truth) as those making trading and funding decisions. Credit, market, liquidity, and operational risk all can be managed in conjunction with optimization though this adds new layers of complexity to the task.

The legal department's focus will remain on the terms of master agreements, and its direct contribution to advancing collateral optimization stems from reviewing and renegotiating terms of master agreements (e.g., global master repurchase agreement or GMRA, CSA, etc.) that pertain to eligible collateral, re-hypothecation, and substitution rights to identify optimization opportunities. Staff in the legal department will likely work closely with risk and operations personnel to ensure dynamic changes are monitored and operationalized. Like all participants in a mature optimization model, the legal function requires the same version of the truth as its organizational brethren. A keen front office trader armed with the same accurate, timely, and concise agreement data as legal staff is more likely to exploit collateral assets. Latent liquidity likely lurks locked and lost in legal agreements. In addition to being a great alliteration, it's also a call for legal, risk, front office, operational and technology teams to explore master agreements in pursuit of greater liquidity.

Operational efficiency and collateral optimization are inextricably linked. Successful collateral optimization requires seamless integration of many enterprise operational components with supporting technology. Effective collateral optimization considers inventory management, collateral tracking, and complex analytics delivered with automation and STP. Securities lending, repo, listed, and OTC derivative trading collateral needs must be matched, in real time, to multiple collateral channels. These channels include cleared, bilateral, tri-party, funding, and regulatory. As a result, collateral operations will have to transition from a line of business resource to an institutional resource. Enterprise inventory management is a critical part of a revised operational mandate. Creating one global view of collateral inventory and eligibility not only enables collateral optimization but also enables operational efficiency, reduces operating cost, and supports revenue growth. At the same time a common inventory pool will create conflicts among stakeholders vying for the same piece of collateral. These conflicts can be addressed by a combination of simple communication protocols and advanced technology solutions.

Ultimately, the heart of collateral optimization is technology. Collateral rules, optimization algorithms, and what-if analysis engines will sit at the center of an organization to provide and receive critical data. Collateral rules consider eligibility, coupon, locations, haircut, disposition, concentration limits, and substitution eligibility. Algorithms consider a securities credit curve, issuer, and maturity against optimization scenarios ranging from cheapest to deliver to maximizing liquidity to reacting to volatility by holding high-quality collateral. A what-if analysis engine will consider various stress scenarios, including downgrades of security, counterparty as well as the organization itself. Together, they will work to provide the data necessary to meet the organization's liquidity and risk and regulatory goals in both the short and long term.

Vendor packages are commonly used as collateral optimization engines. Even sophisticated users with a culture of custom technology development may integrate a vendor module to meet optimization requirements. Optimization engines should be flexible, intuitive, and relatively easy to install and maintain. The logic contained in the best solutions is complex and requires considerable research and development. As the organization moves through various levels of maturity in optimization, the engine of choice is a commodity and it is hard to justify a custom-build for an optimization algorithm. As a result, competitive advantage will be determined by the implementation of an optimization operating model and seamless technology integration of the optimization engine with other up and downstream processes.

IMPROVED LIQUIDITY AND INCREASED COLLATERAL EFFICIENCY: A CASE STUDY

As the demand for collateral and liquidity grew, due in part to global regulatory initiatives that mandate and/or encourage collateralized trading and lending, a global bank searched for solutions to efficiently deploy all of its available collateral (while also recognizing that improving funding costs by even one basis point would yield significant savings). Specifically, the bank endeavored to achieve a more efficient use of a fractured collateral inventory in order to free liquidity in that pool, reduce and/or optimize posted collateral, and reduce the need for unsecured funding. At the same time, the bank wanted to increase operational efficiency (and eliminate duplicative tasks) by consolidating operations through the deployment of merged operating models with common supporting technology platforms. Further, the bank did not want to impact any core business as a result of consolidation. While staff reduction was not a goal of the efficiency effort, the bank also endeavored to redeploy staff to more value-added tasks.

The bank focused on merging the fixed-income repo and prime finance functions, recognizing that there were natural synergies between these groups that could be used to affect enterprise objectives. In particular, the fixed-income repo desk was already fairly well aligned with treasury and was progressing toward a model where it determined the portions of the bond inventory that would be used to satisfy short-term obligations. With the introduction of the prime finance function (and collateral pool), the matching of margin obligations to funding sources would be made that much more efficient.

Project goals and objectives were further refined and placed within one of four priority categories: unlocking latent liquidity, improving risk management, enabling operational and technology efficiency, and enhancing the client proposition. Specific goals and critical success factors within those categories were numerous. Unlocking latent liquidity contained perhaps the most impactful goals. Among these goals was the desire to optimize collateral by enabling a shared view use of a common collateral pool. Additionally, the bank wanted to begin pledging equities (formerly held within the prime finance collateral pool and not available to the fixed income repo function) in place of fixed-income securities to eligible counterparties, CCPs, and other intermediaries. Finally, and in keeping with emerging industry trends, the bank wanted to better leverage its stock borrow/stock loan process to identify evergreen securities and upgrade trade opportunities, while at the same time developing a more efficient and collaborative process to cover short positions less expensively.

This shift towards efficiency and greater convergence of related processes is known as internalization in the industry vernacular. Internalization is predicated on the cross-trading desk model similar to that implemented by the bank. As it operationalized its processes to support the new operating model for the merged function, internalization would allow the bank to identify and deploy internal assets (otherwise hidden in silos) before considering more costly outside funding sources. Limiting expensive unsecured funding (i.e., limiting balance sheet expansion) is critical when confronting ever increasing capital rules (e.g., Basel III). Though the merged function could never be fully self-funded, internalization could help the bank to limit the need for borrowing cash. In subsequent phases, the OTC swaps desk and support functions (and a sizable collateral pool) would be incorporated. The larger central collateral pool would offer more opportunities for internalization, and would be particularly important as more OTC swaps related collateral is segregated from banks for both cleared and bilateral trades.

The goals articulated for enhancing risk management included a better understanding of concentration limits, an improved crisis management response, and improved credit risk management. The bank also wanted to consider the impact of common counterparties on the combined function, as opposed to the silo view in the current state. Operational and technology efficiencies included the elimination of manual tasks, reduction of settlement costs for internal trades, and realization of the benefits of increased scale from the larger user base that was created through the partnership. Finally, the bank defined "enhancing the client proposition" as providing cohesive financing offerings, identifying cross-selling opportunities, and providing a one-bank approach to clients.

With the problem, goals, and critical success factors identified, the bank applied practical, best practice project management principles to guide the effort. Additionally, the bank established several core principles for the pending partnership. Chief among these was that any solution would entail the use of small, achievable, incremental steps that would avoid reliance on distant, costly, wholesale reengineering efforts. The bank would begin with an end state in mind, both operationally and in terms of supporting technology, and incrementally progress to the target model. This incremental, phased approach was also applied to the global implementation, as rollout would occur by region, with subsequent implementations leveraging the lessons learned from prior implementations. Other core partnership principles included the sharing of a P&L. This principle was established to modify silo staff behavior to emphasize enterprise benefit in place of local P&L benefit. Finally, any solution needed to be compliant with all legal and regulatory requirements.

The bank's goals were consistent with the industry trend to consolidate functions in order to gain operational efficiencies while also optimizing the use of enterprise assets (e.g., collateral). Adhering to project management best practices and realizing that achieving this goal would require stakeholder input from across the organization, the bank assembled a cross-functional team that was composed of users from the front, middle, and back offices as well as the treasury function. This was a critical step as stakeholders in the cross-enterprise collateral and liquidity efforts needed to align themselves with the support of senior management and retain a strong sense of solution ownership.

Merging the fixed-income repo and prime finance functions to meet funding, liquidity, and efficiency goals required a transformation execution roadmap that detailed each step of the incremental merger. An impact assessment was performed prior to placing any tasks on the roadmap. This assessment considered the impact to people, processes, and technology using a simple scale of low, medium, and high. The impact analysis provided the data needed to prioritize the tasks and place them on the timeline in a manner that conformed with other ongoing efforts. Relatively simple tasks that yielded measurable results were generally executed first, while more complex tasks were placed toward the end of the roadmap. Over the course of two years, the bank slowly, yet inexorably, migrated towards its target end state.

The process began with the simple step of co-locating staff. This included bringing each function's trading, liquidity management, and funding functions together at the same physical location. Once the staff was co-located, tactical changes were made to each function's technology platform to provide a common inventory view (eliminating the immediate need for a complex common inventory solution implementation). Subsequent steps included leveraging and reducing custodian accounts, aligning the settlement function, and implementing collateral optimization. After approximately twelve months, all tactical steps were implemented and the organization was able to realize tangible, measurable results from a relatively modest capital investment. At the same time the bank now had a stable operational and technical infrastructure, as well as a culture of cooperation and success. These successes were vital to launching more strategic changes that were needed to support a truly merged and optimized function, such as finalizing and implementing the merged target operating model, redeploying staff, implementing a single front office trade capture platform and common margining tool, and migrating to a single settlement platform.

Organizations of similar size and geography could use this same approach to achieve similar goals. More regional organizations that are aligned by functional silo could also use a similar approach. Organizations will have choices on strategic technology decisions (vendor versus proprietary systems) and on specific operating models, leading to distinct approaches for developing improvements. However, sell-side organizations, as in this case study, will eventually be structured to maximize liquidity through optimal collateral while minimizing operating expenses.

CONCLUSION

Convergence, compliance, one version of the truth, efficiency, and optimization each are hallmarks of successful participation in capital markets post financial crisis. The industry will continue to be reshaped by global regulation in ways both intended and unintended. Over time, regulations will be modified, as they were for Markets in Financial Instruments Directive (MiFID) 2.0, for example. Additionally, the manner in which participant behavior changes in the face of new regulation greatly influences subsequent regulation. This is not unique. Historically, financial markets have evolved, as a result of the crisis, through a cycle of regulation, implementation, and revision. Ultimately, pendulums swing both ways. Political change, economic environment, and financial services industry innovation will likely influence when pendulum swings occur, as well as the length of travel; alas, the only certainty is change. However, if history portends future events, then it is likely that the pursuit of financial gain will be strong enough to allow participants to improvise, adapt, and eventually overcome any challenge. The exact manifestation of change will likely vary by participant with each adapting according to its culture and objective. Yet irrespective of approach, all participants will share common goals if they are to be successful in a radically new environment. These goals will share common themes of improved efficiency, risk management, and liquidity. Affecting these goals will require convergence within the organization, as well as within the broader financial services community. Convergence will be achieved incrementally and likely more slowly than required. Still, its advent is inexorable, resulting in the creation of a new world that even at the point of inception is being influenced by yet more change, poised for its next incarnation.

- **Transacting with collateral necessitates active collateral management.** Consistent with the industry trends, collateral management strives to consolidate functions in order to gain operational efficiencies as well as optimize the use of enterprise assets. The creation of cross-functional teams, the merging of operating models with a common set of technology platforms, and the elimination of duplicative as well as manual tasks are key steps in implementing a collateral management program.
- **Collateral optimization is achieved with an enterprise operating model and supporting technology.** Driven by the desire to source, fund, and allocate collateral efficiently, optimization can be attained only after proper collateral management processes are in place. With optimization, market participants can realize the greatest possible yield from each asset, minimize the cost of borrowing, and eliminate over-collateralization, all while never leaving collateral, and thus, potential liquidity idle.
- **Collateral and liquidity are two sides of the same coin.** As a result of regulatory requirements, increased demand for collateral, and pressure to reduce operating costs, organizations are eager to exploit the inextricable link between collateral and liquidity. With greater focus on liquidity, potential institutions are better able to meet the demands of increased margin calls, organizational funding requirements, and regulatory capital mandates.

REFERENCES

State Street Corporation. 2012. "Charting New Territory: Buy-Side Readiness for Swaps Reforms." VisionFocus, State Street.

Galper, J. 2013. "Large OTC Derivatives End-Users on Clearing and Collateral: A Finadium Survey." Finadium LLC.

Koszewski, C. 2013. "Capital Requirements for Pension Funds in the Wake of Dodd-Frank." Line of Sight, Northern Trust.

CHAPTER 6

Early Warning Indicators

Bruce Choy and Girish Adake[1]

EARLY WARNING INDICATORS: MECHANISM TO SIGNAL UPCOMING LIQUIDITY CRISIS

As an integral part of liquidity risk management (LRM), bank leadership has the responsibility to both identify and manage underlying liquidity risk factors. One of the critical aspects of a bank's LRM involves first devising and then monitoring a set of indicators to enable the risk identification process to spot the emergence of new or increasing vulnerabilities. Negative trends serve as early indicators that may warrant an assessment and also a potential response by management in order to mitigate a bank's exposure to any emerging risk.

This chapter provides an overview of the key aspects associated with early warning indicators (EWIs).

Introduction: Dashboard and Beyond

Dashboard. EWIs may be viewed as analogous to warning lights on an automobile dashboard. The turning signals, low oil, and check engine lights alert the driver of driving conditions. Continuing this analogy, a turn signal or "blinker" indicates an intentional risky activity of making a purposeful directional change. In the realm of LRM, this might mean, for example, running a deposit special to raise rate-sensitive liabilities. A low engine oil light indicates to the driver that direct action may be needed in the near future to prevent the engine from seizing up. Again in an LRM context, this is analogous to noticing that the bank's Liquidity Coverage Ratio (LCR) has

---

[1]Bruce Choy is a director in PwC's New York office, and Girish Adake is a manager in PwC's McLean office.

dropped below a specified threshold. A check engine light indicates further investigation is warranted for a yet to be determined reason; the application of this aspect of the analogy may mean, for example, that a dramatic increase in call center volumes may portend a shift in the bank's liquidity position.

Most importantly EWI triggers are used to initiate management discussions and actions that should be formally documented. This could be as simple as an acknowledgment that the bank's treasury is aware that a deposit campaign is underway by one of the business lines so it can orchestrate a corrective action, for example, by increasing the high quality liquid assets buffer in a cost-efficient manner and continuing to comply with LCR requirements.

Beyond. Holding liquid assets to ensure a bank can meet its financial obligations is ultimately a cost-benefit decision. The protection from the catastrophic impacts of not having enough liquidity is offset by a significant drag on earnings if the buffer is too high. A minimum standard for the liquidity buffer is set in accordance with the risk appetite of the bank. However a basic "set and forget" approach does not allow for the strategic management of this risk against a dynamic market.

Increasing buffers before times of stress can extend the survival horizon in a cost-effective manner as a bank does not want to be caught short of liquidity when the market freezes. Indeed, being in a strong balance sheet position during times of stress opens opportunities for significant gains in market share as well as acquisitions that may not be otherwise available in the normal course of business. Strongly positioned companies can take advantage of rare instances of market disruption. The management tool that gives rise to this strategic advantage is the LRM EWI framework.

Regulatory Emphasis in Recent Times

The global financial crisis of 2007–08 has put the spotlight on LRM. The Basel Committee on Banking Supervision (BCBS) issued its "Principles of Sound Liquidity Management and Supervision"[2] (Sound Principles) in September 2008, followed closely by details on standardized metrics such

---

[2] BCBS, "Principles of Sound Liquidity Management and Supervision," Sept 2008, Early Warning Indicators.

TABLE 6.1 BCBS Recommended EWIs (EWIs may include but are not limited to the items listed below)

Rapid asset growth, especially when funded with potentially volatile liabilities
Growing concentrations in assets or liabilities
Increases in currency mismatches
Decrease of weighted average maturity of liabilities
Repeated incidents of positions approaching or breaching internal or regulatory
    limits
Negative trends or heightened risk associated with a particular product line
Significant deterioration in the bank's financial condition
Negative publicity
Credit rating downgrade
Stock price declines
Rising debt costs
Widening debt/credit-default-swap spreads
Rising wholesale/retail funding costs
Counterparties requesting additional collateral or resisting entering into new
    transactions
Drop in credit lines
Increasing retail deposit outflows
Increasing redemptions of CDs before maturity
Difficulty accessing longer-term funding
Difficulty placing short-term liabilities

Source: BCBS, "Principles of Sound Liquidity Management and Supervision," Sept 2008, Early Warning Indicators

as the LCR and the Net Stable Funding Ratio (NSFR). This overarching framework includes the use of EWIs.

Table 6.1 is a non-exhaustive list of EWIs recommended by the BCBS. It includes key indicators that are both qualitative and quantitative in nature.

Key Supervisory Guidelines

National regulators have started to benchmark financial institutions against these sound principles. The regulatory expectations for banks have gone up as a result. In particular, the data needed to support a modern LRM framework, in terms of quantity, quality, and timeliness, is an expensive investment. The responses from banks span a range from those who aim to minimize the cost of compliance to those who believe it can become a strategic tool to guide future management decisions.

Table 6.2 summarizes key supervisory guidelines, which should act as one of the core guiding principles for EWI selection and monitoring at a bank.

Risk Identification and EWIs

It is important to ensure that EWIs align to and are a natural extension of the enterprise LRM framework.

According to Federal Reserve Board Supervisory Letter (FRB SR) 12-7 requirements, the LRM framework should be end-to-end and ensure that the bank will "sufficiently capture the banking organization's exposures, activities, and risks."

A comprehensive LRM framework begins by identifying liquidity and funding risks that are inherent in the business activities of the institution (Figure 6.1). These risks are then memorialized in the firm's liquidity risk inventory and subjected to a risk assessment process that includes the businesses, corporate treasury, the independent risk management function, and other relevant stakeholders. Once the institution has assessed its liquidity risks, including their sources and drivers, the firm can then develop a framework for measuring and monitoring these risks, consisting of stress tests, EWIs, and a limit and response framework.

Framework Components: M.E.R.I.T.

The EWI framework can be summarized as M.E.R.I.T. (Measures, Escalation, Reporting, Integrated systems, and Thresholds). While an appropriate set of measures is the first essential building block for a robust EWI framework, it will be a mere academic exercise if the framework is eventually not linked to escalation processes. The journey from measures to escalation is facilitated by timely reporting with the support of integrated systems and data as well as relevant and properly calibrated thresholds.

Measures Principle 5 from the BCBS' Sound Principles articulates the hallmarks of EWIs. The principle states that "to obtain a forward looking view of liquidity risk exposures, a bank should use metrics that assess (a) the structure of the balance sheet, as well as metrics that (b) project cash flows and future liquidity positions, taking into account (c) off-balance sheet

TABLE 6.2 Key Supervisory Guidelines

OCC - 2012[3]	BCBS - 2008[4]	BCBS - 2012[5]	SR 10-6[6]
■ A bank should have EWIs that signal whether embedded triggers in certain products (i.e., callable public debt, OTC derivatives transactions) are about to be breached, or whether contingent risks are likely to materialize. ■ Early recognition of a potential event allows a bank to enhance a bank's readiness. EWI's may include: ■ A reluctance of traditional fund providers to continue funding at historic levels ■ Pending regulatory action (both formal and informal) or CAMELS component or composite rating downgrade(s) ■ Widening of spreads on senior and subordinated debts, credit default swaps, and stock price declines ■ Difficulty in accessing long-term debt markets ■ Reluctance of trust managers, money managers, public entities, and credit-sensitive funds providers to place funds ■ Rising funding costs in an otherwise-stable market ■ Counterparty resistance to off-balance-sheet products or increased margin requirements ■ The elimination of committed credit lines by counterparties	■ A bank should design a set of indicators to identify the emergence of increased risk or vulnerabilities in its liquidity risk position or potential funding needs. ■ Early warning indicators can be qualitative or quantitative in nature and may include but are not limited to ■ Rapid asset growth, especially when funded with potentially volatile liabilities ■ Growing concentrations in assets or liabilities ■ Increases in currency mismatches ■ Decrease of weighted average maturity of liabilities ■ Repeated incidents of positions approaching or breaching internal or regulatory limits ■ Negative trends or heightened risk associated with a particular product line	■ Intraday liquidity monitoring indicators include: ■ Daily maximum liquidity requirement ■ Available intraday liquidity ■ Total payments ■ Time-specific and other critical obligations ■ Value of customer payments made on behalf of financial institutions customers ■ Intraday credit lines extended to financial institution customers ■ Timing of intraday payments ■ Intraday throughput	■ Institution management should monitor for potential liquidity stress events by using early-warning indicators and event triggers. The institution should tailor these indicators to its specific liquidity risk profile. ■ Early recognition of potential events allows the institution to position itself into progressive states of readiness as the event evolves, while providing a framework to report or communicate within the institution and to outside parties. ■ Early-warning signals may include, but are not limited to: ■ Negative publicity concerning an asset class owned by the institution ■ Increased potential for deterioration in the institution's financial condition ■ Widening debt or credit default swap spreads ■ Increased concerns over the funding of off-balance-sheet items

[3]OCC: Liquidity booklet of the OCC's Comptroller's Handbook (2012)

[4]BCBS: Basel Committee on Banking Supervision, "Principles for Sound Liquidity Risk Management and Supervision" (2008)

[5]BCBS: Basel Committee on Banking Supervision, "Monitoring Indicators for Intraday Liquidity" (2012)

[6]Interagency Policy Statement on Funding and Liquidity Risk Management (2010)

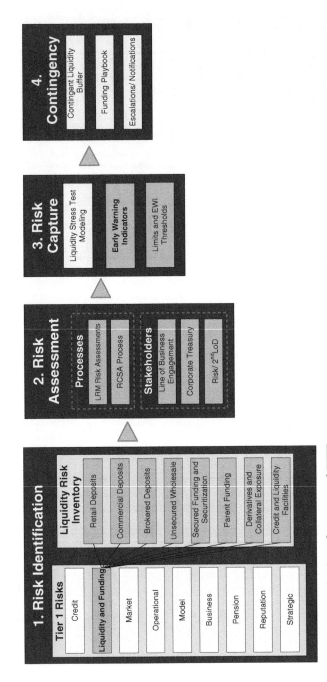

FIGURE 6.1 Risk Identification and EWIs

risks." These measures should span vulnerabilities across business-as-usual and stressed conditions over various time horizons."[7]

Forward Looking Bias/View A suite of EWIs that includes internal and external metrics is required for prudent risk management. These measures ideally need to be leading (forward looking) and sharp (sufficiently granular).

A leading indicator is one that will provide information and signal potential stress prior to the occurrence of an actual event. This is particularly important in preparing for systemic scenarios. Rather than using lagging indicators which report on events that have already occurred, such as government reported GDP figures, a bank can develop proxies for the performance of the general economy from internal loan portfolio metrics.

The granularity and specificity of a particular indicator as it pertains to an institution's profile is known as its sharpness. Sharp indicators are signals that do not go unnoticed within the mass of data. For example, detecting a drop in overall deposit balances is an acceptable EWI; however, detecting drops in deposit balances of more volatile segments, such as high-net worth customers or rate-sensitive products balances, brings into focus that certain important classes of customers are leaving the bank.

Developing EWIs that are both sharp and forward looking allows more time for management to take corrective or mitigating actions; it also helps to ensure that managers have a better understanding of risk drivers and trends than broad, lagging indicators may otherwise provide.

In additional to developing sharp leading indicators, banks should also strike a balance between external and internal measures (Figure 6.2). Internal measures are customized to the bank's balance sheet and activities while external measures signal systemic changes in the economy or market.

It is important to recognize that liquidity events can start either within the bank or may be influenced by external elements resulting from the environment within which the bank operates. For example, an idiosyncratic deposit run may result from either the disclosure of poor performance or due to a systemic failure. EWIs should be positioned to capture emerging internally-driven stress events before they become public knowledge, for example, through monitoring of loan performance, planned significant accounting adjustments, and operational losses. Alternatively, a systemic crisis such as a sovereign default or banking system crisis may trigger

---

[7]BCBS, "Principles of Sound Liquidity Management and Supervision," Sept 2008.

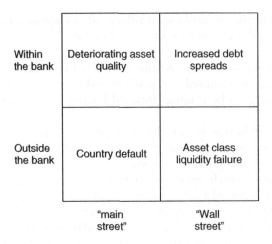

	"main street"	"Wall street"
Within the bank	Deteriorating asset quality	Increased debt spreads
Outside the bank	Country default	Asset class liquidity failure

FIGURE 6.2 Early Warning Indicator Dimensions

liquidity dislocations in parts of the financial market system, disrupting the funding of any institutions that are exposed to those markets.

Environments, Both Normal and Stressed EWIs are meant to provide signals or to act as a heads-up for an upcoming potential disaster. Tracking appropriate EWI metrics during a business as usual environment is essential as any deterioration in these metrics will alert the bank's leadership of weaknesses in the bank's balance sheet or of the emergence of challenging circumstances in the markets that the bank operates within.

In addition, institutions should include stressed measures and limits into their EWI lists in order to gauge the adequacy of the firm's liquidity buffer for a stressed environment. Additionally, stress testing results may also expose previously unidentified or emerging concentrations and risks that could threaten the viability of the institution.

Spanning Various Time Horizons EWI coverage cannot be static and needs to reflect various time horizons in order to match the institution's unique balance sheet needs as well as the market and economic conditions under which it operates.

Typical cycle time horizons that match banking forecasts and business operations tend to be daily, weekly, or monthly. An indicator that is not updated for a period of more than a month is unlikely to satisfy the "early" aspect of the EWI. Certain EWIs may even be monitored on an intraday basis, as warranted by business conditions or required by regulators.

Escalation   Although escalation criteria are bespoke to a bank, an effective escalation policy should ensure that limit breaches are escalated to the appropriate level of management with the authority to undertake corrective actions. Modest responses such as increasing the liquid asset buffer may usually be done within the delegation of the corporate treasurer; however, an EWI that signals a potentially large cash outflow may require the asset-liability committee (ALCO) to authorize a check on future asset growth. The most extreme cases may require management to initiate the bank's contingency funding plan (CFP).

EWIs will have a tangible and favorable impact on LRM governance only when they are linked to a clearly defined escalation plan. The governance overseeing the escalation of EWI triggered actions must be formalized and documented as part of the liquidity risk management framework and be included in the institution's CFP.

Reporting   EWI reporting needs to be timely in order to provide management with sufficient lead time to make adjustments in response to potential crisis events. It is common practice to have the EWI dashboard reported on a daily basis. While most institutions perform some level of daily liquidity reporting, leading institutions are moving toward intraday reporting of certain measures. Firms with a significant trading focus are more likely to use intraday reporting as a result of their increased exposure to external market conditions.

Reporting also needs to strike a balance between being (a) broad enough to provide wide coverage, and (b) specific enough to communicate only key messages.

Integrated Systems   Metrics and reporting are feasible and meaningful only when they are backed by the bank's ability to calculate the selected metrics, and report them consistently.

Integrated data and systems within the bank are essential in providing liquidity managers with the capability to ensure that reported metrics are (a) accurate, and (b) in sync with each other. For example, deposit volumes feeding into liquidity stress tests, and their resulting measures, should be derived from the same source system used to produce non-stressed measures, such as week over week declines in deposit funding. This level of automation and integration is particularly important as EWI frameworks increasingly supplement traditional market-based metrics with a larger array of internal indicators.

Thresholds Firms generally use a stoplight system in representing and communicating their performance against the thresholds of their EWIs. A green indicator means that the measure is within normal bounds. A measure that is classified as amber according to the threshold framework should be investigated further while a red indicator should be a source for significant concern and may warrant an immediate response. The threshold boundaries for which an EWI moves from green to amber should not be so wide that movements go undetected and the metric constantly indicates that the economic and internal environments are healthy and unchanged. Institutions should also be careful not to set boundaries that are so narrow as to force constant investigation of its movements, desensitizing management to its impact and creating a "boy who cried wolf" circumstance.

Historical data analysis is commonly used to estimate the volatility of an EWI and to calibrate its thresholds. The length of the calibration time series needs to be sufficiently long in order to be significant but should also capture recent events to ensure that it represents the current operating environment. If possible, the time series should include a period of stress, such as during 2007-08, to more accurately assess the performance of the metric under stressed conditions. When available, a historical time series of at least one year will be used for calibration. The threshold should be subjected to back-testing to determine if recalibration is needed and a management override, based on historical judgment, is warranted (e.g., historical analysis of the volatility of the Fed Fund rate is informative; however, triggers may be more appropriately set using the FOMC specified target range).

Industry Practices Over the last few years, banking institutions have increased the attention and resources devoted to developing and maintaining EWI dashboards and their overarching governance. The added emphasis in recent years can be largely attributed to supervisory demands in the form of matters requiring attention (MRAs), exams, etc. In certain instances, the credit should also duly be given to self-initiatives from the bank leadership to launch projects to enhance its liquidity management solidifying risk reporting.

As an illustration, we have included lists of EWIs typically reported in the banking industry (Tables 6.3 to 6.9). Please note that the list is non-exhaustive.

Illustrative EWI List

TABLE 6.3 Market Indicators I

EWI Type	Actual Indicator
Credit Rating	Moody's Standard & Poor's Fitch Ratings Changes in ratings
Equity Markets	DJ STOXX 600 Banks DJIA S&P 500 S&P TSX NASDAQ FTSE 100 NIKKEI 225 VIX (Stock market volatility)

TABLE 6.4 Market Indicators 2

EWI Type	Actual Indicator
Rates/MM trends	1M LIBOR 3M LIBOR 6M LIBOR 12M LIBOR OIS LIBOR/OIS Spread Euribor vs. Eonia (bp) 10 yr Benchmark Treasury 2Y/10Y U.S. Spread 3M T- 2yr T spread 3M U.S. Tsy 6M U.S. Tsy 12M U.S. Tsy FED Open FED EFF Federal Reserve Rates (Discount Rate) Federal Reserve Rates (Fed Funds) Global Treasuries Bank O/N Rate – Fed Effective > 10 bps Overnight Positions Net MM Fund Outflows NAV <1.x for MM Funds

TABLE 6.5   Market Indicators 3

EWI Type	Actual Indicator
Other Indicators	USD/CAD foreign exchange rate
	USD/CAD FX Spot Rate
	BKX Index (Banking Sector Health)
	Unemployment Rate
	GDP Growth Rate-QoQ Change
	Crude
	Economic indicators forecasting recession
	Political interference in bank regulation/supervision, leading to reduced capacity at FHLB or discount window
	Internal due diligence activity related to a material acquisition
	ABCP/LIBOR Spread
	State ISMs
	Case-Shiller HPIs
	NCREIF CRE Transaction Price Index
	BBB Option-Adjusted Spread
	Repo Spread

TABLE 6.6   Bank Specific Indicators 1

EWI Type	Actual Indicator
Credit Risk	Bank 5yr CDS(bp)
	S&P Sr. Credit Rating
	Moody's Sr. Credit Rating
	Fitch Sr. Credit Rating
	S&P Bank ST Credit Rating
	Moody's Bank ST Credit Rating
	Fitch Bank ST Credit Rating
	FHLB Credit Rating
	CAMELS rating
	DBRS Sr. Credit Rating
	Bank CDS spread higher than Barclays Capital Aggregate Index
Counterparty Concentration	Total Outstanding 3rd Party Borrowings
	Top 5 3rd Party Borrowings (% per institution)
	% of OIS CDs with Top 10 counterparties
	Total 3rd Party Borrowings (% per business sector)
	% of Total Wholesale Borrowings (per counterparty)
	% of Total Wholesale Borrowings (per business sector)
	Total Outstanding 3rd Party Repo

TABLE 6.6 (*Continued*)

EWI Type	Actual Indicator
Counterparty Concentration (*continued*)	Top 5 Total 3rd Party Repo (% per institution) % of Repo CDs with Top 10 counterparties Total 3rd Party Repo (% per business sector) Breach of tactical liquidity limits Largest Fund (Single) providers Funding Sources as a percent of total average assets

TABLE 6.7 Bank Specific Indicators 2

EWI Type	Actual Indicator
Credit Performance	Credit Card Net Losses Credit Card Industry Avg Net Losses Credit Card 30 + Day DQ Card Excess Spread
Funding Need	Total Deposits Variance to Plan (MM) Total Loans Outstanding Variance to Plan (MM)
Liquidity Metrics	RWAs Total Plc CD/CP LOC - 1 Week / 1 Month. 3 Months CP (term) ($mm) Next Days Maturities WAM of Outstanding CP Unsec Borrows from PLC - Term Unsec Borrows from PLC - O/N Total Unsec from PLC O/N Non Traditional Repo (Ex Equities) Total Available Liquidity I/C Reverse Repo (Ex Equities) Repo/Rev Repo Mismatch (per protuct type) % cumulative RE financed Limit - % Repo to Total Financed % Reverses over repo Limit - Reverses over Repos Prelim TPAs (ex Deriv MTM) Balance Sheet (U.S. GAAP)

TABLE 6.8 Bank Specific Indicators 3

EWI Type	Actual Indicator
Liquidity Metrics	Disc Window Collateral
	Due from % of 3rd Party Liabilities
	Short term market cash
	Total cash at FRB
	Payments
	Receipts
	Closed Fed Balance
	Collateral at Fed
	Daylight OD Usage
	Daily Highlight Comments
	Other Immediate Potential Cash Outflows:
	Anticipated Cash Inflows
	More Liquid Assets
	Total Gross Operational Risk Losses / 12 Month Revenue
	Contingency Funding Plan Activation
	Bank Unsecured Capacity reduced by 10% or more MoM
	Bank Retail Loans greater than 30 days Delinquent
	Criticized Credits > 7% of Total Commercial Loans
	EPS Stress Test Ratio/EPS Branch Stress Test Ratio
	Repo Haircut
	Increased spread paid for uninsured debt issuance
	Decline in earnings and or capital levels

TABLE 6.9 Bank Specific Indicators 4

EWI Type	Actual Indicator
Market Sentiment	Share Price
	Bank vs BKX Index
	Decline in stock price relative to the change in stock prices of peers
	Trading loss risk
	% of outstanding shares
	UMich Index of Consumer Sentiment
Maturity Concentration	% of Total Gross Repo in Overnight
	Overnight Repo Average vs market
	% Total Outstanding Unsecured Borrowing (single day)
	% Total Outstanding Unsecured Borrowing (5 day)
	% Total Outstanding Unsecured Borrowing (10 day)
	% Total Outstanding Unsecured Borrowing (10 day)
	National Market Funding- Maturity Time Horizon

TABLE 6.9   (*Continued*)

EWI Type	Actual Indicator
Stress Testing Results	Liq Scenarios Liq Stress Test +/− 3M Cumulative Parent Liquidity Scenario U.S. LCR NSFR
Other Indicators	Quarterly Net Income Severely Adverse Parent Forecast Disclosure Committee Trigger Gross Impaired Loans & Loan Formations Retail W/W Change in Deposits Bank Credit Turndown of Significance Bank classified ratio

CONCLUSION

Over the years after the 2007-08 financial crisis, banking institutions have significantly increased their reliance on EWIs to avert any potential liquidity crisis. Nonetheless, supervisors as well as risk managers within the banks are constantly looking to expand and refine their EWIs so that the list stays relevant both to the internal changes that the bank may be undergoing and to the dynamic, ever-changing macro-economic landscape.

Regulatory focus is expected to remain elevated, and supervisors are likely to scrutinize idiosyncratic EWIs as these are more tailored to the bank's specific vulnerabilities. Liquidity risk managers at the bank must ensure that EWIs are governed as a part of the holistic risk management function within the organization. It is critical to ensure that EWIs are updated and aligned with other core aspects of the LRM framework, such as:

- Risk inventory
- Liquidity stress testing assumptions
- Cash flow—actuals and projections
- Business plans—Short-term/tactical and long-term/strategic
- Contingency funding plan
- Stakeholders—business lines/treasury/risk (second line of defense)

EWIs will likely aid in managing the risk and averting the crisis only if the reporting mechanism is highly efficient. Thus, liquidity risk managers should ensure the quality and timeliness of the data that feeds into the EWIs. A relevant and reliable EWI list will not only alert the leadership during or ahead of a crisis, but also will likely complement the overall risk management capabilities of the institution.

CHAPTER 7

Contingency Funding Planning

Chi Lai and Richard Tuosto[1]

ACTIONS IN A LIQUIDITY CRISIS

A contingency funding plan (CFP) serves as a logical connection to its companion, the liquidity stress testing framework, by linking the stress test results and other related information as inputs to the CFP governance, menu of contingent liquidity actions, and decision framework.

Contingent liquidity events can be categorized by their level of estimated adverse impact and probability. Institutions manage one end of the spectrum—the low-impact, high-probability events—as part of their business-as-usual (BAU) funding and liquidity risk management activities but use CFPs to address the other end of the spectrum associated with high-impact low-probability events. CFPs provide a structured approach for developing and implementing the institution's financial and operational strategies for effectively managing such contingent liquidity events during periods of severe market and financial stress.

This chapter provides a brief overview of the CFP's evolution and recent changes, design framework and key considerations, and implementation considerations.

EVOLVING CAPABILITIES AND ENHANCEMENTS

Formalized CFPs have gained greater traction and importance over the past decade as market disruptions have become more common and concerns for the survival of institutions in crisis have drawn sharpened attention. Progress has been made in formalizing and standardizing CFPs; however, there remain notable differences among institutions with respect to the level of coverage

---

[1]Chi Lai is a director in PwC's New York office, and Richard Tuosto is a manager in PwC's New York office.

and detail. In general, smaller institutions have typically included their CFPs as part of their broader business continuity plans, while larger institutions have established more formalized CFPs. Larger, more complex firms may also have several CFPs to address the specific challenges and options for different subsidiaries and legal entities.

The European Banking Commission's 2008 report, "EU Bank's Liquidity Stress Testing and Contingency Funding Plans," which highlighted the practices of 84 surveyed institutions, noted recommendations on areas for enhancements, and provided guidance to supervisors and central banks on areas of focus for their evaluation of the institutions' CFPs. Since that time, supervisors have released additional guidance pertaining to CFP design and implementation requirements. More recently, the Federal Reserve, in its "Enhanced Prudential Standards for Bank Holding Companies and Foreign Banking Organizations" guidance, required that banking organizations operating in the U.S. with $50 billion or more in assets establish and maintain a CFP to set out the company's strategies for addressing liquidity needs during liquidity stress events.

As part of this guidance, supervisors have indicated that CFPs should have defined policies and procedures that address the governance, roles and responsibilities, liquidity measures and triggers, menu of contingent actions, and communication protocols. Further, an institution's CFP, or collective set of CFPs, should be tailored to the specific business and risk profiles of the institution, covering the different set of businesses, subsidiaries, legal entities, products/asset classes, and geographic and foreign exchange (FX) coverage in which the institution operates. Finally, institutions should also regularly test their CFPs to ensure operational effectiveness.

In addition to the specific guidance on CFPs, other supervisory guidance on capital management, liquidity risk management, and recovery and resolution planning have impacted how institutions design their CFPs. In particular, the Federal Reserve's Comprehensive Liquidity Assessment and Review (CLAR) and the daily liquidity regulatory reporting requirements have linkages to the CFPs' governance and liquidity measures. Additionally, CFPs are often referenced as part of and aligned to an institution's recovery and resolution planning activities, as liquidity risk is often one of the key drivers of the potential institution's failure and a critical resource needed to effectively support the execution of the institutions' resolution strategies'. In this capacity, the CFP serves as an important bridge between the institution's BAU liquidity risk management practices and the recovery and resolution planning activities, where specific parts of the institution must be resolved.

DESIGN CONSIDERATIONS

While no universal CFP exists that can cover all types of institutions and situations, there are several CFP key design considerations that firms should be mindful of in designing or refreshing their CFPs. These considerations include the following:

I. Aligned to business and risk profiles
II. Integrated with broader risk management frameworks
III. Operational and actionable, but flexible playbook
IV. Inclusive of appropriate stakeholder groups
V. Supported by a communication plan

I. Align to Business and Risk Profiles

CFPs should be considered in the context of the institution's specific business and risk profiles, including the scope of business activities, products/asset classes, geographic and FX coverage, and legal entity structures. Institutions should ensure consistency by aligning their risk appetite statement to the CFP framework, through quantifiable early warning indicators, limits, and escalation levels.

A CFP should be refreshed accordingly as the institution's business and risk profile changes over time; both internally as corporate and business strategies change, new products and services are introduced, as well as externally, as the macroeconomic and market environments evolve. In addition to the periodic updates to the CFP, leading institutions are taking a more proactive stance on the development of the CFP by incorporating it as part of, or in parallel with, their strategic planning exercises, thereby positioning the CFP to be more forward-looking and flexible.

II. Integrate with Broader Risk Management Frameworks

The CFP is not a stand-alone tool, but rather, an integrated part of the institution's liquidity risk management and firm-wide risk management frameworks, including enterprise risk management (ERM), capital management, and business continuity and crisis management. This integration of the CFP to other components of the ERM disciplines increases the CFP's effectiveness and consistency by enabling it to leverage and reference established controls and processes.

The CFP should be explicitly linked to the liquidity risk measurement framework and the liquidity stress test, in particular through its limit structure and escalation levels. For example, the liquidity risk measures used in the institution's BAU risk management activities serve as a foundation from which the CFP defines its early warning indicators (EWIs). Additionally, linkages to the business continuity and crisis management frameworks will reinforce key operational and communication protocols during times of crisis.

III. Operational, Actionable, but Flexible Playbook

As a playbook, the effectiveness of the CFP lies in its operational readiness. In a crisis, the ability to convene management and start to develop contingent strategies and a plan of action would likely prove highly challenging without prior planning. As such, it is important for the CFP to include a menu of possible contingency actions that management can undertake in different stress scenarios and at graduated levels of severity. These graduated stress levels should be aligned to EWIs, triggers, and contingency actions. Through this process, the institution will have a structured roadmap, outlining potential liquidity risks and associated management actions that can be calibrated for different stages of the liquidity crisis.

By virtue of the fact that the CFP cannot anticipate all possible situations that may lead to a liquidity crisis, effective CFPs strike a balance between specifying recommended contingency actions while enabling management sufficient flexibility and discretion to make informed decisions as the crisis evolves over time.

IV. Inclusive of Appropriate Stakeholder Groups

Developing operational readiness in a CFP requires a thorough understanding of both strategic and tactical aspects of the institution. This assessment begins with scenario design, contingency planning, and communication strategies, and continues through execution, where timely coordination and communication are critical to ensuring that internal and external stakeholders remain confident in the institution's financial strength.

For these reasons, the involvement of appropriate stakeholder groups, including various management committees (e.g., asset-liability committee (ALCO), risk and capital committee, investment committee), business units, finance, corporate treasury, risk, operations and technology, is needed to capture the appropriate elements of the CFP as part of the design and to ensure successful coordination from an execution standpoint. In practice, involvement of the various stakeholder groups provides a strong forum in which potential issues or challenges can be openly discussed and addressed.

V. Supported by a Communication Plan

As in any crisis, the coordinated and timely communication of information to stakeholders is critical—a key lesson that resurfaced in the recent financial crisis. In addition to the need for the institution to be internally coordinated, external communication to clients, analysts, counterparties, and regulators with timely and accurate information is critical as it helps to reinforce confidence in the institution and mitigate potential risk that rumors and fears do not further precipitate and adversely impact the institution.

FRAMEWORK AND BUILDING BLOCKS

With these key design considerations in mind, institutions can develop their CFPs using an integrated framework that addresses the people, process, data, and reporting dimensions, keeping in mind that the CFP framework should be tailored to its business and risk profiles, including the scope and scale of its business activities, products/asset classes, geographic and FX coverage, subsidiaries, and/or legal entities.

Key components of a CFP framework include the following:

1. Governance and oversight
2. Scenarios and liquidity gap analysis
3. Contingent actions
4. Monitoring and escalation
5. Data and reporting

Governance and Oversight

An effective CFP requires both well-defined roles and responsibilities and a strong communication strategy that ensures timely coordination and communication among internal and external stakeholders. Both the organizational roles and communications plan need to be supported by well-defined policies and procedures, and reinforced through CFP periodic testing and simulation exercises.

Stakeholder involvement, roles, and responsibilities A well-designed CFP requires representation from a variety of stakeholder groups across the institution. Front office and business groups can provide insights into how their businesses perform under different business environments and stress scenarios; corporate finance, treasury and risk management groups can provide perspectives on how funding and liquidity risk profiles are managed, both in BAU and in crisis situations, and the tools afforded as the liquidity crisis escalates; and operations can describe the collateral and cash management processes and how they manage the inflows and outflows of liquidity.

While the specific CFP roles and responsibilities of different groups may vary across different institutions, there are several groups that play a pivotal role in the CFP design and implementation, including corporate treasury, the liquidity crisis team, management committee, and board of directors. The following descriptions should serve as a starting point for institutions in defining specific CFP roles and responsibilities. Institutions should be mindful that these roles should be tailored to address institution-specific organizational structure, capabilities, and coverage/responsibilities:

Corporate treasury. As part of its BAU activities, corporate treasury monitors the ongoing business, risk, funding, and liquidity profile of the institution. The treasurer, in consultation with the CFO and others, may invoke the CFP and convene the liquidity crisis team (LCT) based on a review of the markets, industry, institution-specific conditions, and liquidity stress testing results.

Liquidity crisis team. The LCT serves as the central point of contact and is responsible for the continuous monitoring of the institution's liquidity profile. The LCT will also provide recommendations on CFP actions, working closely with corporate treasury and the management committee. In performing this function, the LCT helps ensure effective coordination and communication across the organization as well as with external stakeholders. The LCT should be composed of senior members of the institution's business and supporting functions, including C-level executives, and heads of business segments, geographies, and legal entities. Generally, the LCT is responsible for designing the CFP and submitting it to the senior management group for review and approval.

Management committee. During a crisis, the senior management of an institution provides oversight of the LCT and consults with the board of directors, monitoring the institution's liquidity risk profile and reviewing specific recommendations for and coordination of CFP actions.

Board of directors. The board of directors should be actively engaged, in coordination with the management committee and LCT teams, during the crisis and serve as an advisor and counsel to them. A strong understanding of the contents of the CFP will enable board members to be actively engaged with the management committee in evaluating CFP actions being considered, particularly if the institution's liquidity position continues to worsen, and strategic actions, such as large asset and/or subsidiary sales, need to be taken.

For institutions that have complex business models that include multiple business segments, geographies, and/or legal entities, it is important that the overall organizational structure be well defined at the parent level and the operating subsidiaries. This helps ensure a proper chain of command where decisions are well coordinated and aligned across the institution as a whole.

Communication and coordination CFPs should include a communications strategy and plan to ensure proper notification, coordination, issue reporting and escalation. The different groups across the institution must work in concert, relying on each other to ensure information is available on a timely basis to support management decision-making. Additionally, an effective communication strategy and plan promotes confidence. Confidence is critical, as demonstrated time and again in financial services industry, most recently during the financial crisis of 2007-08.

In any crisis situation, clear and timely communication helps the institution demonstrate a sense of control and confidence that management understands the challenges ahead and has a plan of action. This is important to both internal and external stakeholders, including employees, clients, counterparties, shareholders, ratings agencies, and regulators, as the loss of confidence can quickly spiral downward when rumors start to take over news headlines—whether such headlines are grounded on reality or not.

Communications with respect to messaging and content should be centrally managed. Everyone should be working off the same page. However, the bidirectional communication and coordination with the stakeholders should reside with those executive and management teams that have existing working relationships. For example:

- Business units—clients, counterparties
- Corporate treasury—regulators and supervisors, rating agencies, clearing banks
- Investor relations—investors, analyst community, public media
- Legal and compliance—regulators and supervisors

These coordination points may differ across institutions, depending on their size, complexity, and organization structure. Additionally, institutions may already have existing communication plans, as part of their BAU and/or business continuity activities. As such, institutions should look to leverage existing practices as part of their CFP design and make appropriate enhancements, where appropriate.

Policies and Procedures Institutions should document their CFPs and ensure alignment with other risk management, business continuity, and recovery planning-related policies and procedures. Documentation should include all aspects of the CFP, including the governance structure, processes, data, and reporting activities. An illustrative example of a CFP policy outline is as follows:

- Introduction
  - Overview and purpose of the CFP
  - Related policies including CFPs across business segments, geographies and legal entities, resolution and recovery planning, and business continuity policies
- Governance
  - Roles and responsibilities
  - Review and approval
  - Periodic review
- Stress testing and scenarios overview (likely covered in detail in separate document)
  - Methodology
  - Scenario design
  - Inputs, outputs, and calculations
  - Key assumptions
  - Data control
  - Model validation
- Monitoring and escalation
  - Regular monitoring and risk management
  - Liquidity gap analysis
  - Contingent actions
- Reporting
  - Reporting frequency
  - Briefing decks and reports

The CFP policy should be consistently applied, whether it is a single CFP or multiple CFPs, and should be reviewed and updated periodically to ensure continued alignment to the institutions current and forecasted business activities and risks exposures.

Testing and Readiness Assessment   On a periodic basis, institutions should evaluate their CFP operational readiness and test targeted elements of their CFPs to ensure relevance and execution effectiveness in times of stress, particularly given changing market dynamics and the institution's business and risk profiles. While certain contingent activities, such as business divestitures, large asset sales, and use of Federal Reserve borrowing, may be impractical or unavailable for testing, there are some market activities such as debt issuances, brokered deposits issuances, and limited securities sale of the investment portfolio to generate additional liquidity that may be appropriate to test.

Additionally, institutions should evaluate the CFP's operational effectiveness: Such activities should include the CFP's governance, escalation process, communication, coordination, and reporting. Leading institutions that perform frequent exercises that best simulate the potential liquidity crisis environment will improve the CFP's operational effectiveness and response times, aspects that are critical during a crisis. Further, the test simulations may also identify potential gaps and/or improvement opportunities that would otherwise be undetected if the CFP were left purely as a theoretical design exercise.

Scenarios and Liquidity Gap Analysis

Institutions should align their CFP stress scenarios to those in its liquidity stress testing framework, as well as to other frameworks such as the recovery and resolution plans. The liquidity stress testing scenarios will cover both systemic (general market) and idiosyncratic (institution-specific) risks and address both market (asset) liquidity and funding liquidity, over short-term and prolonged stress periods. The liquidity stress testing framework should ensure that effects of these stresses on the institution's liquidity profile is appropriately measured and monitored. The CFP in turn should provide a tactical mechanism for escalating a developing crisis to management's attention and ensuring actionable responses are available.

In addition to incorporating the outcomes of the institution's liquidity stress testing, the CFP itself may contain additional liquidity-related stress scenarios. These additional scenarios, while outside the institution's broader liquidity risk monitoring and limit structure (as contained within the liquidity stress test), ensure effective contingency plans are in place in the event of certain events that could potentially impact liquidity. For example, the CFP might include scenarios in which its intraday debit cap with Fedwire is exceeded, specific counterparties fail, or Federal Home Loan Bank funding becomes unavailable.

Contingent Actions

Based on the liquidity gap analysis, institutions can develop contingent actions/capital recovery actions, including a spectrum of business scoping activities, pricing initiatives, disposition actions, and potential expense control actions, that will help strengthen the institution's liquidity position. In general, the applicability and appropriateness of such contingent actions should be considered in the context of the nature and severity (amount) of capital shortfall, associated timing and pattern of the expected capital shortfall, estimated capital relief from the contingent action, and the institution's ability to execute internal or external/market activities associated with such contingent actions.

Examples of contingent actions include, but not are limited to the following:

- Maintaining lines of credit that allow borrowing without major restrictions on use and reasonable rates
- Increasing underwriting standards and dialing back lending
- Adjusting pricing strategies to increase premiums paid on deposit products in order to entice investors to place deposits with the institution
- Changing investment strategy to roll off reinvestment of securities at maturity
- Shifting allocation from short-term funding to longer-term funding sources
- Increasing issuance of brokered CDs or direct to consumer deposits
- Securitizing retail assets (e.g., mortgages, credit card receivables, loans, auto leases)
- Pledging of assets through the Federal Reserve discount window
- Selling liquid assets/investments
- Drawing down on securitization conduits
- Issuing subordinated debt
- Reducing asset growth through reduced balance transfers
- Issuing at-call loans (which can be recalled to provide cash when needed)
- Selling consumer loans and/or credit card receivables
- Selling business or business units
- Raising equity funds through asset sales or issuance
- Reducing capital distributions
- Curtailing discretionary spending and expenses

The availability and potential impact of these contingent actions is dependent on the systemic and/or idiosyncratic nature and severity of the stress events. For example, a general freeze-up or withdrawal of credit in the financial markets could prevent access to existing lines of credit for rolling over short-term obligations. Lenders may restrict or outright refuse to extend credit based on perceptions of the institution's financial strength and exposures to risks. Asset liquidity may decrease precipitously, leaving the institution challenged to fund certain business activities and commitments.

In general, a number of market factors can impact the institution's ability to take contingent actions including, but not limited to the following:

- Shutdown of securitization markets
- Restricted access to repo funding due to solvency issues, credit downgrades, or reputation damage
- Ratings downgrade and subsequent increase in collateral/margin requirements
- Predatory margin and collateral practices by counterparties
- Increased cash deposit requirements with custodian banks
- Increased cost-of-funding (i.e., debt yields)
- Deposit runoff
- Collapse of interbank market and wholesale funding concentration
- Counterparties not willing to roll over funding

Management should try to anticipate these challenges as well as the implications they may have on its liquidity responses. Where possible, the CFP should document mitigating actions that management would consider taking to address such challenges.

Market signals and reputational impact In the early stages when an institution experiences liquidity stress, it may elect to curtail certain businesses activities, tighten its credit and lending standards, and/or limit its exposure to higher risk counterparties to strengthen its liquidity profile and resources. While these responses will provide some measure of improved liquidity, such actions may send inadvertent signals to the market and thereby impact the external perception of the institution's financial strength and reputation, adversely limiting the availability and/or effectiveness of future contingent actions as the crisis evolves.

For example, borrowers who believe that the institution has spurned their business will likely look to other lenders. Counterparties, such as hedge funds, which rely on credit from prime brokers or trading counterparties, could cease their relationship with the institution and seek other trading partners or intermediaries. Certain debt holders that have strong business relationships with the institution could "force" a debt buyback, and the institution in agreeing to such buyback will likely reduce its liquidity; however, refusing to do so could raise questions regarding the institution's viability.

A change in the market's perception of an institution's viability could have rapid and severe impacts on its liquidity. For this reason, certain actions could cause more harm than benefit depending on the severity of the stress and the institution's financial strength, as already noted.

At various stages of liquidity stress, management must consider the signals that its actions convey to the markets, its lenders, clients, and counterparties. Depending on the specific timing, certain contingent actions, while they may provide short-term liquidity, may ultimately leave the institution worse off, depending on the reactions of its external stakeholders. For example, attempts to access a sovereign lending facility or other emergency source of funds may lead counterparties and lenders to immediately withdraw existing credit out of concern that the institution will fail. The sale of certain businesses or a suspension of activities, such as reverse repo or other customer funding operations, could be perceived as signs of distress. These contingent actions may be necessary during the later stages of the crisis; however, at earlier stages, perceived signals of weakness may actually precipitate a liquidity crunch for the institution.

Monitoring and Escalation

The CFP should leverage the institution's liquidity risk monitoring and measurement framework. This framework should include a portfolio of measures to monitor both the current liquidity profile and the anticipated effects of potential liquidity events. These measures can be organized as market and business measures (external and internal) and liquidity health measures (internal), and represent factors that affect—directly or indirectly—the institution's liquidity position. Collectively, these measures form a set of key risk indicators or Early Warning Indicators (EWIs) that provide advance signaling of potential liquidity problems on the horizon, enabling management to evaluate and take measured steps as the crisis escalates.

Early Warning Indicators   Market and business measures reflect the market environment and institution-specific business strategy and activities. These indicators, such as significant changes in levels and volatility of the equity markets, severe drop in institution's stock price, and dramatic changes in the business' revenues from a certain geographic area, can prompt management to evaluate how changing market conditions and institution's business strategy may be adversely impacted and thereby proactively take actions in advance of oncoming market disruptions.

Liquidity health measures serve as indicators of the institution's liquidity base and strength. While the market and business risk measures should be evaluated within a broader context, the liquidity health measures, such as short-term funding as a proportion of total funding, deposits-to-loan for depository businesses, and the firm's credit rating, are more targeted in that deterioration in these metrics reflect a direct and adverse impact on the institution's current and/or projected liquidity profile and strength.

Both types of measures are important for informing management of the potential effects of different liquidity stress scenarios. Internal and external

EWIs should be selected in concert so that the institution can identify emerging liquidity risks and the nature of these risks as idiosyncratic, systemic, or some combination of the two. The combination of EWIs and escalation levels enable the institution to anticipate and manage the liquidity crisis as it unfolds over time.

Market and Business Factors Institutions will need to define EWIs using external and internal information in order to monitor trends in the market as well as among the institution's peer group. Such information can include a combination of macroeconomic measures, industry measures, and institution-specific measures.

Macro-environment factors may not directly correspond to individual liquidity challenges that an institution may face; however, they can provide insight into general market distress and a systemic withdrawal of liquidity, similar to the freezing of the repo markets during the financial crisis. Macro-environment measures should focus on risks that are specific to the financial system and its general liquidity. Examples may include repo spreads, asset haircut trends, and movements in credit default swap (CDS) spreads.

Industry factors include trends in the profitability of the financial sector, recent rating agency action, banking industry capital adequacy, S&P financial institution sector movement, and other factors. Competitor analysis can also be applied to evaluate the trends in the industry to detect potential performance problems in an institution's peer group.

Institution-specific measures help management to assess the market's perception of the institution's financial strength and the likelihood of a liquidity crisis through external information. Internal measures provide greater insight into the operations of the institution and their potential impact on its liquidity position.

Examples of EWIs encompassing market and business factors include:

- Significant and unexpected drop in stock market indices
- Downgrade of U.S. Treasury or other sovereign debt rates
- Spike in market volatility (e.g., VIX)
- Unexpected catastrophic events (e.g., September 11, 2001, earthquakes)
- Rapid asset growth funded by potentially volatile liabilities
- Real or perceived negative publicity
- A decline in asset quality
- A decline in earnings performance or projections
- Downgrades or announcements of potential downgrades of the institution's credit rating by rating agencies
- Cancellation of loan commitments and/or not renewing maturing loans

- Wider secondary spreads on the institution's senior and subordinated debt, rising CDS spreads and increased trading of the bank's debt
- Increased collateral requirements or demand collateral for accepting credit exposure to the institution from counterparties
- Counterparties and brokers unwilling to deal in unsecured or longer-term transactions
- Requests from depositors for early withdrawal of their funds, or the bank has to repurchase its paper in the market
- Calls by debt holders for the institution to buy back its debt or CD issuance
- Volatility in foreign exchange markets, particularly in the currencies in which the institutions has exposure to and/or requires as part of its liquidity risk management

Such EWIs are generally most useful before or at the onset of the liquidity crisis, and during the early stages of the CFP escalation levels; however, their usefulness and applicability are aligned to the specific stress scenario and the institution's specific business and risk profiles.

Liquidity Heath Measures While the review of macro-economic and industry measures provide advance signaling of a potential pending liquidity crisis, institutions should also monitor a suite of liquidity health ratios to help quantify the impact of the liquidity risks and to support decision making on CFP actions being considered. These metrics will typically be detailed in the institution's liquidity risk management policy and referenced by the CFP. Key liquidity health measures include, but are not limited to, the following:

- **Projected net funding requirements to current unused funding capacity.** Measures the funding and borrowing needed to finance the institution's increased lending activities and banking activities, and provides an approach to assess the institution's future lending obligations in proportion to the total funds available at the institution.
- **Non-core funding to long-term assets.** Measures the proportion of long-term funding needs that are supported by less stable sources of funding. A higher non-core funding dependency ratio is indicative of a high dependence on volatile funding sources that, during times of financial stress, may have limited availability or may only be available at a much higher cost.
- **Overnight borrowings to total assets.** Measures the reliance on overnight funding to fund the institution's assets as the use of this volatile source of funding can expose the institution to increased liquidity risk.

- **Short-term liabilities to total assets.** Measures the funding levels that will need to be rolled over within a predetermined short-term time period (e.g., under 30 days, 60 days, 90 days) to support the institution's assets.
- **Funding sources concentration.** The concentration of funding sources for an institution is an important measure for understanding which counterparties are most likely to cease providing liquidity during a stress event. Liquidity providers that comprise a substantial proportion of an institution's funding needs could cause serious harm to liquidity during times of stress, should they decide that their exposure to the institution is too large and decrease that exposure. Managing concentration and establishing a variety of liquidity providers will likely lessen the impact of the loss of any single provider and give the institution additional sources of liquidity to tap in the case of a shortfall.
- **Funding maturity profile.** In addition to managing the concentration of funding sources, institutions should also evaluate the concentration of maturities for their funding. Large concentrations in funding maturities can threaten an institution's liquidity position, particularly when a concentration in maturity is accompanied by a reliance on short-term funding. Institutions should assess the maturity horizon of their funding sources in tandem with the concentration of funding sources and with significant consideration to the institution's reliance on short-term funding.
- **Used capacity to total borrowing capacity.** Measures the borrowing capacity available to the institution, based on the used capacity relative to the total borrowing capacity, where the used capacity represents the amount of funding currently being utilized across all funding channels (core funding, interbank markets, and funds generated by institutional sales).
- **Liquid assets to volatile liabilities.** Measures the basic surplus or cushion that liquid assets provide over required funding needs and can be used to monitor the level of liquid assets available to offset volatile funding.
- **Unpledged eligible collateral to total assets.** Measures the institution's ability to sell assets or use assets as collateral to obtain funding to meet future requirements. The ability to quickly identify and understand the liquidity of unencumbered assets will help it optimize its management of the collateral, particularly during periods of market stress.
- **Loans to commitments.** Measures the exposure to credit facilities that may be required at some point in the future. As these commitments are drawn down, utilization increases, prompting further need for funding to meet the obligations.

For institutions with more advanced liquidity risk management capabilities, these liquidity health measures will also include daily liquidity position reporting, the Basel III Liquidity Coverage Ratio (LCR) and the Net Stable Funding Ratio (NSFR) measures.

These liquidity health measures should be monitored continuously over the course of the crisis; however, their importance is related to their associated limits. As these liquidity health measures start to reach predefined limits, management should start to evaluate what contingent actions are appropriate. Similar to the market and business measures, the usefulness and applicability of liquidity health measures are dependent on the institution's scope and complexity of business activities.

Escalation levels In designing their CFPs, institutions establish a series of escalation levels properly aligned to the scenarios, contingency actions, and liquidity measures, including EWIs and health measures. While there are no specific guidelines in the number of escalation levels required in CFPs, three to five escalation levels are common industry practice. For illustrative purposes, here are descriptions of the different escalation levels, using three levels:

- **Level 1.** This is the initial escalation level and represents elevated monitoring over market conditions and the impact to the institution's business segments and performance. Level 1 could be triggered by stress test results indicating a greater decline in liquidity than the institution's risk appetite targets and/or a shift in the market's perception of the institution.

  The convening of the LCT prompts closer coordination and communications among the various stakeholders internally and a communication plan is executed to keep external stakeholder properly informed and aware of the institution-specific issues and challenges, and actions being contemplated. Monitoring should remain focused on forward-looking measures of the institution's liquidity health and the general market perception. Business activities that are expected to impact the business and risk profile of the institution will likely be closely monitored with increased frequency and scrutiny.

- **Level 2.** At this escalation level, the institution has experienced noticeable markets and/or idiosyncratic events that are adversely impacting its business and liquidity risk profile. The institution should monitor indicators of its current liquidity position and any causes of deterioration more closely, with a focus on how the institution's peers and counterparties react to the changing market dynamics.

As the crisis continues to worsen, management's attention is on recovery while sustaining business and financial performance; however, the focus is more attuned to the immediate and short-term horizon. The LCT and management committee activities are taken to actively enhance the institution's liquidity position, likely curtailing business activities, and limiting the extension of additional and new credit facilities.

In addition, the institution may take steps to improve its liquidity through strategic sales of less liquid portfolio investments and assets, in addition to evaluating the feasibility of significant CFP contingent actions, such as larger asset sales, business divestitures, and discontinuing certain business activities, given the evolving market conditions.

▪ **Level 3.** At the later stages of the crisis, the institution would have taken dramatic steps to stabilize its liquidity position, potentially including significant curtailing of liquidity intensive business activities or disposition/sales of businesses.

At this point, the institution's focus is primarily on survival. In this situation, the market environment, state of the institution, and potential CFP actions show similarities to the circumstances contemplated as part of the institution's recovery and resolution planning activities.

Events that trigger the status of the escalation level should be analyzed to understand the cause of the trigger event(s) and the association to capital adequacy; findings should be summarized and communicated, along with specific recommendations. The movement from one escalation level to another—whether up or down—should be explicitly considered and approved by the LCT. While the CFP provides a structured outline for the expected levels and trend of EWIs and liquidity risk measures, the importance of management's expert judgment and ability to put together the mosaic of the different challenges and decide on a proper course of action should not be understated.

At each escalation level, notification, review and approval requirements should be defined to ensure appropriate communications and reporting, in alignment and concert with the defined CFP governance structure, roles and responsibilities. For example, the Level 1 escalation level, which represents heightened management monitoring, may require only notification and periodic update to senior management, CFO, CRO, etc.; contingent actions taken at this level may require ALCO and/or the Treasurer. At the Level 2 or 3 escalation levels, where contingency actions typically involve more severe actions, notification as well as approvals for certain contingent actions will inevitably involve senior management and/or the Board.

Additional information on EWIs can be found in Chapter 6—Early Warning Indicators.

Data and Reporting

When ensuring that the institution's liquidity risk monitoring and measuring framework adequately supports the objectives of the CFP, one should consider the frequency with which various measurements utilized to monitor and manage liquidity risk are generated, assessed, and reported. While daily reporting of the liquidity profile to the treasury function and the funding desks is prevalent at many institutions, there are a number of institutions that could benefit from increasing the frequency of liquidity management reporting, especially to other areas of the institution (such as senior management group, ALCO and other risk committees, and the board). This broader reporting of liquidity management should have the contextual information and qualitative guidance to support senior management in its approach to understanding the institution's liquidity profile.

Reports should convey the methods used to determine liquidity coverage for upcoming liabilities and funding needs and elaborate on the level of coverage predicted by these measures. In addition, institutions should ensure that existing reports capture intraday liquidity positions, track exposure to contingent liabilities, and monitor capacity usage in funding sources.

Consideration should be given to the dissemination of liquidity risk reports within the institutions, how these reports are used by management and the board in making decisions, and the appropriateness of the information contained within the reports, given their audience.

ADDITIONAL CONSIDERATIONS

Different Types of Institutions

As noted earlier, the scope and depth of the CFP will be dependent on the type of institution. Depository institutions will primarily focus on their deposit base and potential runoff, while institutions that rely more on wholesale funding will look to lines of credit and funding markets. Insurance companies primarily derive their funding from the liabilities of their policies and have historically focused on cash flow matching more than banking institutions. These unique characteristics should be reflected in the CFP's design, monitoring tools, and menu of contingent actions.

Institutions must also recognize the risks inherent in their business practices. Lending institutions that specialize in revolvers and other open commitment loans should incorporate the potential liquidity drain from obligors drawing down on unfunded commitments. Prime brokers and broker dealers can experience a decline in the funding coverage of their assets as clients withdraw their accounts from the institution. Counterparties may also make collateral calls, where they previously did not, on positions that have moved in their favor or refuse to post collateral. Institutions that rely on wholesale funding may also experience higher margin requirements and collateral haircuts as their creditworthiness comes under question.

Organizational Structure of the CFPs

An effective CFP properly addresses the institution's suite of businesses, geographies, and legal entities. However, it is unlikely that a single CFP document can properly cover all these elements in a clear and concise manner. More practically, institutions have developed a portfolio of CFPs. This portfolio of CFPs consists of individual CFPs that address business-specific segment, products/asset classes, geographic and FX coverage, and legal entities. In aggregate, the portfolio of CFPs provides a comprehensive view and coverage of the institution's business activities.

Depending on the nature and scope of the institution, separate CFPs may be necessary to address regulatory requirements. For example, ring-fenced entities that are supervised by a different regulator than that of the institution's regulator at the holding company have separate CFPs. Some industry participants have taken the opportunity to align CFP coverage to also include legal entities classifications associated with their recovery and resolution planning strategies. Other institutions that have large FX business and coverage may develop a currency CFP that analyzes the currency exposures across its legal entities.

Liquidity and Capital

The advancement of capital and liquidity practices, guided both by enhanced expectations from supervisors as well as internally-driven initiatives, has been notable; however, there is still work to be done. Historically, capital and liquidity management practices have been highly siloed; however, most recently, institutions have started to bring a more integrated approach and view to these areas. This integrated approach will help bring a common set of EWIs, a more comprehensive view of the impact of liquidity specific stress test results, and proposed response actions on capital positions and vice versa. Further, it should strengthen the alignment of the integrated liquidity and capital stress testing and contingency plans to other enterprise-wide applications, including recovery and resolution plans, capital management, enterprise risk management, and other related capabilities of the institution.

CONCLUSION

While institutions have made measureable progress in their CFPs, there are nevertheless opportunities for improvement. Regulatory focus will likely remain elevated in the area of liquidity risk management, and expectations will likely only increase. Consequently, institutions need to demonstrate their CFPs are well designed, aligned with the institution's target business and risk profiles, and are actionable. As such, institutions should review their CFPs to ensure that the key elements that constitute an effective CFP include the following attributes:

- Strong management involvement and participation from the enterprise
- Alignment to other capital and risk management frameworks
- Evaluation of a wide range of possible scenarios
- Clearly documented management action plan
- Communication plan with coordination to internal and external stakeholders

Institutions should be mindful that the CFP is a playbook—and as such, it requires updating on a regular basis. Strong CFPs will not only provide a menu of options during a time of crisis, but also enhance the overall strategic, business, and risk management capabilities of the institution, ultimately helping to establish further credibility and confidence from the institution's external stakeholders.

REFERENCES

European Central Bank. 2008. "EU Bank's Liquidity Stress Testing and Contingency Funding Plans," European Central Bank

SR 10-6. "Interagency Policy Statement on Funding and Liquidity Risk Management," 2010. OCC, FRB, FDIC, OTS, NCUA

Basel Committee on Banking Supervision, 2008. "Principles for Sound Liquidity Risk Management and Supervision, Bank for International Settlement—Basel Committee on Banking Supervision"

Office of the Comptroller of the Currency. 2012. Comptroller's Handbook, "Safety and Soundness—Liquidity," June 2012, Office of the Comptroller of the Currency

R. Bryant. "Contingency Funding Plan: Banking Busywork or Essential Management Tool?" Federal Reserve Bank of Atlanta

CHAPTER 8

Liquidity Risk Management Information Systems

Saroj Das, Shyam Venkat, and Chi Lai[1]

Treasurers of banks and financial institutions are seeking to improve visibility of the sources and uses of liquidity across their operating entities; move towards greater centralization of liquidity management activities; and implement more robust stress testing and liquidity contingency plans. Their key objectives are to gauge potential threats to the liquidity position of the firm, estimate and strategically address funding requirements, facilitate continued operation within acceptable risk tolerance limits, and provide timely and transparent reporting to internal and external stakeholders. To achieve these objectives, an effective liquidity risk MIS is required; however, as most institutions can attest to, this is easier said than done, as firms face a number of challenges, including:

- Evolving regulatory rules and heightened regulatory expectations for data reporting granularity and frequency
- Increasing focus on collateral management and intraday liquidity
- Expanding requirements for granular data spanning multiple subsystems
- Disparate systems of record resulting in lack of data quality
- Manually intensive data management process and ad-hoc data retrieval
- Assembling position data at pre-aggregated levels, resulting in lack of granularity
- Reconciling LRM metrics with underlying data and books of records due to lack of transparency and an audit trail
- Complex data classification and aggregation rules across many regulatory and organization dimensions over large volumes of data
- Lack of computational flexibility to run complex calculations and advanced analytics over large volumes of data
- Extensive use of spreadsheets and other end user computing applications

---

[1]Saroj Das was formerly a director in PwC's Atlanta office; Shyam Venkat is a principal in PwC's New York office; and Chi Lai is a director in PwC's New York office.

141

- Non-standard reporting infrastructure for disseminating information across multiple constituencies

LRM has shifted from traditionally falling under the purview of the treasury function's asset and liability management (ALM) mandate to an enterprise-wide, holistic process warranting a more integrated and consistent risk management framework. This requires close collaboration among the firm's treasury, business units, and other functions to understand the nature of the institution's business strategies, balance sheet requirements, and liquidity positions. An expansive liquidity risk MIS should include robust data and analytics infrastructure as well as have the architectural agility to respond to changing business needs quickly. Important capabilities that define a leading liquidity risk MIS include:

- **Integrated operating environment.** The liquidity risk MIS infrastructure design and implementation should be well integrated with asset-liability management, funds transfer pricing (FTP) including the allocation of liquidity costs, hedging and diversification of funding sources priorities, business forecasting, and capital planning to enable strategic decision making and optimization of return and risk considerations.
- **"Golden source" of data.** The disparate data sources that often make up the composition of liquidity data present significant challenges. To develop a comprehensive and integrated view of the institution's liquidity profile, the relevant liquidity data needs to be sourced, aggregated, normalized, standardized, and integrated.
- **Unified data management.** The data management process should be supported by governance and controls ensuring standardization, conformance, quality, reconciliation, traceability, auditability, and flexibility to add and change data.
- **Computational flexibility.** The calculation and analytics engines for measuring liquidity risk should be flexible and provide for complex quantitative modeling capabilities that can provide cash flow projections, generate and run complex stress scenarios, and enable the implementation of rule changes fairly quickly.
- **Adaptive reporting and information monitoring (IM) engine.** The reporting and IM engine should support intraday, daily, weekly, and monthly liquidity monitoring; survival horizon analyses; report-level calculations and validation rules; regulatory metrics and templates; audit trails; access to granular data; and timely implementation of changes.
- **Flexible information architecture.** The information architecture should have a flexible architecture that is forward-looking, enabling changes and enhancements to the data structure, elements, and relationships, as well as linkages to external data sources.
- **Information readiness.** Basic information should be readily available for day-to-day liquidity and funds management and during times of stress.

LIQUIDITY RISK MIS REFERENCE ARCHITECTURE

The MIS plays a critical role in establishing a well-integrated, automated, and sustainable LRM operating platform that can facilitate timely decision support by transforming raw on- and off-balance sheet position data into meaningful liquidity risk measures and information that can support management decision making.

The liquidity risk MIS architecture requires the organization of functional requirements and logic for enterprise-wide LRM processes, workflows, analytics and stress tests, and IT capabilities. Accordingly, the MIS architectural design and implementation should be viewed as a strategic, rather than a technical, exercise with a vision of driving optimum business value from the IT capabilities. The design of the MIS should be scalable and flexible and allow the operating platform to attain architectural maturity over time by transitioning into a standardized use of technology components that can readily incorporate potential changes in liquidity regulatory rules and business decisions.

In developing liquidity risk MIS infrastructures, firms should evaluate the considerations and key architectural components illustrated in Figure 8.1 and explained in the following list:

Position and reference data collection. Within similar product classes and/or cash flow categories, the data collection templates should be standardized to eliminate duplication. Upstream data transformation that is native to the subsystems should be handled by the subsystems to derive target fields.

Data integration. A normalized treasury data warehouse (TDW) should be developed by integrating position and reference data at its most granular level while keeping the native business entity relationship (i.e., master entity to transaction entity) as close as possible to the actual business processes; in defining this data relationship, one should consider using a normalized data architecture technique and reconcile position data to the general ledger and other important financial systems of record.

Data classification and aggregation. A denormalized LRM data mart will help to capture and stratify cash flow positions by the required data aggregation dimensions and regulatory classification buckets (i.e., Basel III and U.S. Federal Reserve classification rules). This can be achieved by using a set of shared and conformed internal organization dimensions, including asset/liability (A/L) product charts of accounts, high quality liquid asset (HQLA) classes & regulatory dimensions, and fact constellation (i.e., an individual flat table for each A/L instrument) configuration.

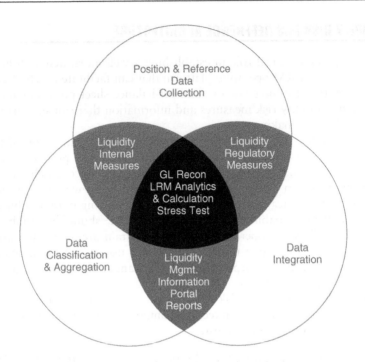

FIGURE 8.1 Liquidity Risk MIS Architecture Components

Liquidity internal measures, reports, and LRM information portal. A set of metrics and reports to support liquidity managers' day-to-day needs for liquidity monitoring and decision making (e.g., liquidity ratios and limits, mismatch, concentrations of large fund providers, etc.) should also be developed and included within the periodic reporting packages for management committees, including the asset and liability committee (ALCO). Furthermore, developing an enterprise-wide LRM information portal will enable senior management to access a single view of the firm's global liquidity position as well as a forecasted liquidity survival horizon.

Liquidity regulatory measures. Capabilities should be developed to support the calculation of the Basel III Liquidity Coverage Ratio (LCR), HQLA buffer, and other U.S. Federal Reserve daily liquidity position reports. The reporting capabilities should be enhanced to show aggregated and details views, including holding company level as well as drill down to legal entity, line of business (LOB), currency, jurisdiction, and other granular dimensions required by regulatory mandates.

An agile and adaptive approach should be established for the design, implementation, operation, and management of the liquidity risk MIS infrastructure (e.g., componentization of data stores, analytical engine, analysis and reporting platform). This approach reduces the risk of a single point of failure, further enhancing the architecture's resilience and sustainability. The core components to design and implement a robust liquidity risk MIS include:

- LRM information portal and reporting
- LRM analytical engine
- LRM data mart—data classification and aggregation
- GL reconciliation
- TDW—data integration
- Source data collection and staging

Liquidity Risk Management Information Portal (MIP) and Reporting

As enterprise-wide active liquidity management importance continues to grow, financial institutions seek better and easier tools to manage liquidity. Banks are responding with new tools such as a one-stop-shop MIP, where CFOs, corporate treasurers, risk managers and other members of management can access and monitor not only a consolidated view on global liquidity position but also a forward-looking view of the firm's liquidity profile. A liquidity MIP provides an integrated platform for liquidity information, planning, and analysis.

Achieving revenue and earnings potential requires managing a bank's balance sheet in a holistic manner by linking risk, funding, contingency planning, and customer-facing decision making to a consistent understanding of liquidity behavior. The liquidity MIP acts as an accelerator to catalyze improved visibility into underlying liquidity characteristics within the business operating network. One should define clear business objectives and capabilities to design a robust liquidity MIP. An illustrative list of business capabilities includes:

- Control over day-to-day liquidity
- Transparency into cash holdings and forecasted flows on a daily and intraday basis
- Analysis of new products and their effects on liquidity
- Visibility of crucial information, which facilitates the development of key performance indicators (KPIs) such as overdrafts and idle balances
- Effective management of funding levels and variances to forecasts

- Monitoring of trends in the volume and pricing of assets, liabilities, and off-balance-sheet items that may significantly impact liquidity
- Enterprise-wide visibility of global financial information (cash and investments) aggregated within a single service
- Analysis of cash flow and funding mismatch gaps over different time horizons, early warning indicators, and regulatory liquidity ratios
- Monitoring of a survival horizon under stress conditions, and of unencumbered collateral positions on a daily and intraday basis
- Reduction in short-term external funding needs by monitoring funding concentration and wholesale funding

In order to satisfy the aforementioned business capabilities, a well-integrated liquidity MIP framework should enable online analytical processing (OLAP) functionality for LRM that enables dynamic multidimensional analysis of consolidated enterprise liquidity information, supported by end user analytical and navigational activities (e.g., multidimensional views of the liquidity risk measures and metrics by organizational hierarchies, trend analysis and comparisons over sequential time periods, and cash flow forecasting and analysis over a range of time buckets).

Liquidity risk reporting package framework   It is important to create a reporting management framework that can support accurate and timely reporting at multiple levels. In this regard, business stakeholders at all levels should be involved early on to define their functional requirements, liquidity decision-making data points, and reporting needs to drive the reporting package configuration. Determination of the reporting hierarchies, frequency, selection of measures and metrics, and the level of aggregation play a vital role in enabling the LRM reporting engine to generate a consistent set of reports, and allow flexibility for ad-hoc report requests.

The increased oversight and emerging regulatory mandates have prompted LRM practices within financial institutions to produce a varied spectrum of different reporting packages with narratives on market conditions, internal liquidity metrics and KPIs, stress test results and early warning indicators, peer financial institution benchmarks, and executive dashboards and heat maps. To help improve efficiency and effectiveness, these packages should be produced as standard reports prepared on a recurring basis supported with additional flexibility to respond to ad-hoc queries. The key elements involved in designing and implementing a robust liquidity reporting management framework are detailed in Figure 8.2 and detailed further in the following paragraphs.

Information readiness. Reports containing certain basic information should be readily available for day-to-day liquidity and funds management

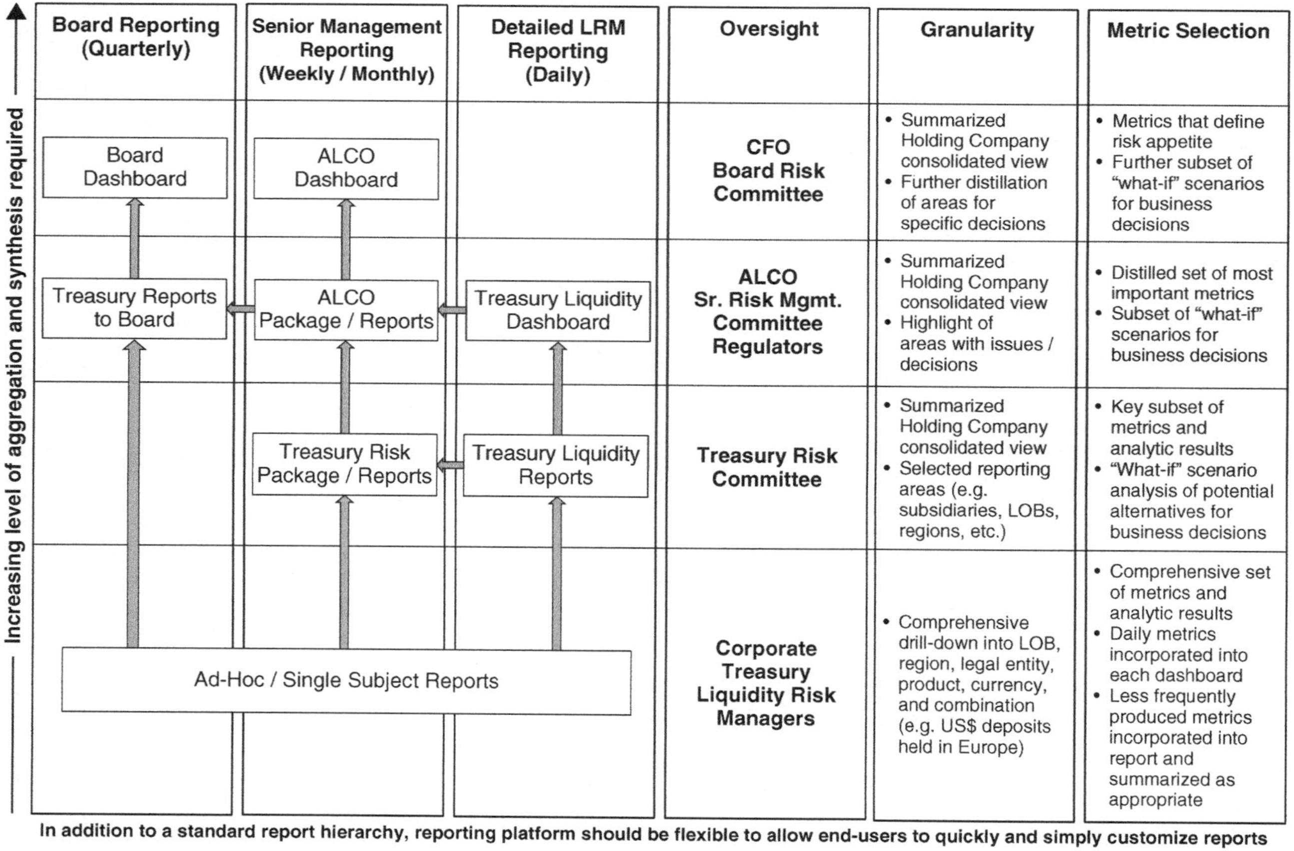

FIGURE 8.2 Liquidity Risk MIS Liquidity Reporting Package Framework

◄———— Increasing level of aggregation and synthesis required ————

Board Reporting (Quarterly)	Senior Management Reporting (Weekly / Monthly)	Detailed LRM Reporting (Daily)	Oversight	Granularity	Metric Selection
Board Dashboard	ALCO Dashboard	Treasury Liquidity Dashboard	CFO Board Risk Committee	• Summarized Holding Company consolidated view • Further distillation of areas for specific decisions	• Metrics that define risk appetite • Further subset of "what-if" scenarios for business decisions
Treasury Reports to Board	ALCO Package / Reports	Treasury Liquidity Reports	ALCO Sr. Risk Mgmt. Committee Regulators	• Summarized Holding Company consolidated view • Highlight of areas with issues / decisions	• Distilled set of most important metrics • Subset of "what-if" scenarios for business decisions
	Treasury Risk Package / Reports		Treasury Risk Committee	• Summarized Holding Company consolidated view • Selected reporting areas (e.g. subsidiaries, LOBs, regions, etc.)	• Key subset of metrics and analytic results • "What-if" scenario analysis of potential alternatives for business decisions
	Ad-Hoc / Single Subject Reports		Corporate Treasury Liquidity Risk Managers	• Comprehensive drill-down into LOB, region, legal entity, product, currency, and combination (e.g. US$ deposits held in Europe)	• Comprehensive set of metrics and analytic results • Daily metrics incorporated into each dashboard • Less frequently produced metrics incorporated into report and summarized as appropriate

In addition to a standard report hierarchy, reporting platform should be flexible to allow end-users to quickly and simply customize reports

and during times of stress. Report formats and their contents will vary from bank to bank depending on the characteristics of the bank and its funds management methods and practices. As illustrated in Figure 8.2, a standard LRM reporting framework should typically encompass the operational liquidity needs of core business areas, the sensitivity of fund providers to both systemic and institution-specific trends and events, economic conditions affecting other aspects of the bank's assets and liabilities, and regulatory reports and metrics:

Technology platform consideration. Reporting and the MIP engine should support liquidity monitoring over various horizons (e.g., intraday, daily, monthly, quarterly) and report-level calculations and validation rules, regulatory metrics and templates, and audit trails. Additionally, it should provide access to granular data to enable drill-down reporting capabilities. In light of frequent regulatory rule changes as well as internal stakeholders' requests for ad-hoc information, the reporting and MIP platform should be scalable and flexible to enable the addition, subtraction, or other changes of data elements quickly.

There are several business intelligence and reporting tools readily available in the marketplace; however, given the large volume of data and complexity involved in LRM reporting and the MIP, firms should consider using server-based advanced business intelligence technologies that support ample amounts of cache and in-memory data manipulation and analytical operations, as well as multiple OLAP techniques. These business intelligence platforms offer a range of advanced features such as server-based cache mechanism, framework manager–based multidimensional OLAP design, reports and dashboard design, portal design, drill-down and drill-through techniques to access the underlying data, Java-based web-server integration, and web-based MIP. The regulatory metrics and templates required for liquidity risk reporting can be developed and customized using these business intelligence applications. Additionally, there are leading treasury risk management vendor applications that provide out-of-the-box reporting and MIP capabilities. Many of these vendor applications also pre-package Basel III multi-jurisdiction liquidity risk reporting and U.S. Federal Reserve regulatory reporting templates.

Both regulatory and internal liquidity risk reporting are data intensive in nature and warrant asset and liability position data to be classified in accordance with the regulatory guidance prior to the metrics calculation and aggregation. For the most part, this level of data transformation and business rules association would require the classification scheme to be developed outside of the reporting engine irrespective of whether one chooses to proceed with a homegrown application or an off-the-shelf vendor product.

Liquidity Risk Management Analytical Engine

The LRM analytical engine should encompass analytics data sets, calculations, and the stress test engine, and have capabilities that can run complex quantitative models to project cash flows, generate advanced stress scenarios, perform the stress tests over multiple time buckets, and compute regulatory calculations over large volumes of data. The use of a common analytical engine for ALM interest rate risk, liquidity risk management, fund transfer pricing, and capital management would help provide consistency of contractual and behavioral assumptions, accounts and products hierarchy, and reporting across all treasury functions.

The key elements involved in a comprehensive treasury risk analytics engine design and implementation are detailed in Figure 8.3. Components of the liquidity stress test analysis engine are elaborated to illustrate the multi-dimensional nature of the liquidity stress test, degree of complexity involved, and an approach to implement.

As depicted in Figure 8.3, the analytical engine data foundation can be developed using a set of flat analytics base tables (ABTs). The construction of the ABTs should follow the data stratification structure as required by the position data mapping from the LRM data mart to the analytical engine;

The LRM analytical engine should encompass analytics data sets, calculations, and stress test engine, and must be robust enough to run complex quantitative models to project cash-flows, generate advanced stress scenarios, perform the stress test over multiple time buckets, and compute regulatory calculations over a large volume of data.

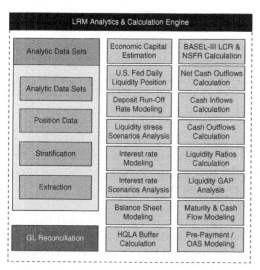

FIGURE 8.3 LRM Analytical Engine

the LRM analytical engine should provide a standard set of data exaction and stratification rules to capture data from the LRM data mart and stratify it into the ABTs. These ABTs are the suitable candidates to offer low data latency and high input/output (I/O) throughput that can significantly augment the overall performance of the analytical engine; a feedback loop should be built between the analytical engine data foundation and the LRM data mart to capture analytics outputs for history and reports.

The LRM analytical engine should support advanced quantitative methods for modeling of instrument valuation, cash flow projections, stochastic term structure of interest rates, net interest income, economic value of equity, deposit run-off rates, and stochastic stress scenarios. Additionally, the analytical engine should provide integration support for external models and market data.

Liquidity Stress Test Analysis Engine

The severe liquidity shocks witnessed during the financial crisis demonstrated a balance sheet feature that could work to amplify the effects of a small negative shock into large losses resulting in a two-way liquidity spiral (i.e., market liquidity and funding liquidity) and the equilibrium disorder. The contagion disrupted wholesale funding markets and interbank lending markets. As a result, a number of bank runs occurred as the banks failed to cover their obligations. The contagion also led to core deposit (i.e., demand deposits) runoff and a new phenomenon of an excess in noncore institutional deposit (i.e., hot money) inflows. In the light of these observations coupled with regulatory mandates, the liquidity stress test has taken center stage. Banks and financial institutions are required to gauge their liquidity position under various stress scenarios on a regular basis and formulate a tangible contingency plan to mitigate the risk.

The key elements involved in designing and implementing a thorough LRM stress test analysis engine are detailed in Figure 8.4.

It is important to employ an agile LRM stress test framework by designing and implementing a workflow driven stress test engine. Regardless of whether the stress test application is built in-house or a vendor product is selected, the application should offer user interfaces (UIs) for the end users to execute the test using a set of key workflow components, including:

- **Analyze and create a base case.** This entails analyzing on/off balance sheet asset and liability instruments with contractual, indeterminate, and behavioral cash flows to create a base case that reflects the concentration of the assets and liabilities. This workflow step should allow the end-user to design relevant stress scenarios that can cause erosion of liquidity.

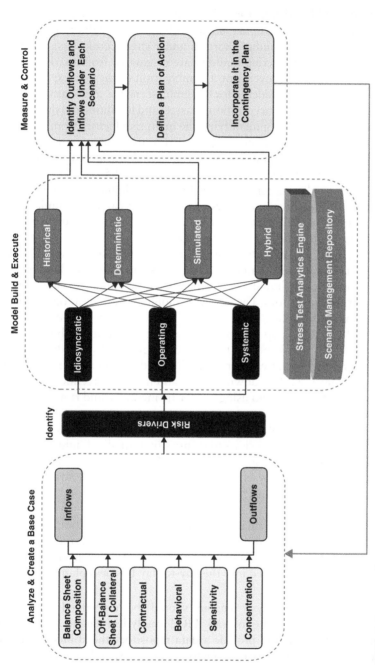

FIGURE 8.4 Liquidity Stress Test Analysis Engine

- **Identify liquidity risk factors.** This requires identifying a set of liquidity risk factors or drivers in alignment with asset and liability instruments that can manifest liquidity shortfall under stress conditions. Normally, the risk factors impacting liquidity are originated from market, credit, and operational risk events or a combination of these risks; hence, the risk factors to be considered for designing scenarios are relatively larger. The analysis of the concentration of assets and liabilities and their behavioral profile will aid in identifying the main risk factors from the larger population. Techniques such as principal component analysis (PCA) can help in reducing the number of factors to be considered for designing stress scenarios, by choosing those which explain 95% or 99% of historically observed variations. This workflow step should allow the end-user to identify a set of stress factors or drivers that can cause liquidity erosion, and map these factors to the individual instrument or to a group of instruments defined in the base case.
- **Model, build, and execute.** Banks are required to design scenarios taking into consideration both idiosyncratic stress and system-wide stress. The stress test model should support deterministic and stochastic scenario generation capabilities. The scenarios should be built by adopting historical, simulated, and hybrid methods. This workflow step should allow the end-user to set up dimensionalities (e.g., asset and liability regulatory category, legal entity, LOB, currency, geography, product, etc.) to configure the base case; enter manually the deterministic stress scenario assumptions (i.e., drawdown, runoff, and haircut percentage); generate advanced stress scenario using stochastic methods; and run the test and capture results.
- **Measure and control.** This comprises measuring the stress test results using multidimensional views to secure a high-quality liquid asset buffer as a counterbalancing strategy under different scenarios to control the liquidity shortfall. This workflow step should allow the end-user to analyze the stress test result by generating multiple views and dashboards using a combination of different dimensions; determine what stress factors affect the balance sheet the most, given the composition, concentration and the behavioral profile of assets and liabilities, and if possible, determine early warning indicators; and formulate contingency planning that can be incorporated into the day-to-day business planning.

The stress test analysis engine should be embedded as a core sub-component within the overall LRM analytical engine. The stress test analysis engine should provide a data repository the ability to capture the liquidity stress test's base case, factors, or drivers, and their corresponding mappings to the base case, scenarios, assumptions, test results, and early warning and risk indicators. The stress test data repository can be developed using ABTs as outlined earlier. The liquidity stress test application should allow the end-user to be able to add, subtract, or change the composition of the asset and liability instruments, corresponding stress factors, and scenario assumptions.

Technology platform consideration The LRM analytical engine should ensure flexibility in order to run complex quantitative models to project cash flows, generate and run complex stress scenarios, and implement rule changes fairly quickly. Advanced stochastic models and Monte Carlo simulation over large data sets often require high-performance computing. As a standard practice, average balance sheet management systems run approximately 2,000 to 10,000 trials to ensure model accuracy. The technology platform to implement the LRM analytical engine should offer high-performance distributed computing and multithreading, low latency data transmission and parallel I/O, and load balancing and fault tolerance. The technology platform can be configured using an array of blade servers with high-speed interconnections.

Depending on the size and the complexity of the banks and financial institutions, the in-house development of a comprehensive analytical engine and stress test application can be a significantly time-consuming endeavor. Therefore, it is important to conduct a buy-versus-build analysis before proceeding.

In addition to the previously stated analytical application development platforms, there are leading treasury risk management vendor applications that offer an out-of-the-box LRM analytical engine. Many of these vendor applications also pre-package liquidity stress test capabilities; however, some vendors may lack the required level of maturity. Therefore, a thorough vendor selection process with a light proof-of-concept analysis is extremely important before selecting a vendor application.

Liquidity Risk Management Data Mart—Data Classification and Aggregation

This is a data layer that should be designed and implemented to support A/L cash flow segmentation based on regulatory classification schemes (i.e., Basel III LCR, U.S. LCR, and FRB 5G rules), data aggregation, and LRM analytics and reports.

Many banks use a spreadsheet-based LRM approach to collect and aggregate cash flow positions. The data management process is largely manual and data is aggregated at multiple levels before the final metrics are compiled leading to data quality and sustainability issues. In such a scenario, it becomes extremely challenging to collate enterprise-wide liquidity positions.

Raw transactional data is critical for operational liquidity management and regulatory reporting—raw reference data attributes are used to formulate cash flow classification rules stipulated by the regulators. Therefore, as a first step to the LRM data layer design, granular details pertaining to transaction, client, product, cash flow, contract, maturity, and market reference data sets should be normalized and integrated within a central data warehouse to ensure a single source of truth. The data warehouse is used for data disaggregation, traceability, auditing, and reconciliation, and serves as a central repository for all downstream treasury risk management needs. Subsequently, the data should be migrated to a data mart environment where the data is dimensionalized to interface with the LRM analytical engine, stress test engine, and business intelligence engine including executive dashboards, standard management and regulatory reports, and ad-hoc queries.

An approach would be to implement a LRM data mart by employing a dimensional data structure. The LRM data mart should be used to stratify cash-flow positions by required data aggregation dimensions and regulatory classification buckets. One should consider using a set of shared and conformed internal organization dimensions (e.g., legal entity—cost center rollup, geography, product, etc.), GL chart of accounts, A/L product chart of accounts, HQLA classes and regulatory dimensions, and fact constellation (i.e., an individual flat table for each A/L cash-flow position file) configuration. The facts and dimensions of the LRM data mart model should represent the end-user views (e.g., liquidity reports, executive dashboards, etc.), and should allow rollup and drill-down functionalities; thus, the design should be performed using business use cases and functional requirements.

There are two types of data objects that are used to configure the LRM data mart conceptual data model: dimensional tables and fact tables. If necessary, in order to satisfy regulatory A/L cash flow classification schemes, other types of data objects such as reference data look-up tables, business rule-based tables, and summary tables can also be considered in this data layer. However, the efficient design approach would be to de-normalize these data objects into standard dimensions and facts.

In order to maximize I/O efficiency over the high volume of data, an emerging practice in data mart design has been to decompose certain types of dimensional attributes into fact tables. These attributes are either local to a particular fact or used for intermediate derivations. For example, the dimension or reference data attributes (e.g., deposit type, product type, account type) required for formulating deposit regulatory cash flow classification schemes (e.g., retail, SME, stable deposits, wholesale) can be decomposed into the deposit cash flow position fact table.

Table 8.1 illustrates the composition of the data objects, type of data captured, design concepts, and the data management principles.

TABLE 8.1 Composition of Data Elements

Data Objects	Type of Data Attributes and Usage	Data Management Principles and Design Concepts
Dimension tables	■ The dimension tables are used for data aggregation as required by the regulatory reporting and internal management reporting. The liquidity risk metrics are measured and reported by these dimensions. Some of the Key LRM dimensions are: 　■ Organization dimension 　■ Geographic region/jurisdiction dimension 　■ Customer/counterparty dimension 　■ A/L product chart of account dimension 　■ Remaining term time bucket dimensions 　■ Time period dimension 　■ Currency ■ These dimensions should be treated as a core set of global data aggregation hierarchies by individually associating them with each cash flow position fact table to enable cross-dimension hierarchical views. ■ These dimensions present multidimensional views of the liquidity risk measures by aggregating the metrics at different levels of the hierarchies (e.g., funding concentration or total interest bearing deposits by LOB, legal entity, and holding company).	■ Global dimensions: The key LRM dimensions listed here should be considered as global in nature as they are the standard set of data aggregation hierarchies used by banks and financial organizations. 　■ Standardize these dimensions to ensure conformity within the organization, management and regulatory reporting. 　■ Assign right level of nodes and leaf for adequate drill-down and rollup while designing data aggregation hierarchies to ensure granularity. ■ These dimensions should be individually assigned to each cash flow position fact table. ■ These global dimensions should be treated as master data within the scope of master data management in the data warehouse layer, and a slowly changing data (i.e., Type-II SCD) capture method should be used to manage the historical changes of the hierarchies. ■ Unless it is necessary for trends of liquidity-related key performance and risk indicators to be maintained over earlier versions of the organizational hierarchy that

(Continued)

TABLE 8.1 (*Continued*)

Data Objects	Type of Data Attributes and Usage	Data Management Principles and Design Concepts
	Reference data attributes and dimensions required formulating the derivation rules for the regulatory cash flow classification data tags and intermediate calculations for cash-flow aggregation specific to each cash flow position fact table should be captured in the LRM data mart. Some of the local dimensions and reference data attributes are: ■ Deposit type: To classify interest bearing and non–interest bearing deposits ■ Operational deposit tag: To classify wholesale operational and non-operational deposits ■ Security type: To classify types of securities required for HQLA (e.g., cash, Treasury bonds, RMBS, GSE securities, covered bonds) ■ Issuer type: To segment securities issuers that can qualify for HQLA classes (e.g., sovereign, central bank, GSE, financial & non-financial corporate) ■ Regulatory HQLA level tag: A derived data tag to classify Level 1, 2A, and 2B liquidity assets.	may have subsequently changed, it would generally be sufficient to capture only the most recent instance of the global dimensions in the LRM data mart for data aggregation and reporting purposes. ■ Reference data attributes and local dimensions: The reference data attributes and dimensions pertaining to a particular cash flow position, which in general are required for intermediate calculations and/or regulatory classification derivation rules, should be treated as local in nature. As a design and data management principle, these reference data attributes and dimensions should be de-normalized to their corresponding fact tables. For example: ■ Deposit type, deposit account type, purpose, product type, and operational deposit tag etc. should be captured in deposit position fact. ■ Security type, issuer type, and regulatory HQLA level tag, etc. should be captured in securities position fact. ■ The same principle should be applied to position data classifiers and reference data attributes for other instruments (e.g., loans, leases, letters of credit, derivatives, repos/reverse repos, and bank debts).

Fact tables

- The fact tables are used for capturing balances for assets and liabilities, cash flow reference data attributes, and cash flow position classifiers. The number of fact tables and their configuration can vary from one bank to the other depending on the on/off balance sheet composition, number of instruments, and type and complexity of the instruments. Some of the Key LRM fact tables are:

  - Securities position fact
  - Cash or cash equivalent position fact
  - Derivatives position fact
  - Bank debt position fact
  - Reserves position fact
  - Repos and reverse repos position fact
  - Loans and leases position fact
  - Letters of credit position fact
  - Credit facilities position fact
  - Deposits position fact

- These fact tables should be designed as periodic snapshot facts at a daily time-period granularity. By design principle, keeping the cash flow fact data at the lowest grain, a row in a periodic snapshot fact table summarizes liquidity metrics measurement events occurring over a standard period, such as a day, a week, or a month.

- End-of-business day cash flow balances and their corresponding reference data attributes originating from on/off balance sheet A/L instruments should be inserted into their respective fact tables on a daily basis.

- If intraday liquidity monitoring is desired, a set of point-in-time snapshot fact tables design can be considered by capturing multiple cash flow and liquidity events during the day.

- It is ideal to design an individual fact table for each A/L instrument, however, if the contractual cash flow characteristics are similar in nature (e.g., maturity terms and type of instruments); in such case, the cash flow positions can be consolidated into one fact table (e.g., loans and leases).

Regulatory Liquidity Reporting Classification Rules and Data Mapping

Basel III and U.S. LCR reports and FRB daily liquidity position reports require A/L cash flow positions to be classified in accordance to regulatory rules in determining haircuts, runoffs, and drawdowns pertaining to HQLA, cash inflows, and cash outflows, respectively. As such, the LRM data mart, data architecture, data transformation process, and data mapping design should ensure the following:

- Classification of A/L position data based on regulatory rules
- Allocation of cash flows into the right buckets and mapping to the LCR workbook
- Application of haircuts, runoffs, and drawdowns
- Aggregation of cash inflows and outflows, net cash outflows, total HQLA, and LCR calculations

Figure 8.5 illustrates a conceptual view of the Basel III LCR liquidity reporting classification scheme and the data mapping flow.

As depicted in Figure 8.5, the cash flow classification tags are derived based on certain account-level operational or transactional characteristics of the A/L instruments, customer or counterparty segmentations, and product segmentations. For example, the following reference data tags are necessary to determine retail stable deposits: transactional account, established relationship, and FDIC-insured product. Similarly, in case of credit facilities, "facility type" and "facility purpose code" are mapped to determine credit/liquidity facility versus committed or uncommitted facility. Subsequently, these classifications are mapped to their corresponding runoff and drawdown assumptions to estimate a final cash flow position amount.

GL Reconciliation

The regulatory examination process requires that the A/L cash flow position balances presented on a bank's liquidity reports reconcile with its books and records. The goal of the reconciliation process is to identify, record, and remediate variances for subsystems' cash flow position balances related to specific GL accounts. This process ensures that variances resulting from GL posting delays or additional accounting processes done at the GL level are reflected and/or adjusted appropriately in the bank's liquidity risk measurements, calculations, and reporting. These efforts culminate with the consistent and transparent reporting of consolidated numbers between finance, treasury LRM, and other supporting source systems to ensure that the key balances tally with the books of records and any variances can be explained with an auditable data trail.

Basel III Liquidity Reporting Classification Schemes
Cash-Flow Position Data Tagging Process Flow & Dependencies

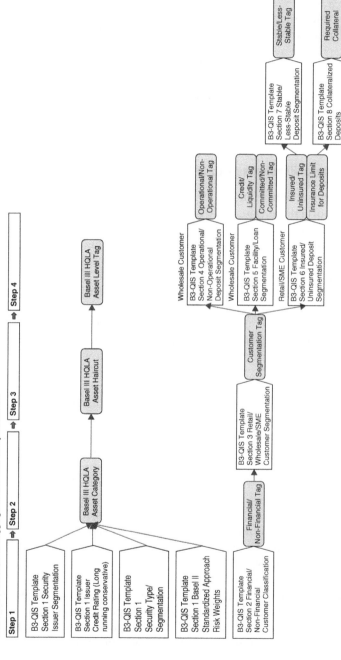

FIGURE 8.5 BASEL III LCR Cash Flow Classification Scheme and Data Mapping Flow

The key elements involved in the GL reconciliation process are detailed in Figure 8.6.

At a conceptual level, the reconciliation process will compare balances obtained at a particular grain available from the GL (e.g., GL account and cost center) to an aggregated balance from the source systems at that same grain. The reconciliation process should not, therefore, be done at an individual instrument level. Additionally, the aggregated level of the GL reconciliation process will result in a fewer number of plug (i.e., forced reconciliation) records, which will significantly reduce reconciliation and adjustments process overheads.

Treasury Data Warehouse—Data Integration

Golden source of data Data at its most fundamental level is required to be collected, normalized, standardized, integrated, and retained within a single data warehouse.

Regulatory guidance has reinforced the importance of well-integrated and high-quality data environments, including consideration for the lowest common denominator of data requirements, so that the liquidity risk measures presented at an aggregated level can be seamlessly reconciled with data sources. The liquidity risk data integration environment should present a granular data warehouse without losing its affinity to the business process relationship to ensure that the data production can be audited over a full data lifecycle—from the origin through the downstream information management.

Data management practices have evolved dramatically since their inception; consequently, there are many methodologies that exist in the banking industry to draw upon. Identifying the right data management methodology, however, is critical to address the challenges just discussed. An approach would be to develop a centralized TDW by integrating transaction, client, product, cash flow position, contract, maturity, and market reference data sets at their most granular level while keeping the native business entity relationship (i.e., master entity to transaction entity) as close as possible to the actual business processes. The construction would be to design a normalized structure by using a third normal form data architecture technique to define the data relationship. The TDW can serve as a common standard data store for all of treasury's risk and analytics needs (e.g., ALM/interest rate risk, FTP, capital planning, stress test, and funding and liquidity risk).

As depicted in Table 8.2 mainly five different types of entities are used to configure the data model: (1) level-1 super-type master entities, (2) level-2 super-type master entities, (3) level-3 sub-type entities, (4) relationship entities, and (5) transaction profile entities. Additionally, there are reference

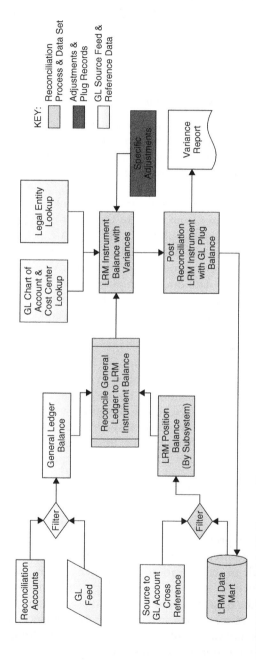

FIGURE 8.6 LRM GL Reconciliation Process Flow

entities to capture internal and external reference data (e.g., market rate data, market reference data, internal organization hierarchy, and product hierarchy).

Table 8.2 illustrates the composition of the entities, type of data captured, their corresponding relationship, and the data management principles.

Sources Data Collection and Staging

Source data collection Liquidity risk management is highly data extensive in nature, which requires collecting granular data from a wide range of transaction systems involving the banking book, trading book, collateral, market reference data, customer/counterparty reference data, general ledger, and other treasury and finance data sets.

Depending on the size and complexity of the banking organization, the number of sources can vary from thirty to fifty back-office transaction systems. For large banks having multiple LOBs with A/L positions involving diverse instruments, there could potentially be more than one transaction system serving the same A/L product, resulting in a disparate source data environment and lack of data interoperability along the transaction lifecycle. More importantly, this disparate source data situation coupled with the complexity involved in normalizing the source data collection process will certainly impact the data integration as some underlying processes may rely on unstructured and inadequate data.

An approach to address this data sourcing challenge would be to implement a standardized data collection process to collect source data in predefined and standardized data templates. For the same A/L product, the data template should be standardized across all source systems. For example, if there are multiple back-office transaction systems in place to service deposit products originating from different LOBs, in such case one single standardized data template should be developed to collect deposit cash flow transaction data from all the source systems.

The standardized data collection templates are designed and developed by:

- Performing a comprehensive source data analysis and profiling based on business data requirements and data dictionary
- Analyzing SOR in collaboration with source system owners to understand the structure, content, relationships and derivation rules, and anomalies of the data, and subsequently to assess data quality
- Developing a source system inventory by A/L products and capturing upstream data unification rules (i.e., rules to unify multiple sources/SOR for the same A/L product), and upstream data conversion rules

TABLE 8.2 Entity Types

Entity Type	Type of Data Attributes and Usage	Data Management Principles and Design Concepts

Level-1 supertype master entities	The Level-1 supertype entities are used to capture attributes related to master data that remains static or changes highly infrequently over the lifecycle. For example:
	
	  Account master
	  Customer/counterparty master
	  Product master
	  Collateral master
	
	All the common attributes with respect to master data that represent related subtypes should be captured in these entities. For example: Common non-changing attributes of deposit and loan accounts should be captured in the Account Master.
		A highly infrequent change data capture (CDC) data management method should be used to manage historical data in these entities.

Level-2 supertype master entities	The Level-2 super-type entities are used to capture attributes related to a common data set shared by a particular group of subtypes that remain relatively static or may change slowly over the lifecycle. For example:
	
	  Deposit account
	  Credit facility
	  Retail loans
	
	All the attributes with respect to a common data set that represent related subtypes should be captured in these entities. For example, common attributes of all deposit accounts, which can only be applied to different deposit types should be captured in the deposit account entity.
		A relatively slow CDC data management method should be used to manage historical data in these entities.

(Continued)

TABLE 8.2 (*Continued*)

Entity Type	Type of Data Attributes and Usage	Data Management Principles and Design Concepts

Level-3 subtype entities	▪ The level-3 subtype entities are used to capture attributes related to a common data set that can represent behavioral characteristics of a particular portfolio/instrument type that may change slowly over the lifecycle. For example:
	
	  ▪ Money market deposit account (MMDA)
	  ▪ Revolving line of credit
	  ▪ Mortgage loan
	  ▪ All the attributes that are common to a money market deposit and can represent the behavioral characteristics of a MMDA should be captured in the MMDA subtype entity. The same principle applies to the other type of instruments (e.g., auto loan, student loan, commercial line of credit, letter of credit, and leases).
		▪ A slow CDC data management method should be used to manage historical data in these entities.

Relationship entities	▪ The relationship entities are used to define one-to-many or many-to-many relationships between two master entities by using the relationship type as a classifier. For example:
	
	  ▪ Collateral master to credit facility
	  ▪ Customer master to account master
	  ▪ Product to account master
		▪ A slow CDC data management method should be used when relationship type changes.

Transaction profile entities	The transaction profile entities are used to capture daily end-of-the-day and/or monthly end-of-the-month contractual cash flows balances, accrued interest, and other amounts pertaining to instrument level transitions. For example: ■ Demand deposit account cash flow profile ■ MMDA deposit cash flow profile ■ Installment loan cash flow profile ■ Mortgage loan cash flow profile ■ Commercial line of credit cash flow profile ■ Leases cash flow profile	■ These transaction profile entities should be treated as insert-only snapshot—each time insert a new record by taking a snapshot of daily or monthly balances.
Reference entries	■ The reference entities are used to capture internal and external reference data (e.g., market rate data, market reference data, internal organization hierarchy, product hierarchy, and GL data).	■ Reference/master data management methods should be used to manage these entities.

- Developing a data-mapping matrix by matching target business data elements with source data
- Standardizing SOR for each A/L product by leveraging the results from the source data analysis and mapping exercise

The SOR standardization process should be performed in collaboration with the source system owners. Additionally, in order for the source system team to build the interfaces to produce the data collection templates, a comprehensive set of interface specifications and data mapping rules should be captured by the source data analysis team. The final data collection templates should be reviewed and approved by the combined project team prior to the commencement of the interface development. The main benefit of collecting source data in standardized data collection templates is efficiency (e.g., a fewer number of data files to integrate for downstream data production, source data cleansing and data conversions are performed upstream, less complex data staging layer construction).

Data staging layer The source data extracted from the back-office transaction systems serving A/L products should be loaded into a data staging layer prior to the downstream data integration. The data loading process to the staging layer should be a straight through ETL process as the source data is captured using predefined data collection templates. The data staging layer should be used to validate, standardize, apply data quality control rules, and prepare the data to generate load ready files for the TDW load. Some calculated or derived data fields pertaining to the regulatory cash flow classification data tags may be added (e.g., Basel III HQLA level tag, Retail/SME/Wholesale tag, and Operational Deposits tag), and some fields may be parsed into a single target data field as needed by business transformation rules.

LIQUIDITY DATA GOVERNANCE AND QUALITY CONTROL FRAMEWORK

As discussed earlier, regulatory agencies require banks to have high-quality data environments, considering the lowest common denominator of data requirements so that the liquidity risk measures presented at an aggregated level can be seamlessly reconciled with the source. In today's disparate system landscape in the banking industry, data accessibility and quality are significant obstacles, especially when generating timely and accurate regulatory reports. As such, banks and financial institutions need to institute an effective and measurable data governance discipline at the program level to produce LRM data in a controlled environment.

Data governance ensures improved data reliability so that the data can be trusted by the internal and external stakeholders. There should be a process put in place under the data governance guidance to produce data audit metrics in a timely manner as well as an on-demand basis to satisfy regulatory data quality requirements. A well-integrated data governance framework also ensures data stewardship and custodian accountability so that those who are responsible for back-office transaction data and the downstream data sets related to the liquidity risk MIS can be held accountable for any adverse event that occurs due to low data quality.

Large organizations may form an enterprise-wide data governance framework offering high-level guidelines; however, such guidelines and standards may not properly be translated down to the local programs. Thus, these guidelines need to be made both actionable and tailored to the liquidity risk MIS development program. The key tenets of a strong data governance discipline that is critical to a liquidity risk MIS program include:

- Data dictionary management with standardized business definitions and rules
- Data management policy
- Data quality (DQ) control

Data Dictionary Management

The data dictionary is a tool to define common business taxonomy for liquidity risk MIS data requirements, which provides improved conformance across user groups within the organization. The approach would be to capture a comprehensive list of business data elements up front satisfying the liquidity risk MIS functional requirements to construct a liquidity risk data dictionary. Additionally, these data elements and their corresponding business definitions and derivation rules should be standardized to establish a single source of truth. Once finalized, the standardized data dictionary should be approved by the business stakeholders, and subsequent changes thereafter should be managed through a change control process under the LRM project data governance committee.

Data Management Policy

The data management policy constitutes a set of guiding principles based on which the TDW and LRM data mart are designed, built, implemented, and managed over the LRM information lifecycle. The key principles are as follows:

- Data should be modeled using a structured approach, and maintained close to the source in the data integration layer.
- A data aggregation layer should be designed and implemented to facilitate analytics and information delivery.

- Metadata (i.e., underlying business definition and rules) should be recorded and utilized.
- Data should be accessible with a service level agreement (SLA) that ensures efficiency.
- Data should be reconciled with a set of predefined controls and acceptance criteria.

It is important to develop internal guiding principles pertaining to metadata management, data accessibility via an SLA, and data reconciliation controls and acceptance criteria. The data management policy should be approved and supported by the senior management (i.e., both business and IT department heads) as the governing body for adherence and implementation.

Data Quality (DQ) Control

With respect to liquidity risk regulatory expectations, controlling data quality through the establishment of a comprehensive audit trail is a critical requirement. The source data needs to be quality checked and certified at the point of extraction, transformation, load (ETL), integration, and aggregation to ensure that it meets or exceeds the standards established by its intended consumers. The data quality check is all about wrapping a set of DQ controls around these data production processes.

Two sets of interdependent processes are used to accomplish the desired DQ check: off-line and in-line. The off-line DQ process is run outside of the automated data production process, while the in-line DQ process is run in with the automated data production process.

Off-line DQ process   The off-line DQ process is used to perform the initial data quality assessment of the input sources and is executed periodically thereafter. The controls used to manage the off-line DQ process are:

- Data profiling
- Data standardization
- Data validation

Data Profiling: Liquidity risk management is an extremely data intensive exercise. Depending on the size and complexity of the on/off balance sheet instruments, the number of cash flow positions, and its corresponding reference data attributes could range from 900 to 1,200+ data elements. Data profiling is an exploration exercise used to analyze and understand the input source data in the context of the business data requirements. This exercise should be performed up front to analyze these business data elements by comparing them against the source systems serving A/L products to further evaluate the structure, content, relationships and derivation rules, and anomalies of the data, and subsequently to assess data quality.

This process step should be aimed at generating a set of metrics depicting a profile of the source data and a list of candidate errors. One should consider using descriptive statistics to profile the input source data population. Additional metadata information obtained during data profiling could be data type, length, discrete values, uniqueness, occurrence of null values, typical string patterns, and mandatory data fields' (e.g., index rate, index type, maturity date, term type, spread rate, interest rate, book balance) population ratios.

Data profiling analysis results should be used to formulate remediation rules that are then used by the in-line DQ process. The benefit of the data profiling is to improve data quality, shorten the implementation cycle of the LRM projects, and improve understanding of data for the users. Discovering business knowledge embedded in the data itself is one of the significant benefits derived from the data profiling exercise. Data profiling is one of the most effective technologies for improving data accuracy in the LRM database.

Data Standardization: Standardization of data is a prerequisite to achieving semantic interoperability within asset and liability products and is a key element of a robust LRM data foundation. The goal is to attain conformity of the input source data for each asset and liability product by mapping it to a standard business data element matrix and creating consistent business definitions. The standardized data sets are built based on the interpretation of the data and corresponding business definitions during the source data preparation stage of the data production process. Standardized data is important for several purposes, including enhanced data matching, consistency in the output data and business definitions, data duplication, and uniqueness.

Standardization looks at individual data elements and puts them into a standard representation. The definition of the input source data elements within the same data class can vary from one A/L system to another. These input source data elements should be conformed to a standard target business data element. The rule should be: If the data elements present a uniform business definition across the asset and liability products within the same data class, then the source data elements that represent the uniform domain value should be conformed to one target data element.

A synopsis of the data standardization rule is illustrated in Table 8.3.

Once the data standardization process is completed, a conformed master data element list with A/L product matrix should be maintained for change control management over the lifecycle of the LRM information delivery. This data element matrix also serves as the LRM data dictionary and the metadata for business process cross reference.

TABLE 8.3 Data Standardization

Data Class (Business Definition)	Deposit Input Source-1	Deposit Input Source-2	Loan Input Source-1	Loan Input Source-2	Security Input Source	Conformed Target Data Element
Market Rate Index used in interest rate calculation	Index Name	Index Used	Index Type	Index	Market Index	Base Rate Index
Index Rate used to calculate interest rate	Index Rate	Base Rate	Base Rate	Market Rate	Yield Rate	Base Rate

Data Validation: This is the most critical and final quality assurance (QA) step in the data production process before the source data is migrated to the user acceptance test (UAT), and subsequently to the production environments. Data validation ensures clean, correct, and useful data sets in the TDW and LRM data mart QA environments, as well as serves as entry criteria for the UAT process to commence —the business users should approve and sign off on the data validation results. One should consider loading and validating three to six months of source data into the TDW and LRM data mart QA environments in an iterative manner.

For liquidity risk MIS application development and implementation, data validation can be defined through procedure-based business rules—the rules that are used to transform the source data via ETL process to populate the TDW and the LRM data mart. Data that does not conform to these rules will negatively affect the LRM functional/business use case execution. Therefore, data validation should start with the business process definitions and rules and/or test cases within this process. Rules can be collected through the requirements capture exercise.

Two sets of independent processes are used to accomplish a concrete data validation check:

- Validation of cash flow balances by key dimensions used in balance aggregation; and
- Validation of each cash flow reference data element provisioned in the TDW and LRM data mart.

Validation of cash flow balances: Cash flow position balances and other key financial figures (e.g., book balance, daily/monthly average balance, interest income) should be validated against books of records (i.e., statutory financial statements) and/or GL by the following dimensions:

- Time period (monthly or daily)
- Holding company (top-of-the-house)
- Legal entity (LE)
- LOB
- Cost center
- GL chart of account#A/L products (as defined for balance sheet cash flow aggregation)

The balance aggregation rule for validating the cash flow positions balances should follow the same aggregation principle as it is used in banking organizations' statutory financial statements. Consider using four aggregation levels:

- **Level 1.** At time period, A/L products, and holding company level
- **Level 2.** At time period, A/L products, and legal entity level
- **Level 3.** At A/L products, legal entity, LOB, cost center, and GL chart of account# level
- **Level 4.** At source system, A/L products, cost center, and GL chart of account# level

The aggregation granularity below the holding company level will generate multiple rows/data points, and each data point should be compared against its corresponding data point from the bank's books of records or GL. Subsequently, potential variances between the two data points should be compared against the acceptance threshold, and if the validation result meets the acceptance criteria, then accept it for UAT; otherwise reject it for further investigation and resolution.

It is important to validate the cash flow position balances using granular aggregation levels (i.e., Level 3 and Level 4 on the list) as at these levels the numbers can be compared and reconciled with the general ledger numbers.

Validation of each cash-flow reference data element: The LRM position data classification and cash flow modeling warrant substantive reference data attributes to execute the required analytics (e.g., behavioral and stressed cash flow, deposit modeling, regulatory and internal metrics calculation and aggregation). Depending on the size and complexity of the balance sheet, as well as the investment portfolio, the number of reference attributes can range from 500 to 700+ data elements. These data elements are required to be validated against the QA test data sets (i.e., three to six months of the real source data) for consistency, accuracy, completeness, and integrity before migrating to the UAT and production environments. The steps involved in validating the reference data elements are:

- **Completeness and consistency check.** Checks that the input data carries valid values to populate the corresponding mandatory (i.e., Not Null) data fields in the target (e.g., Index Rate, Index Type, Maturity Date, Term Type, Spread Rate, Interest Rate, and book balance should have valid values). Also checks that there is a consistent population of the non-mandatory target data fields (i.e., at least 85% to 90%).
- **Data type and format check.** Checks that the input data carries numeric values to populate the corresponding numeric data fields in the target (e.g., if the Account# is defined as a numeric field in the target, then the input source supplying "AC0001" as a data value is unacceptable—this will cause an error in target data load). Also, checks for input sources supply data values in the specified format (e.g., dates have to be in the format DD/MM/YYYY).
- **Range check.** Checks that the input data values fall within the acceptable range (e.g., Month of the Maturity Date lies between 1 and 12, or Interest Rates, Rate Lock Period, Teaser Rates, CLTV, and FICO scores are not out of range).
- **Limit check.** Checks that the input data values conform to the specified limit (e.g., Spread Rate <= .05).
- **Logic check.** Checks that the input data values do not yield a logical error causing a Zero Divide issue in the calculation (e.g., Accrual Rate and Accrual Period cannot be Zero).
- **Integrity check.** Checks that all the key data fields in the target have unique values (e.g., Account#, Customer#, and Source System keys are populated with unique input data values).

These data validation steps are important in implementing a set of DQ controls that can be automated via standard ETL (refer to "In-line DQ process") as a straight-through data production process.

In-line DQ process The in-line DQ process is run synchronously with the automated data production process each time when the input source data is populated. The controls used to manage the in-line DQ process are timeliness, completeness, accuracy, integrity, and reconciliation.

DESIGN AND IMPLEMENTATION CONSIDERATION

Key LRM capabilities such as having visibility into liquidity characteristics, enterprise-wide liquidity position monitoring, measuring internal and external liquidity stress, contingency planning, decision strategy, and liquidity regulatory reporting are critical to the business operating network within banking organizations. Such capabilities should be available to LOBs, product and portfolio management, corporate finance and treasury, ALCO, funding operations, liquidity risk managers, regulatory reporting, collateral managers, corporate risk managers, and the board of directors. Accordingly, it is critical to involve key stakeholders and the business process owners from these functional areas over the lifecycle of the liquidity risk MIS solution design and implementation.

Liquidity Risk MIS Solution Design

As a first step to the solution design approach, the MIS project team should clearly define business process work streams, identify work stream leaders, and subsequently capture liquidity risk management business objectives, capabilities matrix, and business use cases. The key considerations are as follows:

- Define liquidity risk management business objectives with regard to contractual, behavioral, and stress cash flows; static and dynamic liquidity ratios; scope of the analysis (i.e., banking book), granularity of data required; and frequency of the analysis (i.e., daily versus monthly)
- Develop a capabilities matrix, business use cases and process workflows with regard to:
  - Contractual and behavioral cash flow modeling and projection
  - Structural liquidity gap analysis by maturity buckets both for contractual and projected cash flows
  - Fund transfer pricing, cost of liquidity and liquidity pricing
  - Predictive analytics to model deposit segmentation and runoff rate percentage
  - Basel III liquidity ratios (i.e., LCR and the Net Stable Funding Ratio or NSFR) reporting across various regions and currencies
  - Basel III liquidity asset classification rules to allocate the Bank's asset positions into Level 1, 2A, and 2B liquid asset categories and haircut/runoff assumptions for cash inflows and outflows to estimate Basel III net cash outflows
  - Liquidity stress events and cash flow projections based on scenarios spanning internal portfolio stress events, idiosyncratic/firm specific stress events, and systemic/market stress events; and contingency funding analysis
  - U.S. LCR and daily liquidity position reports
  - Liquidity monitoring and capital regulation
  - Funding concentration analysis

- Intraday liquidity and collateral management
- Company-level liquidity and capital dashboard
- ALCO liquidity dashboard/ratios with corresponding limits
- Consolidated collateral report

The business objectives, capabilities matrix, and business use cases should be developed involving each business work stream lead. Subsequently, the capabilities matrix and business use cases can be used as key drivers to formulate:

- LRM solution development scope
- Business and functional requirements
- LRM vendor application selection
- Conceptual and detailed solution design and prototype
- Phased implementation roadmap
- User acceptance criteria and test cases

LRM solution design and architecture should be vetted against the capabilities matrix and business use cases and signed off by the business work-stream leads.

Conceptual Solution Design and Prototype

In the conceptual design, the feasibility of meeting the management objectives for the MIS is assessed and a broad picture of the system is analyzed. Liquidity risk MIS needs should be defined by outlining management's objectives, business capabilities matrix, and use cases; linking critical success factors to their measure; and then translating these components into a conceptual solution design and prototype. The early system prototype prior to commencing a full-scale development offers tangible proof of concept to the business stakeholders and enables the project governance committee to build trust among the businesses. The conceptual design paves the foundation for the detailed system design and implementation.

Developing comprehensive output formats (e.g., UI, MIP, LRM metrics and KPI screens, reports, and graphical dashboards display) early in the conceptual design is extremely important to the accuracy of the detailed system design and eventual acceptance by management. These formats let the system builders graphically demonstrate the capabilities of the new liquidity risk MIS. The prototyped dashboards and reports should be vetted with the business stakeholders as a part of conceptual design.

Additionally, the process of conceptual design also answers complex data requirement questions. A line-by-line determination of which information (e.g., liquidity asset buffer by HQLA category, deposit concentration, deposit runoffs, unfunded commitments and drawdowns, net cash outflows) to include in the prototype helps identify problems or concerns about how specific data elements should be gathered. The conceptual design should also include description of essential information required to produce the reports, flow charts, and descriptions of the flow of data from the source application. For example, the deposit cash flow position data should be sourced with detailed account qualifiers (e.g., deposit type, customer type, insured flag, account type, purpose) to determine whether the deposit is operational or non-operational to classify cash flow positions and apply runoff assumptions as stipulated by the BASEL III and U.S. LCR rules.

The conceptual design should also enforce that the system should be implemented in a manner that is as agile and adaptive as possible. For instance, if the Basel III and U.S. LCR rules with regard to HQLA and cash flow classifications and/or runoff assumptions changes in the future, the data analytics components involved in the liquidity risk MIS should be able to adapt to such changes fairly quickly. The designer has several tools to enhance the overall flexibility. They include table-driven maintenance, business rule-based table design, modular sub-functions, parameterized stored procedures, and support for powerful ad-hoc access and reporting tools.

Current application simulation software offers the opportunity to quickly develop prototypes of reports and screen displays, using test data that will bear a strong resemblance to real conditions. This technique can be highly valuable, especially with systems that emphasize electronic delivery. It speeds up the refinement of the conceptual design into more detailed specifications that can be quickly programmed and will require minimal modification during acceptance testing.

Detail Solution Design

Once business stakeholders have approved the conceptual design, the next step is to develop detailed system requirements and solution design. The detailed solution design translates the functional design requirements into a detailed set of system requirements that are required to construct the application. The detailed set of system requirements and solution design includes:

- Preparing a detailed liquidity risk MIS data dictionary by each A/L products and reference data subject area
- Defining the data source inventory/system of records (SOR) and source data treatments
- Outlining the process, data, and system flows
- Creating a data collection template design for the cash flow position, reference data, and collateral source feeds

- Creating a data staging layer design and data mapping to the Treasury data warehouse (TDW) as well as a TDW design and data mapping to the LRM data mart
- Designing the LRM data mart logical and physical design and cash-flow segmentation, classification, and aggregation dimensions design
- Tagging the cash flow position data logic and workflows to satisfy Basel III and U.S. regulatory classification schemes
- Generating a GL reconciliation process
- Designing a LRM analytical engine for cash flow modelling and liquidity stress test, and a LRM management and regulatory reporting engine design
- Creating a liquidity risk MIS end-to-end physical architecture for platforms and security
- Developing application components and integration specification, and application prioritization and a deployment roadmap

The detailed system design describes how the system will behave (from a user's point of view), and how the system will meet the requirements developed in the definition component. If a design requirement is dependent on other systems, development activities, procurement, or efforts outside of this project, it should be documented at this point in the design process.

It is important to ensure that the design meets the business and functional requirements. An effective approach to achieving this would be to conduct joint sessions with treasury and IT to drive detailed functional requirements and solution design as well as to eliminate inconsistencies of understanding early in the process. Additionally, it saves overall time as teams can move into functional design more rapidly with a greater understanding of the overall requirements. Furthermore, consider instituting a Design Authority and Architecture Review Council—this council should be used to coordinate and facilitate end-to-end future state architecture design, review the solution design for accuracy, and finally approve the detailed design.

Liquidity Risk MIS Program Implementation Approach

The LRM MIS implementation is a multidisciplinary program that involves close collaboration between the project governance, business, and technology teams. As discussed in the solution design section, the scope and the requirements of the liquidity risk MIS can stem from a broad array of users and business operations leading to a complex liquidity monitoring framework; therefore, before an institution actually begins designing and implementing the MIS capabilities, it needs to examine its information network from a business perspective; that is, it needs to look at the scope of the liquidity risk management and its requisite information systems not individually but as a component of an overall business information support system. Often while executing a complex MIS program to address multifaceted business functions and technology delivery, implementation challenges arise from differences in understanding of requirements between the business and the IT teams. Therefore, it is important to design and deploy a cohesive program delivery structure ensuring proper alignment between the key stakeholders, functional work stream leads, and IT work stream leads. Figure 8.7 illustrates a standard liquidity risk MIS implementation program delivery structure.

Additionally, the project management team should consider developing a detailed project work breakdown structure by laying out key activities for the individual work stream that could run in parallel while keeping a continuous interaction between the business and the technology team. It is critical to institute the project plan in order to organize resources, deliverables, priorities, key milestones, day-to-day activities, and tracking the progress. The following are key program implementation elements to consider:

- A clear future state vision, scope and delivery roadmap (e.g., technology roadmap), and obtain business stakeholders buy-in.
- A program governance model, execution structure, communication strategy, and project performance metrics to ensure continuous progress.
- Engagement of business users early in the process and conduct joint solution design sessions to drive functional requirements and technology solutions.
- A clear understanding of the data complexity, challenges, remediation strategy, governance and quality assurance, and corresponding business process treatments.
- Organization of the project by breaking the entire delivery into iterative waves, and sharing the results early in the delivery process with the business users for early gap detection and remediation. Maximization of resource throughput by educating staff on business subject knowledge, harnessing their strength with appropriate skill-to-task alignment.

Once the business capabilities are clearly outlined and approved, the work streams depicted in Figure 8.7 can be run as parallel tracks. The most time consuming component of the liquidity risk MIS solution design and implementation is the data discovery and analysis process (i.e., to determine requisite data element, data sources, and transformation rules). Therefore, this work effort should commence immediately after the completion of the business use cases, or can be staggered with the business requirements and prototype design.

Governance

Steering Committee	Design Authority	Program Implementation Team
• Steering Committee will be chaired by the Group Treasurer or Group CFO and will have representation from Divisional CFO or Head of Treasury / ALM. • Approve project objectives, scope, resource and cost estimates, governance framework, and target operating model. • Ensure alignment with other in flight strategic change programs in the Bank.	• Design Authority will comprise of Funding and Liquidity leads from all the Business Units, Group Treasury, and IT Lead. • Approve high level design principles, business requirement, functional and technical specification. • Review and approve standard and customized reporting requirements for group and local regions.	• Responsible for day-to-day operational project management, including project resources and cost tracking. • Ensure appropriate engagement and allocation of resources across business work-streams. • Ensure implementation and tracking of design authority decisions and escalate issues and deviations. • Provide a monthly status update to the Steering Committee and Design Authority.

Program Structure

Internal Stakeholders: Treasury Management / ALM · Group / Division Finance · Liquidity Risk Management Committees · Cash & Collateral–Operations · Line of Business and Portfolio Managers

	Governance, Policies, Processes & Methodology	Liquidity Data Management	IT–Hosting, Build, Configuration & Support
WS1: Management Reporting & Analytics			
WS2: Liquidity Risk Analytical Engine			
WS3: Stress Testing & Scenario Analysis			
WS4: Regulatory Reporting			
WS5: Liquidity Risk Data Foundation			
WS6: Funds Transfer Pricing			
WS7: Intra-Day Liquidity and Collateral Management			
WS8: Risk Appetite, Strategic Funding and Contingency Planning			

Phases: Enhancement · Initial Implementation

FIGURE 8.7 Liquidity Risk MIS Implementation Program Delivery Structure

Testing

The liquidity risk MIS implementation is data-intensive by nature and requires a number of test cycles. Each interface should be tested as a unit, along with each of the data transformation logic, calculation processes, and reports. Once the unit testing has been certified, the individual components should be tested as a group in what is known as an integration test. This is accomplished by having the development team run the entire production cycle using test scripts with a subset of data prepared for this purpose, much as it would occur in production. An approach would be to extract a previous cycle data from the current state environment and, where the results or outputs are already established—the test data can be adjusted as per the future state needs. Because the desired results are known in advance, the outputs from the test are compared to the benchmark from the test scripts. This is an iterative process because of the resolution of errors and rerunning of the test cycles.

Once these tests are successfully completed, the A/L position data and the corresponding reference data set provisioned in the TDW and LRM data mart environments should be validated for accuracy and consistency. The A/L cash-flow position balances should be reconciled to the bank's books of records and each individual reference data element should be matched against the desired outcome (i.e., a set of predetermined data acceptance criteria) of the transformation and/or business rules. Data that does not conform to these rules will negatively affect LRM functional/business use case execution. Data validation is an important data QA step in the data production process, which ensures the data can be trusted. The source data should be certified and accepted by the business users before it is migrated to the UAT and subsequently to the production environments. Consider loading and validating three to six months of source data into the TDW and LRM data mart QA environments in an iterative manner. Refer to the subsection on Data Validation for more details around the data validation/QA test.

Upon successful completion of the source data validation and reconciliation, the business users should sign off on the data set provisioned in the TDW and LRM data mart environments as an acceptance or entry criteria to commence UAT. Subsequently, the entire liquidity risk MIS application functional components along with the end-user certified data set should be migrated to a pre-production environment—ideally the configuration of the pre-production environment should replicate the real production setup. This is where real data is processed through normal production cycle by the organization that will administer it in production.

UAT test cases should be linked to one or more use cases. The business users should assign success criteria to accept the test case. It is at this stage that the high-level results are reviewed against external sources (e.g., with the current production results and/or financial statements) and the basic integrity reviews of the standard LRM KPI & KRI metrics (e.g., key deposit ratios and LCR) are formed.

The UAT should be performed using three to six months of real production cycle data to ensure consistency in the UAT test results. Once this test is successfully completed, the business users sign off on UAT and release the system for production rollout.

As part of the production rollout preparation, an end-to-end system performance and regression test should be conducted to ensure that the SLAs signed between the business and the IT stakeholders are met—the liquidity risk MIS application should operate within the performance time window as prescribed by the business stakeholders. These SLAs are required to be developed as a joint effort engaging both business users and the IT team. The IT team should guide the business stakeholders on what should be reasonable system performance expectations given the business-as-usual operational parameter and technology infrastructure used for the production environment.

These performance guiding principles apply to all the components involved in the LRM MIS application such as data layer (i.e., TDW and LRM data mart), analytical engine, and results/output layer. Each of these components should be performance tested in the production environment using real production data. The test results should be measured against the system performance metrics and throughputs defined in the SLA. Once the SLA requirements are successfully met, and the business users are satisfied with the test results, the system should go live by commencing the end-user on-boarding process and training, and subsequently the source data history conversion should begin if necessary.

UAT test cases should be developed using the capabilities matrix, business use cases, and functional requirements. The test cases should be approved by the business users for accuracy, and the UAT results should be measured against the business use cases to ensure that they are satisfactory.

CONCLUSION

The 2007-08 financial crisis has shown that the current LRM capabilities needs further enhancements to effectively operate in a changing and difficult macroeconomic environment. Heightened by both internal and regulatory oversight, the LRM has shifted from the traditional ALM treasury risk space to a key risk measurement component within the enterprise-wide risk management framework. Given that the elements of the liquidity risk affect all functional areas of the organization, achieving holistic operational liquidity management capabilities requires visibility into underlying liquidity characteristics within the business network. The regulatory oversight process requires a bank's liquidity risk measurement process to be commensurate with its size, complexity, and liquidity risk profile.

In the light of these challenging demands, it is critical for the business stakeholders to identify, monitor, measure, and mitigate the liquidity risk position embedded within the portfolio and the business operation while responding to the internal business needs and to regulatory inquiries in a timely manner. The liquidity risk MIS plays a pivotal role to enable these functional capabilities within the organization's overall liquidity risk management practice.

Overcoming the data and analytics challenge is a prerequisite for the successful implementation of a sound liquidity risk MIS framework. Risk monitoring and decisions should be based on comprehensive, accurate, consistent, and timely information.

CHAPTER 9

Recovery and Resolution Planning—Liquidity

Pranjal Shukla and Daniel Shanks[1]

The management of systemic risk and mitigation of "too big to fail" concerns have been a major focus of macro-prudential regulatory policy in the wake of the recent financial crisis. Recovery and resolution plans are two important tools that have been developed as part of prudential regulatory frameworks to address these concerns, and are currently being implemented at large global financial institutions. Primarily led by the U.S. and Europe, regulators across the globe are requiring the largest, most systemically important firms within their jurisdictions to produce and periodically refresh formal recovery and resolution plans. Additionally, the Financial Stability Board (FSB), which has been established as the coordinator among various national regulators and international standard setting bodies and is charged with developing and promoting the implementation of effective regulatory, supervisory, and other financial sector policies, has published guidance papers on recovery and resolution planning.[2] These guidance papers are aimed at assisting local regulators in defining recovery and resolution requirements and assisting firms in developing their recovery and resolution plans. In the U.S., the resolution plan requirement is set forth

---

[1]Pranjal Shukla is a principal in PwC's New York office, and Daniel Shanks is a manager in PwC's New York Office.

[2]Financial Stability Board. "Recovery and Resolution Planning for Systemically Important Financial Institutions: Guidance for Developing Effective Resolution Strategies," July 16, 2013, http://www.financialstabilityboard.org/wp-content/uploads/r&uscore;130716b.pdf, viewed May 18, 2015; Financial Stability Board. "Recovery and Resolution Planning for Systemically Important Financial Institutions: Guidance on Identification of Critical Functions and Critical Shared Services," July 16, 2013, http://www.financialstabilityboard.org/wp-content/uploads/r& uscore;130716a.pdf, viewed May 18, 2015; Financial Stability Board. "Recovery and Resolution Planning for Systemically Important Financial Institutions: Guidance on Recovery Triggers and Stress Scenarios," July 16, 2013, http://www .financialstabilityboard.org/wp-content/uploads/r&uscore;130716c.pdf, viewed May 18, 2015.

in Section 165(d) of the Dodd-Frank Wall Street Reform and Consumer Protection Act[3] (the DFA) and has been implemented in a final rule adopted jointly by the Board of Governors of the Federal Reserve System (the Board) and the Federal Deposit Insurance Corporation (FDIC). Recovery planning requirements, on the other hand, have been primarily driven by the Board as part of its supervisory process.

While recovery and resolution plans are often grouped together by practitioners and regulators as similar concepts, there are key differences between them. Recovery and resolution plans are both tools for managing risk at different points along the "strategic continuum," which defines different stages of a firm's financial position and viability. This continuum extends from business as usual, where the firm is financially sound and viable, through severe stress and "recovery" conditions where the viability of the firm is in question, and ultimately to resolution where the firm has reached the point of non-viability and fails. In the context of this continuum, a recovery plan is a contingency plan for conditions of severe stress—essentially a playbook for management that outlines the various options for helping restore the financial condition of the firm. A resolution plan, on the other hand, outlines an overall strategy along with specific steps that regulators can follow to effectively resolve the firm once it has failed while minimizing systemic disruption in the financial markets.

Ensuring adequate liquidity is among the most important considerations for the development of both recovery and resolution plans, as insufficient liquidity has proven historically to be a major driver of financial institution failure as well as a major constraint to the orderly resolution of such institutions. From a recovery perspective, it is essential that firms' plans incorporate a comprehensive framework of liquidity measures and triggers that can be used to effectively monitor the financial condition of the firm and escalate issues and concerns on a timely basis. Building on this framework, recovery plans must also incorporate an analysis of the potential impact of funding and liquidity actions that could be executed in order to respond to periods of severe liquidity stress. From a resolution perspective, the firms' plans must ensure that surviving legal entities would have sufficient liquidity available to continue systemically important functions for as long as required to prevent market disruption.

In light of these conceptual requirements for both recovery and resolution planning, it is also crucial for financial institutions to have the ability to develop accurate and granular funding and liquidity projections under a variety of scenarios stretching from severe financial stress to failure. The purpose of these financial projections is to enable firms to sufficiently assess and

---

[3] 12 U.S.C. §5365(d).

plan for the management of potential liquidity needs under different scenarios; additionally, such preparations provide assurance to key stakeholders, including regulators, as to the firms' abilities to manage liquidity effectively.

The remainder of this chapter provides a detailed discussion of liquidity-related requirements, considerations, and leading practices, including liquidity projections, in the context of recovery and resolution planning.

LIQUIDITY REQUIREMENTS IN RECOVERY PLANNING

Recovery Planning Overview

As described earlier, a recovery plan is a playbook that the management of a financial institution can use during periods of severe financial distress to assess the firm's condition and restore liquidity and capital strength. The core components of a recovery plan should include: (1) measures, triggers, and early warning indicators that a firm uses to identify, monitor, and assess conditions of severe stress and determine appropriate response actions; (2) recovery actions at the firm's disposal to recover from severe financial distress; and (3) an analysis of potential scenarios depicting conditions of severe stress which demonstrates the firm's ability to recover—this analysis should incorporate financial projections illustrating the firm's financial condition both before and after the execution of various recovery actions. Key requirements and considerations for each of these three core components of recovery planning are discussed in detail next.

Measures, Triggers, and Early Warning Indicators

As stated in the FSB guidance on recovery triggers and stress scenarios, "The aim of triggers in recovery planning is to enable firms to maintain or restore financial strength and viability before regulatory authorities see the need to intervene or enforce recovery measures. Such triggers are generally understood as a pre-identified point in time, situation, or marker, which requires the firm to notify senior management or its board and its supervisory authority that a triggering event has occurred."[4]

Triggers incorporated in the recovery plan are generally based on capital and liquidity measures that have already been established and are used

---

[4]Financial Stability Board. "Recovery and Resolution Planning for Systemically Important Financial Institutions: Guidance on Recovery Triggers and Stress Scenarios," July 16, 2013, http://www.financialstabilityboard.org/wp-content/uploads/r& uscore;130716c.pdf, viewed May 18, 2015.

as part of a firm's business-as-usual risk management practices. Typically, firms include both quantitative and qualitative triggers. Some examples of the liquidity measures used as recovery planning triggers include:

- Macroeconomic, market, and internal early warning indicators that are indicative of a developing idiosyncratic or system liquidity event
- The Liquidity Coverage Ratio or other similar measures for assessing short-term liquidity needs under stress
- Ratios/measures related to cash/liquid funds at the parent level
- Collateral eligible to be pledged to the Federal Reserve
- Liquid asset buffer
- Central bank deposits
- Various measures/ratios related to deposits and other sources of funding
- Percent renewal of wholesale financing
- Withdrawal of deposits and other primary sources of funding

Recovery Actions

As noted previously, one of the core components of a recovery plan is a comprehensive inventory of feasible recovery options that a firm has at its disposal to respond to severe financial distress. Such recovery actions can be organized into three main categories:

- **Capital actions.** Actions related to preserving existing capital and raising new capital
- **Contingency funding and liquidity actions.** Actions related to preserving existing liquidity and funding and accessing contingent funding sources
- **De-risking actions:** Actions related to selling portfolios of assets or businesses in order to de-risk the balance sheet and thereby preserve capital

In order to develop a comprehensive set of contingency funding and liquidity actions, firms have typically leveraged actions described in their existing contingency funding plans. Some examples of contingency funding and liquidity actions include the following:

- Entering into repo contracts and reducing reverse repo activity
- Selling of liquid and illiquid securities
- Increasing fed funds purchased and reducing fed funds sold
- Borrowing from interbank market
- Issuing commercial paper and other sources of short-term funding
- Issuing medium- and/or long-term debt
- Borrowing from central banks

- Utilizing unencumbered securities as collateral for other short-term secured borrowing
- Reducing placements with banks

A detailed analysis is required for each of the identified contingency funding and liquidity actions to assess feasibility and impact. Such an analysis should address the following aspects:

- Feasibility under different market conditions
- Timing and duration
- Order of execution
- Pre-conditions to execution and other requirements
- Potential impediments and related mitigants
- Likelihood of success and other credibility considerations
- Approval and implementation process

Finally, it is important to keep the inventory of recovery actions relevant by periodically revisiting the actions identified and refreshing the supporting analysis; this is particularly important given potential changes in the firm's business and risk profiles and/or market environment.

Scenarios and Liquidity Projections

Firms are required to contemplate at least two different extremely severe scenarios as part of their recovery plan—a systemic scenario where the overall financial market is impacted, and an idiosyncratic scenario where the stress is primarily firm-specific. For each of these two scenarios, detailed funding projections are required in order to assess the funding needs of the firm. Such funding projections should include detailed projections covering all of the firm's major sources and uses of funds and the resulting net funding position. The projection horizon is usually two years, with projections on a daily or weekly basis over the initial three to six months and then on a quarterly basis thereafter.

In order to produce these projections, firms must develop various assumptions concerning the likely behavior of depositors, clients, and counterparties; anticipated reactions of various financial market utilities (FMUs), agent banks, and correspondent banks; anticipated reactions of primary borrowers and lenders; and anticipated responses from regulators across different jurisdictions. Assumptions in these areas are required as part of resolution planning projections as well. Further details on the development of such assumptions are provided within the next section of this chapter.

Additionally, projections of funding sources and uses are required not only at the top of the house, but also at the material legal entity level. To the extent possible, projections should be segmented by jurisdiction as well as by line of business, at least for those critical operations of the firm that perform systemically important functions.

Ultimately, in order to develop projections that are meaningful and relevant, firms should ensure that three underlying critical issues are addressed. These include: (1) ensuring accuracy and reliability of the data used for the projections, (2) ensuring appropriate granularity of the projections, and (3) ensuring consistency across the underlying assumptions and methodologies. With respect to the first two items, data, systems, and technology enhancements should be contemplated to ensure accuracy and reliability of data as well as the ability of the firm to produce projections with the appropriate granularity (as described before). With respect to the third item, ensuring consistency of underlying assumptions and methodologies will require significant involvement and close coordination across a number of relevant functional areas and lines of business in the projections process, and may also require significant enhancements to the overall financial projections process.

LIQUIDITY REQUIREMENTS IN RESOLUTION PLANNING

Resolution Planning Overview

As noted in the introduction to this chapter, the requirement for certain financial institutions to produce resolution plans, or "living wills," is set forth in Section 165(d) of the DFA[5] and is implemented in a final rule adopted jointly by the Board and the FDIC.[6] In concept, a resolution plan is a detailed document that provides potential strategies for how an institution could be wound down or otherwise resolved in a manner that minimizes risk to the broader financial markets and economy. Such plans, which also include a variety of financial data and analysis supporting these potential strategies, are intended for use by regulators when determining how to carry out resolution authority in the event of the failure of a major financial institution.

As described in the final rule, Section 165(d) of the DFA "requires each nonbank financial company supervised by the Board and each bank holding company with total consolidated assets of $50 billion or more (each a

---

[5]12 U.S.C. §5365(d).
[6]The final rule was originally published in the Federal Register at 76 FR 67340, Nov. 1, 2011, and is now codified at 12 CFR 243.

'covered company') to periodically submit to the Board, the Corporation, and the [Financial Stability Oversight Council ('Council')] a plan for such company's rapid and orderly resolution in the event of material financial distress[7] or failure."[8] The final rule defines "rapid and orderly resolution" as " ... a reorganization or liquidation of the covered company ... under the Bankruptcy Code that can be accomplished within a reasonable period of time and in a manner that substantially mitigates the risk that the failure of the covered company would have serious adverse effects on financial stability in the United States."

One of the key aspects of a rapid and orderly resolution is providing for the continuance of so-called "critical operations," which are defined in the final rule as " ... those operations of the covered company, including associated services, functions and support, the failure of discontinuance of which, in the view of the covered company or as jointly directed by the Board and the Corporation, would pose a threat to the financial stability of the United States."[9] Generally, these critical operations have been identified by the Board and the FDIC and communicated to covered companies, and represent the functions or services performed by a company that are critical to the ongoing stability of the broader financial markets.

Specific services provided by a given institution are more likely to be designated as critical operations if that institution has a high degree of market share in those business areas. Critical operations may include, among others, market-making activities for certain types of securities, custody services, and payment clearing activities. Covered companies are expected to develop resolution strategies which provide for the continuation of designated critical operations. Additionally, covered companies are required to " ... not rely on the provision of extraordinary support by the United States or any other government to the covered company or its subsidiaries to prevent the failure of the covered company." That is to say, in developing their resolution strategies, institutions should not anticipate that the U.S. government or any government will provide extraordinary support to prevent their failure.

---

[7]The final rule determines "material financial distress" to exist with regard to a covered company when: "(1) The covered company has incurred, or is likely to incur, losses that will deplete all or substantially all of its capital, and there is no reasonable prospect for the company to avoid such depletion; (2) The assets of the covered company are, or are likely to be, less than its obligations to creditors or others; or (3) The covered company is, or is likely to be, unable to pay its obligations (other than those subject to a bona fide dispute) in the normal course of business." This definition is provided in 12 CFR 243.2.

[8]12 CFR 243.4.

[9]12 CFR 243.2.

In the event that a covered company experiences material financial distress or failure, the potential lack of sufficient liquidity available to the company or its subsidiaries during resolution proceedings is a major impediment that may arise in ensuring the continuance of that company's critical operations. As such, liquidity analysis, including projections of potential liquidity needs and available resources during resolution proceedings, is a crucial part of developing effective resolution strategies, allowing for the continuation of critical operations, as well as improving the credibility of the resolution plan overall. Such liquidity analysis will be the focus of the remainder of this chapter, which will discuss regulatory expectations and best practices for liquidity analysis in the context of resolution planning and how such analysis can be integrated with existing liquidity risk management processes.

Liquidity Analysis in Resolution Planning

As noted earlier, a key aspect of effective resolution planning is developing resolution strategies that allow for the continuance of critical operations during resolution proceedings, in order to mitigate risks to the stability of the broader financial markets. In order to demonstrate that a given resolution strategy will support the continuance of critical operation, a covered company must demonstrate, among other things, that it and its subsidiaries will have access to sufficient liquidity to support these critical operations throughout the timeline for the execution of the strategy.

With respect to liquidity analysis, the final rule specifies that each covered company's plan must include a strategic analysis describing "funding, liquidity and capital needs of, and resources available to, the covered company and its material entities,[10] which shall be mapped to its critical operations and core business lines,[11] in the ordinary course of business and in the event of material financial distress at or failure of the covered company."[12] Additionally, the plan must describe the covered company's "strategy for maintaining operations of, and funding for, the covered company and its material entities, which shall be mapped to its critical operations and core

---

[10] As specified in the final rule, a "material entity" refers to " ... a subsidiary or foreign office of the covered company that is significant to the activities of a critical operation or core business line." (See footnote below for definition of "core business line.") 12 CFR 243.2.

[11] "Core business lines" are defined in the final rule as "those business lines, including associated operations, services, functions, and support that, in the firm's view, upon failure would result in a material loss of revenue, profit, or franchise value." 12 CFR 243.2.

[12] 12 CFR 243.4.

business lines."[13] In other words, the rules require covered companies both to (1) examine the funding and liquidity needs of their key functions and businesses in the normal course of business as well as material financial distress or failure scenario, and (2) to describe their strategies for maintaining sufficient funding for such key functions and businesses throughout the resolution timeline. Subsequent to the rule, there have been additional guidance instructing banks how to address funding and liquidity as a potential obstacle, with the central component being the development of a set of "liquidity needs schedules" which project liquidity needs and available sources over time for each resolution strategy presented in the plan. The liquidity needs schedules should be consistent with the assumptions and timing of each resolution strategy and should demonstrate the firm's ability to maintain continuance of critical operations over the scenario horizon.

The precise format and structure of these schedules are not specified in the guidance, but institutions have generally sought to leverage their existing liquidity stress testing and/or contingency funding plan (CFP) framework, both to reduce effort and demonstrate the integration of resolution planning with ongoing risk management activities. The schedules are usually presented as projected liquidity needs against available sources, with a calculation of net available liquidity to demonstrate that the institution, or its material entities, would not require extraordinary government support to meet ongoing needs during the execution of the resolution strategies.

The subsections below address key considerations for performing liquidity analysis in resolution planning including with respect to scenarios and the development of projection assumptions that are especially important in a resolution context.

Scenario considerations In developing resolution plans, institutions must establish a scenario or set of scenarios which describe the forward-looking economic environment during the time period in which the resolution strategies would be executed. The scenario should describe the nature in which the economic and market environment will impact the funding, liquidity, and capital needs and available resources of the company in resolution, and will also impact the receptiveness of other market participants to proposed strategic actions. As mentioned before, while the chosen scenario or scenarios impact all aspects of resolution strategy, extending beyond just the liquidity analysis element, the nature of the scenario is particularly important to the construction of liquidity needs schedules.

---

[13] 12 CFR 243.4.

Resolution Scenario Timeline While the projected macroeconomic conditions over the resolution strategy horizon are generally consistent with those that are forecasted as part of supervisory scenarios, institutions must develop an overall timeline and sequence of events to complete the full scenario, which generally includes an idiosyncratic stress to the firm that precipitates failure. This subsection discusses key considerations related to the overall structure of a resolution plan scenario, which can be divided into five key components: (1) starting point, (2) resolution trigger, (3) runway period, (4) entry into resolution proceedings, and (5) resolution strategy horizon.

1. *Starting Point*
   Covered companies must decide, in coordination with their regulators, the appropriate "as of" date for financial data provided in their plans. In many cases, this date is consistent with the most recent quarter-end or year-end period in which financial information was publicly filed, though in practice could be any point in time. For simplicity and ease of analysis, most institutions have chosen to use this "as of" date as the starting point for the resolution scenario. The starting point of the scenario essentially represents the last period in which the institution was operating in a "business-as-usual" state, and is immediately prior to the occurrence of a resolution trigger or to the runway period, both of which are described in more detail later. The starting point of the scenario also dictates the "beginning balances" (i.e., the initial balances for cash flow and balance sheet line items) used for liquidity projections.

2. *Resolution Trigger*
   The resolution trigger is generally an event or loss that occurs and depletes the institution's capital or liquidity resources beyond recovery. Examples of triggering events include an operational event, such as a major firm-specific systems failure, or a major contingent liability that becomes a payable for the institution. Traditionally, many institutions have not chosen a specific trigger, but instead provided a number of options which could, in theory, lead to material financial distress or failure, more recent regulatory guidance requires the firms to be more specific in defining their resolution trigger events. For purposes of the resolution plan scenario, such an event could occur immediately following the starting point, or after a short period during which the firm may have advanced warning of a potential event. The impact of the event, on both capital and liquidity as appropriate, should be incorporated into the financial projections developed in support of the resolution strategies. That is to say, if an institution experiences a $10 billion loss resulting from the resolution trigger, this loss should be subtracted from the projected available financial resources of the institution.

3. *Runway Period*
   Covered companies are allowed to assume a runway of up to 30 days prior to entry into resolution proceedings. Covered companies can use this

runway to perform specific actions to increase the resolvability of the institution, and to prepare customers, counterparties, rating agencies, and other stakeholders in advance of the resolution proceedings. Depending on the nature of the selected resolution trigger, this runway period may occur before or after the triggering event. If the runway period occurs before the triggering event, it can be assumed that the institution has some advance warning of the upcoming event, but that the event is unpreventable and will result in immediate entry into bankruptcy proceedings. If the runway period occurs after the triggering event, it can be assumed that the triggering event will not have immediately forced the institution into resolution proceedings, but that it starts the institution on an unavoidable path towards such proceedings, which will commence not more than 30 days after the triggering event.

Covered companies should incorporate estimated impacts during the runway period into their projected liquidity needs schedules. For example, if the triggering event occurs prior to the runway period, the institution is likely to experience significant decreases in available liquidity during the runway period as external counterparties would become increasingly concerned about extending credit further. Covered companies should attempt to project all such impacts during the runway period so that the financial condition of the institution at the time of entry into resolution proceedings is consistent with prior events.

4. *Entry into Resolution Proceedings*

At this stage, the institution is formally unable to continue operating as a going concern, and commences the execution of its resolution strategies. These strategies will differ by institution, but may include entry into Chapter 11 bankruptcy proceedings for some subsidiary entities, attempted sales of other entities, wind down of certain entities, or other approaches including the establishment of a temporary bridge bank for insured depository institutions. As already noted, the projected financial condition of the firm at this point should reflect prior events including the resolution trigger and runway period, and should be consistent with the loss of capital and liquidity that is likely to have occurred during those periods. To the extent that the commencement of resolution strategies involve immediate significant changes to the balance sheet of the institution, such as over a weekend when bankruptcy is declared, these should be incorporated into liquidity needs schedules as appropriate.

5. *Resolution Strategy Horizon*

Finally, the scenario timeline should extend out as far as needed to appropriately capture the time necessary to execute the resolution strategies. The purpose of the liquidity needs schedule analysis is to demonstrate the continuance of critical operations during the execution of the resolution strategies; as such, the scenario horizon should be long enough to properly demonstrate such continuance. Depending on the nature of the chosen resolution strategies, most institutions have employed scenario horizons of one to two years in length.

Key Assumptions for Liquidity Analysis In developing projected liquidity needs schedules, an institution should develop detailed assumptions for how liquidity needs and available resources will change over time throughout the resolution scenario horizon. The institution's liquidity position will be affected by a number of factors, including but not limited to reputational impacts arising from the resolution trigger; general market willingness to transact with the institution under specific terms and conditions; specific actions taken by the regulators on behalf of the institution, such as asset sales or transfers, which may substantially impact the balance sheet and earnings capability of the institution; regulatory/supervisory actions including ring-fencing of entities in a certain jurisdiction; and overall economic conditions.

While existing liquidity stress testing and CFP frameworks will likely have already identified the assumptions that are needed in many of these areas, institutions may need to modify or expand those assumptions to better align them to the resolution context. Additionally, certain assumptions which are not relevant in the ordinary course or severe stress but are important in resolution, such as regulatory ring-fencing, may not be addressed in existing liquidity risk management exercises and will need to be developed for purposes of resolution planning analysis.

In supplemental guidance issued to first-wave resolution plan filers, regulators have directed particular focus to the development of assumptions in the following areas:

- Counterparty and customer responses to resolution (e.g., loss of funding, withdrawal of deposits)
- Contractual provisions triggered by resolution (e.g., identify the impact of guarantees, Qualifying Financial Contracts, off-balance sheet financing and other contracts that will accelerate due to a resolution credit event)
- Identification of the sources of funding for all the identified liquidity needs over time, including adequate liquidity to deal with potential liquidity traps, with the understanding that sources of funding must be consistent with the overall resolution strategy[14]

---

[14]"Guidance for 2013 §165(d) Annual Resolution Plan Submissions by Domestic Covered Companies that Submitted Initial Resolution Plans in 2012." Federal Deposit Insurance Corporation and Board of Governors of the Federal Reserve System, released April 15, 2013.

The subsections below discuss some key considerations related to these assumptions in the context of resolution planning.

Counterparty and Customer Responses Likely behavioral responses on the part of counterparties and customers to the resolution proceedings of a financial institution are a key consideration for liquidity analysis because they directly impact available liquidity sources as well as liquidity needs. While assumptions specifying such behavioral responses should likely already be captured in existing liquidity stress testing and CFP frameworks, the types of responses from counterparties and customers that have been in focus for regulators in the context of resolution planning could include the following:

- Withdrawal of deposits
- Decrease in business activity directed at the institution (e.g., reduction in clearing activity, lower trading volumes)
- Refusal to provide the institution with access to secured and unsecured wholesale funding
- Increased collateral or other credit support requirements associated with derivatives or secured funding transactions
- Refusal to provide the institution with access to intraday credit, secured or unsecured
- Increased draws on unfunded commitments

The assumptions applied in these areas will heavily influence the forecasted liquidity sources and needs over the projection horizon.

Contractual Provisions Triggered by Resolution In addition to assumptions about the behavioral responses of counterparties and customers, it is important to consider contractual issues which are likely to arise in the event the firm enters resolution proceedings. Contractual issues may include those related to:

- Termination rights in derivatives contracts
- Downgrade triggers requiring additional collateral
- Guarantees and other credit support agreements
- Off-balance sheet commitments
- Other contractual terms and conditions which may result in the outflow of liquidity or customer business in the event of a credit event

In a resolution event, it is likely that an institution would experience a credit rating downgrade of some magnitude or a change in status such that its creditworthiness is called into question in a contractually actionable manner.

Contractual terms and conditions requiring the posting of additional collateral or providing a non-defaulting counterparty with the right to terminate a transaction could create significant outflows of liquidity due to collateral posting or settlement payments, or due to re-hedging costs created by the termination of a material hedging arrangement. Additionally, certain customers could be subject to regulatory or other provisions requiring them to do business only with counterparties or service providers meeting certain credit rating standards. In a resolution event, a credit downgrade may render the defaulting or distressed institution unable to meet creditworthiness standards, which could result in a withdrawal of customer business and potentially a decrease in available and required liquidity.

Trapped Liquidity The potential for liquidity to become trapped in specific legal entities or regulatory jurisdictions, and thus to become unavailable to the rest of the institution, is a critical issue in resolution planning. Due to the global nature of many large systemically important financial institutions, these institutions will have assets and liabilities located in a number of legal jurisdictions around the world, potentially giving rise to conflicts between international regulators as to how to handle the resolution of a particular failed institution. It is possible that, should a regulator in one country attempt to "ring-fence" liquidity in legal entities under that country's jurisdiction, the ring-fenced liquidity would not be available to meet needs in other countries or other parts of the institution. As a result, the potential for trapped liquidity can significantly impact available liquidity resources for an institution. In addressing potential ring-fencing, firms should consider:

- Anticipated timing of insolvency proceedings
- Mitigants to lessen likelihood of ring-fencing
- Mitigants to lessen impact of ring-fencing on critical operations
- Actions that can be taken to avoid or minimize the impact of insolvency proceedings

Availability of Contingent Funding Sources The access of an institution to contingent funding sources could be significantly impacted in a resolution scenario. Contingent funding sources may include:

- Liquidity buffers
- Backstop facilities with external financial institutions
- Federal Home Loan Bank advances
- Foreign central bank advances

The impacts of the specific resolution strategies on the institution's access to these sources of funding should be carefully considered.

CONCLUSION

Recovery and resolution plans are important risk management tools designed to enhance a firm's ability to survive under severe stress and, should the firm prove unable to survive, enhance regulatory authorities' ability to resolve the firm quickly and cost-effectively with minimal systemic impact to the broader economy. Due to the critical importance of liquidity for any financial institution, understanding and planning for potential liquidity needs during severe stress and post-failure is a core component of developing effective recovery and resolution plans. Firms must be able to assess their liquidity under a variety of hypothetical financial distress scenarios, both in the short-term as well as over a one-to-two-year time period. In order to develop meaningful and relevant projections for recovery and resolution planning, firms will need to address three critical aspects: (1) ensuring accuracy and reliability of the data used for the projections, (2) ensuring appropriate granularity of the projections, and (3) ensuring consistency across the underlying assumptions and methodologies.

Major financial institutions in the United States are at varying levels of progress in addressing these three aspects, and none of them have yet reached a state of sustainability in implementing enhanced approaches. Data reliability and accuracy have so far been the primary issue and, in order to address it, firms will need to enhance their technology infrastructure, especially with respect to data related to asset-liability management, deposits, collateral holdings, and intraday liquidity requirements. Technology and infrastructure enhancements will also help address the issue of projection granularity: Firms must be able to develop projections not only at the top-of-the-house level, but also at the level of material legal entities, lines of business, and regulatory jurisdiction.

Finally, in order to address the third issue, ensuring consistency of underlying assumptions and methodologies, firms will have to significantly enhance their governance and processes for developing assumptions related to anticipated client and depositor behavior and expected reactions of major counterparties, creditors, and lenders. Specific methodologies and models should be developed to analyze major sources of funds, including operational and non-operational deposits and intraday and overnight credit provided by FMUs, agent banks, and correspondent banks. Similarly, methodologies and models should be developed and implemented to help firms anticipate and analyze major uses of funds under different scenarios. Further, firms should ensure that relevant representatives from the lines of business are involved in developing funding projections and working closely with treasury and finance personnel to provide business insights and justifications to assumptions.

Ultimately, the requirements and expectations around the assessment of liquidity needs for recovery and resolution planning are closely related to and consistent with those in other liquidity management areas such as LCR reporting and monitoring, liquidity stress testing, contingency funding, intraday liquidity management, and overall liquidity reporting. Through guidance issues across each of these areas, prudential regulators are pushing firms to enhance their abilities to generate more accurate and granular funding projections under different scenarios and assumptions. The end goal is a reduction in systemic risk across the financial system through strengthened liquidity risk management, a process that begins with a focus on capability enhancements at the largest, most systemically important financial institutions.

The Regulatory Environment of Liquidity Risk Supervision

Two

CHAPTER 10

Supervisory Perspectives on Liquidity Risk Management

Kevin Clarke[1]

INTRODUCTION

"Another crucial lesson from recent events is that financial institutions must understand their liquidity needs at an enterprise-wide level and be prepared for the possibility that market liquidity may erode quickly and unexpectedly."[2]

The global liquidity crisis in 2007-08 evidenced challenges faced by banking organizations and renewed banking supervisors' attention to liquidity risk management as they looked to address the emergence of new issues as well as to reemphasize previously highlighted expectations. Since that crisis, banking supervisors have highlighted, in a variety of published documents, how firms failed to take account of a number of basic principles of liquidity risk management when liquidity was plentiful. Subsequently, the reversal of market conditions in 2007 produced a range of lessons learned for both banking supervisors and banking organizations related to liquidity risk management. For banking supervisors, it was not enough that published guidance documents such as banking circulars, supervisory letters, and examination manuals covering the core elements of liquidity risk management were available to supervised firms, but rather their systemic oversight of such controls may have been subject to other priorities. However, the regulators' renewed emphasis on liquidity risk management in regulations such as the Enhanced Prudential Standards (EPS) within the United States and standards issued by the Basel Committee on Banking Supervision

---

[1]Kevin Clarke is a director in PwC's McLean office.
[2]Chairman Ben S. Bernanke of the Board of Governors of the Federal Reserve System at the Federal Reserve Bank of Chicago's Annual Conference on Bank Structure and Competition, Chicago, Illinois May 15, 2008.

(BCBS) have ushered in a set of regulatory and supervisory requirements that complements the quantitative measures implemented under the Basel III framework.

In this chapter we will review the evolution and range of regulatory and supervisory requirements relative to liquidity risk management including firms' governance and internal controls frameworks. We will also review the foundations for these requirements by highlighting the context of the changes in supervisory expectations by U.S. banking regulators and the BCBS and discuss where banking supervisors are headed.

RATING LIQUIDITY RISK MANAGEMENT WITH U.S. BANKING REGULATORS' RATING SYSTEM

With the development of the CAMEL rating system for supervised banks in 1979, the U.S. banking regulators set out a path for a uniform rating system that would be applied across the range of institutions from the largest global firms to the smallest community banks. While the rating system was intended to cover a combination of financial, governance and internal controls measures (Capital–Asset quality–Management–Earnings–Liquidity), the assessment of liquidity risk management practices was highlighted in certain elements of the liquidity and management[3] components as follows:

- "In evaluating the adequacy of a financial institution's liquidity position, consideration should be given to the current level and prospective sources of liquidity compared to funding needs, as well as to the adequacy of funds management practices relative to the institution's size, complexity, and risk profile."
- "Practices should reflect the ability of the institution to manage unplanned changes in funding sources, as well as react to changes in market conditions that affect the ability to quickly liquidate assets with minimal loss. In addition, funds management practices should ensure that liquidity is not maintained at a high cost, or through undue reliance on funding sources that may not be available in times of financial stress or adverse changes in market conditions."

Generally, the board of directors of a bank need not be actively involved in day-to-day operations; however, they must provide clear guidance concerning acceptable risk exposure levels and ensure that appropriate policies,

---

[3] Board of Governors of the Federal Reserve System, SR Letter 96-38 (SUP), "Uniform Institutions Rating System," published December 27, 1996.

procedures, and practices have been established. Through the previous passages, it becomes much clearer that the subsequent releases of supervisory guidance, regulatory requirements, or quantitative measures are not necessarily new but rather intended to address or, in some cases, restrain the emergence of certain practices across supervised banking organizations. One of the more defining elements of the "L" component of the CAMEL rating, albeit somewhat simplistic, is the assessment of management as follows[4]:

> *"The capability of management to properly identify, measure, monitor, and control the institution's liquidity position, including the effectiveness of funds management strategies, liquidity policies, management information systems, and contingency funding plans."*

The cited criteria sets the tone and the framework of regulatory requirements and supervisory expectations that would evolve over time in response to financial market events and define the increased prescriptiveness of banking supervisors' documentary releases.

FOUNDATIONS ESTABLISHED IN BCBS' "SOUND PRACTICES FOR MANAGING LIQUIDITY IN BANKING ORGANIZATIONS"

With the onset of the new millennium, the BCBS issued the paper, "Sound Practices for Managing Liquidity in Banking Organizations," as part of a broader effort by banking supervisors across the globe to strengthen liquidity risk management practices within supervised firms.[5] As highlighted in the paper, global supervisors had observed firms' increased reliance on wholesale funding markets and their utilization of newer financial and technological innovations to fund their activities and manage liquidity exposures. With the liquidity crisis that emerged as a result of the collapse of Long Term Capital Management and the Russian debt moratorium, the observed "flight to quality" produced an unexpected event that prevailing funding models had not accounted for and resulted in a spiraling effect for assets as market participants sought to meet more frequent margin calls. The BCBS paper, which replaced an existing paper on liquidity risk management issued in 1992, focused on a set of fourteen principles that highlight the key elements for effective liquidity risk management within supervised firms.

---

[4]Ibid.
[5]BCBS. "Sound Practices for Managing Liquidity in Banking Organizations," February 2000. http://www.bis.org/publ/bcbs69.pdf.

In the subsequent sections of this chapter, we will highlight the principles established in this paper and how those have evolved through subsequent guidance and regulations issued by banking supervisors.

STRATEGY SETTING AND THE OVERSIGHT ROLE OF DIRECTORS AND SENIOR MANAGEMENT

As noted in "Sound Practices for Managing Liquidity in Banking Organizations" (BCBS 2000), supervisory perspectives on sound liquidity risk management have focused on the need for effectively setting strategies and the monitoring by directors and executed by senior management. Foremost in the opening principles is the discussion of the utilization of quantitative and qualitative targets and ensuring firms' ability to withstand stressed market conditions over both short- and long-term horizons. Moreover the BCBS emphasized that management should understand perspectives and be able to articulate through effective reporting the interactions of risks (e.g., credit, market, operational and liquidity) across the firm.

Since the release of the paper, the role of the board of directors has been an evolving focal point for supervisory directives. While the BCBS paper highlights the board's role in approving a firm's strategy for managing liquidity risk as well as the policies and procedures that identify lines of authority and responsibilities for managing liquidity risk, the paper also notes the role of the board of directors in monitoring exposures relative to the defined strategy. In achieving this objective, the paper noted that the board should review timely and sufficiently detailed information to allow its members to understand and assess the liquidity risk facing the bank's key portfolios and the bank as a whole. While this paper did not designate the frequency by which directors should monitor performance, it did note that firms holding significant funding concentrations or experiencing significant changes in the composition of holdings were expected to have more frequent reviews by their boards of directors. This concept was revisited by the Federal Reserve's Regulation YY (often interchangeably referred to as EPS), which set a prescribed frequency of at least semiannual reporting by the Chief Risk Officer (CRO) or senior management to the full board of directors regarding the firm's exposures relative to its liquidity risk appetite statement.

The role of senior management is highlighted in BCBS 2000 through the discussion of policy decision making and review of liquidity decisions stemming from the authority delegated by the board of directors. The form of this senior management review was left open to allow firms to formalize this oversight process either through a committee structure such as an asset-liability committee (ALCO) or through a specific function, either central treasury or risk management. Regardless of the form of oversight, banks were expected to maintain appropriate checks and balances to ensure the efficacy of the oversight activities. Limit setting is also highlighted in the management process with a series of suggested limits focusing on cash flow mismatches over certain time horizons that include the impact of reduced marketability of certain assets under stressed conditions, the impact of drawdowns on commitments, and the extent of available liquid assets as a percentage of short-term liabilities.

In a subsequent paper issued by the BCBS in 2008, "Principles for Sound Liquidity Risk Management and Supervision" (BCBS 2008), the theme of strategy was expanded to address a bank's need for a liquidity risk tolerance that is appropriate for its business strategy and its role in the financial system along with the requirement that the strategy be approved on an annual basis. This perspective on a firm's role in the financial system was largely indicative of the observed practices during the crisis events of 2007-08. Another principle noted in BCBS 2008 stemming from crisis-related observations was the requirement that firms incorporate liquidity costs, benefits and risks in the internal pricing, performance measurement and new product approval processes for all significant business activities, both on and off balance sheet, thereby aligning the risk-taking incentives of business lines with the liquidity risk exposures that those business lines create for the firm. This theme would become a requirement for banking organizations operating in the United States through the finalization of Regulation YY by the Federal Reserve in 2014.

For U.S. firms, the governance expectations set forth under the BCBS papers were reinforced by U.S. banking regulators in 2010,[6] which also served to harmonize the standards across the various agencies. More specifically, the policy statement noted that the board of directors should ensure that the institution's liquidity risk tolerance is communicated in such a manner that all levels of management clearly understand the firm's approach to managing the liquidity risk rewards versus cost trade-offs. The policy statement also denoted that the board or a delegated committee of board members should oversee the establishment and approval of liquidity management strategies, policies, and procedures, all of which would be subject to annual reviews.

Measuring and Monitoring Exposures

In line with the strategy and the board of directors and senior management oversight objectives that are driving the first set of principles, BCBS 2000

---

[6] "Interagency Policy Statement on Funding and Liquidity Risk Management," March 17, 2010, issued by the Board of Governors of the Federal Reserve System, the Office of the Comptroller of the Currency ("OCC") and the Federal Deposit Insurance Corporation (FDIC).

brought forward the process by which the board of directors and senior management would meet their monitoring responsibilities for the firm's strategy. The BCBS 2000 principles emphasized the measurement and monitoring of exposures and net funding requirements as well as the adequacy of systems to support timely controlling and reporting of liquidity risks to senior management and the board of directors. These principles also addressed an emerging need for firms' stress testing capabilities, including the range of scenarios and the ongoing validation of underlying assumptions to ensure the alignment with emerging market trends as well as inherent risks of products and counterparties.

In the context of management information systems, the principles denote the expectation that, in addition to providing timely information, they should be sufficiently flexible to meet various contingencies and have the ability to calculate positions in all major currencies on an individual and aggregate basis. Furthermore, such systems should support the monitoring of shorter-term horizons on a daily basis, out to five days, and over additional longer-term horizons to enable the monitoring and management of net funding requirements. These systems should also allow management to evaluate trends in the firm's liquidity exposures, and to understand the implications of various stress scenarios that are based on consistent and validated assumptions.

The principles also raised the matter of conservative estimations of the timing of inflows and outflows as well as the application of discounts to assets to reflect their inherent market or price risk. These concepts would become highly relevant in the Liquidity Coverage Ratio (LCR) that would be mandated over a decade later and the coverage of stress testing in the Federal Reserve's Regulation YY. The emphasis on stress testing as a function of exposure monitoring is particularly important given the paper's discussion of internal (i.e., idiosyncratic), external (i.e., market-related), and combined scenarios as well as the utilization of a blended approach to assumptions leveraging historical experience, market conventions, and management judgment. These factors would be prominent in Regulation YY through the specification of these scenarios as minimums and also added time horizon requirements of at least overnight, 30 days, 90 days, and one year.

With respect to assumptions, the BCBS principles noted that the behavioral assumptions used for cash flow estimates under normal conditions as well as stress conditions should be subject to frequent reviews to ensure their continuing validity, particularly given the rapidly changing conditions in banking markets. The one aspect that the paper may have underplayed is the number of assumptions to be made by firms, which BCBS 2000 identified as fairly limited, as well as the observed market practice of firms relying more heavily on a stock of liquid assets to offset greater uncertainty stemming from the behavior of liabilities. As time would tell, the requirements of greater granularity of assumptions to account for heterogeneous funding risks and the need for liquid asset buffers became more the rule through Regulation YY requirements for firms' cash flow estimation processes and collateral management practices.

The BCBS 2008 paper, as well as Regulation YY, built upon these foundations to address the complexity of firms' legal entity structures. Specifically, these requirements focused on the firms' ability to monitor and control liquidity exposures and funding requirements within and across legal entities, business lines, and currencies. Firms were also required to take into account legal, regulatory, and operational limitations that might impede the flow of funding, which would also be a component of the U.S. LCR requirements relative to the transferability of High Quality Liquid Assets (HQLA) buffers between the parent company and its covered subsidiary.

Building upon the principles of BCBS 2000 that addressed assets as cash flow sources, BCBS 2008 and Regulation YY noted that banks should actively manage their collateral positions (segmented by encumbered and unencumbered assets), monitor the legal entity and physical location of the collateral, and understand how that collateral could be monetized in a timely manner. The core driver to this change in requirements was the observed restrictions on cross border asset flows during the period of 2009–10.

Market Access and Contingency Funding

Given the broad tenet of liquidity risk management as the ability to meet financial obligations under normal and adverse market conditions, managing access to diverse funding sources and maintaining contingency funding plans are critical elements in a firm's liquidity risk management framework. In BCBS 2000, this was highlighted through principles addressing a firm's ability to manage the diversification of funding sources and outflows (e.g., liabilities) and the capacity to monetize assets, all of which are core components of contingency funding planning (CFP) for supervised firms. The principle pertaining to CFPs also highlighted the need for firms to establish procedures for addressing cash flow needs in crisis situations.

Given the timing of BCBS 2000, the discussion of access to funding sources provides greater insight concerning concentration matters. The emphasis was on the firms' ability to monitor concentrations by counterparty and instrument type as well as the nature (e.g., potential behavior) of the funds provider and geographic markets, with the latter consideration alluding to regional stress conditions that emerged during the late 1990s.

With respect to CFPs, the concept introduced in BCBS 2000 was further refined in BCBS 2008 and the U.S. regulators' 2010 guidance, "Interagency

Policy Guidance on Funding and Liquidity Risk Management,"[7] as well as, Regulation YY, which set requirements for the CFP's delineation of policies governing how the firm would react to a range of stress scenarios. Furthermore, the more recent pronouncements covered the delineation of roles and responsibilities of management in addressing the crisis, including communications plans, the transparency of plan invocation triggers and escalation procedures, and regular testing of the plan to ensure its continued effectiveness. For U.S. regulators, expectations regarding CFPs also included the concept of early warning indicators (e.g., metrics to identify the emergence of increased liquidity risks or vulnerabilities that would impact the firm's funding capacity); whereas these measures were viewed as requirements for risk measures in BCBS 2008, which also provided a more exhaustive list of recommended measures ranging from concentrations to increased funding costs and capital levels.

FOREIGN CURRENCY LIQUIDITY MANAGEMENT

Recalling the currency problems across several markets that emerged during the 1990s and the resulting liquidity issues that befell global banking organizations, global banking regulators extended the liquidity risk management standards that applied to home currency funding management to address funding requirements related to major currencies in which a given bank engages. This ranged from exposure reporting and cash flow estimations to stress testing and contingency funding planning. While the expectations expanded upon the notion of basis risk across currencies, the BCBS guidance issued in 2008, as noted earlier, extended these requirements to incorporate monitoring and management of liquidity risk exposures and funding needs within and across legal entities, business lines and currencies, as well as taking into account potential legal, regulatory, and operational limitations that may impede the transferability of liquidity across jurisdictions. This requirement was reiterated in the Federal Reserve's Regulation YY, with added emphasis on the firms' data management capabilities to support effective risk reporting to senior management. Lastly, the original concept of currency risks has been emphasized in guidance issued by regulators relative to intraday liquidity risk management and the firms' capacity to manage outflows within jurisdictions on a global scale.

---

[7]"Interagency Policy Statement on Funding and Liquidity Risk Management," March 17, 2010, issued by the Board of Governors of the Federal Reserve System, the Office of the Comptroller of the Currency ("OCC") and the Federal Deposit Insurance Corporation (FDIC).

CORE INTERNAL CONTROLS FOR LIQUIDITY RISK MANAGEMENT

Core internal controls for liquidity risk management and its components within BCBS 2000 focused on the establishment of a strong control environment through policies and procedures, effective information systems, and the continual independent review of adherence to those policies and procedures. While these expectations for internal controls may seem rudimentary nearly fifteen years after their issuance, the citing of internal controls requirements was broadly covered in BCBS 2008 and the U.S. regulators' 2010 interagency guidance. This course of broad expectations was reversed with the release of Regulation YY, which prescribed a range of internal control requirements particularly for independent oversight of liquidity risk management controls. While firms may have developed independent liquidity risk management functions out of existing market risk management frameworks, many of these firms lacked clearly defined roles and responsibilities for these functions, and as a result, the lines between front office activities and independent control functions became opaque, at best, and thus drove the prescriptiveness of Regulation YY.

Another important element in supervisors' rising expectations for independent oversight has been the expertise of staff within those functions. With the evolution of products, modeling methodologies, and underlying assumptions, the increasing complexity has required greater product or activity-specific expertise whereas firms in the past may have relied on internal audit functions to perform these independent oversight responsibilities. While continued reliance on internal audit may be the case for some firms, most firms have enhanced their independent risk functions and now rely upon internal audit to assess the effectiveness of the first and second lines of defense and their adherence to established policies and procedures, banking regulations, and emerging control needs of the organization.

THE DISCIPLINE OF PUBLIC DISCLOSURE

Following the crisis events of the late 1990s, global banking supervisors sought to enhance the firms' disclosure of information concerning the firms' funding risk profile and liquidity risk management practices through BCBS 2000. Global supervisors viewed that such public disclosures would improve transparency, reduce uncertainty in the markets, and strengthen market discipline (through expectations set by counterparties).

Among the standards issued by regulators regarding liquidity risk management, this one received very limited attention by regulators and regulated firms, as evidenced by marginal disclosure improvements prior to the financial crisis. In fact, this principle was repeated in BCBS 2008. With the release of regulatory metrics such as the LCR and Net Stable Funding Ratio (NSFR), firms have been attentive in releasing reports concerning these metrics to assure investors, counterparties, and analysts of their ability to meet supervisory expectations. Supplementing this effort, over the past year the BCBS released disclosure guidelines for the LCR and NSFR; U.S. regulators followed suit in late 2015 with respect to LCR-related disclosure requirements concerning disclosures.

MONITORING ADHERENCE TO BCBS STANDARDS

With the emergence of BCBS 2000, global banking supervisors sought to ensure there was a consistent and effective process for evaluating firms' adherence to these principles across jurisdictions and, more importantly, also to ensure that such standards were enacted by banking regulators. While liquidity risk management had always been an important aspect of the CAMEL supervisory ratings framework, BCBS 2008 provided a shift in supervisors' emphasis of a firm's resilience to liquidity stress given the firm's role in the financial system and its systemic importance. For U.S. regulators, their alignment to this BCBS standard has been evidenced in more stringent requirements of Regulation YY for systemically important banking organizations and the LCR final rule for firms greater than $250 billion in assets. In supplementing this change in regulations, the Federal Reserve has utilized horizontal reviews of liquidity risk management practices and funding profiles of supervised firms (e.g., Comprehensive Liquidity Assessment and Review) for firms greater than $50 billion in assets to assess their adherence to regulatory requirements.

CONCLUSION

While supervised firms have questioned the increasingly prescriptive measures taken by banking supervisors, the previous discussion outlines how regulators have remained consistent to the foundations set forth in the CAMEL ratings framework and BCBS 2000 as they pertain to firms' liquidity risk management practices and controls. That stated, the priorities set forth by regulators have been more pronounced in the quantitative requirements of the LCR and NSFR framework as well as the U.S. implementation of the global systemically important bank (G-SIB) surcharge framework and its inclusion of a short-term wholesale financing component. This emphasis on quantitative metrics has influenced regulatory reviews of the supervised firms' information systems, data quality/capacity, and data management controls to ensure the accuracy of calculated regulatory liquidity ratios.

Another aspect of emerging qualitative requirements by global supervisors has focused on intraday liquidity risk management practices; however, these have largely emphasized home country currency flows and stress testing of these intraday flows. Over the near term, it is likely that regulators will expand their expectations to encompass global exposures and flows for the larger systemically important firms.

CHAPTER 11

LCR, NSFR, and Their Challenges

Claire Rieger and John Elliott[1]

INTRODUCTION

Liquidity risk management is a key aspect of the Basel III reform agenda, and has been subject to increased regulatory scrutiny since the financial crisis. Liquidity has become critical priority for the G20, Financial Stability Board, and regulators worldwide and Basel III is the first time that an internationally harmonized set of liquidity standards has been agreed upon, with the quantitative ratios and metrics broken down in the following way:

- The liquidity coverage ratio (LCR) is a measure of the ratio of available liquid assets to the estimated net cash outflow over a 30-day period stress, based on a number of prescribed cash-flow assumptions, and is designed to ensure short-term resilience against liquidity disruptions.
- The net stable funding ratio (NSFR) is a structural liquidity ratio which aims to ensure the use of stable, longer-term liabilities to fund less liquid and long-term assets.
- A set of monitoring metrics assists supervisors in the analysis of bank-specific and system-wide liquidity risk trends.

The original LCR and NSFR standards were published in December 2010 by the Basel Committee on Banking Supervision (BCBS).[2] That announcement stated that both the LCR and NSFR would be subject to an observation period that allowed for revisions to be made in areas where the

---

[1]Claire Rieger is a director in PwC's London office, and John Elliott was formerly a senior manager in PwC's London office.
[2]BCBS, "Basel III: International framework for liquidity risk measurement, standards and monitoring," 16 December 2010.

TABLE 11.1   BCBS Timeline

	2011	2012	2013	2014	2015	2016	2017	2018	2019
LCR	Observation period		Final standard decided January 2013		60% min requirement	70%	80%	90%	100%
NSFR		Observation period			Final standard decided October 2014			100% minimum standard in place	

standards had been miscalibrated. Subsequently, the rules were finalized[3] in January 2013 for the LCR and in October 2014 for the NSFR.[4]

Table 11.1 provides an overview of the BCBS timeline in relation to LCR and NSFR.

The introduction of the Basel III liquidity ratios will have profound implications for the global banking sector. The need to meet the new requirements will prompt banks to reduce their reliance on short-term wholesale funding in favor of more stable sources such as retail deposits and long-term wholesale funding. The new requirements will also require banks to maintain a larger portfolio of liquid assets.

For many banks the challenge of meeting the new liquidity rules may be greater than the challenge of meeting the new capital rules because there is a limited quantity of stable sources of funding and high-quality liquid assets. The Basel III liquidity ratios could therefore have a profound influence on how banks fund their businesses and how they seek to make money.

Regulatory reporting requirements will also intensify, to enable supervisors to monitor compliance with the new rules. With the increased regulatory scrutiny and conservatism embedded into regulatory quantitative requirements, firms need to carefully assess the impact of these rules to ensure they remain competitive. Despite the extended implementation timeframe, banks will likely want to tackle the balance sheet consequences of the new regime sooner rather than later. Comparisons with peers and the need to disclose numbers to the market are likely to be more important than the formal regulatory timetable.

Firms also need to implement a robust liquidity risk management framework. The implications of not getting liquidity management right can lead to

---

[3]BCBS, "Basel III: The Liquidity Coverage Ratio and Liquidity Risk Monitoring Tools," January 2013.
[4]BCBS, "Basel III: The Net Stable Funding Ratio," October 2014.

oversized derivatives books and mispriced liquidity costs. From a regulatory perspective, poor systems and controls could result in increased quantitative requirements, such as higher buffers of low yielding securities or restrictive funding profiles (access to only certain sources of funding that will probably be more expensive than the current market). Most regulators have already implemented or are currently in the process of implementing qualitative liquidity risk management requirements in their national rule books, largely based on the BCBS's 2008 "Principles for Sound Liquidity Risk Management and Supervision."[5]

This chapter describes the Basel III liquidity requirements, with a specific focus on the LCR, NSFR, and the challenges associated with the implementation of these ratios from a risk management perspective.

LIQUIDITY COVERAGE RATIO

Definition

The 30-day LCR requirement is designed to ensure that a financial institution has sufficient unencumbered, high-quality liquid resources to survive a severe liquidity stress scenario lasting for one month. It accomplishes this by identifying the net cash outflows that a bank could encounter under a short-term stress scenario, using assumptions prescribed by supervisors. The measure also prescribes the type of unencumbered liquid asset that must be held.

The LCR is calculated as follows:

$$\frac{Stock\ of\ high\ quality\ liquid\ assets}{Total\ net\ cash\ outflows\ over\ the\ next\ 30\ calendar\ days} \geq 100\%$$

Scenario Proposed

The scenario underlying this measure combines an idiosyncratic shock with a period of market-wide stress, and has the following characteristics:

- Significant downgrade (three-notch) of the institution's credit rating leading to additional contractual outflows
- Partial loss of retail deposits
- Significant reduction in availability of unsecured wholesale funding
- Partial loss of secured short-term financing with a significant increase in secured funding haircuts

---

[5]BCBS, "Principles for Sound Liquidity Risk Management and Supervision," September 2008.

- Increases in derivative collateral calls and substantial calls on contractual and non-contractual off-balance sheet exposures, including committed credit and liquidity facilities
- The requirement for the institution to buy back debt or fund balance sheet growth arising from non-contractual obligations that might be honored in the interest of mitigating reputational risk

Under this scenario, the Basel III framework provides assumptions for outflow for maturing liabilities, inflow for maturing assets, and haircuts for liquid assets, as discussed in the next section. These drive net cash outflows (which consist of cumulative expected cash outflows minus expected cash inflows; the expected cash inflows are capped at 75% of the expected cash outflows). While most factors are prescribed by the BCBS framework, there are some which allow flexibility for national supervisors and some, such as guarantees and letters of credit that are entirely subject to national discretion.

LEVEL PLAYING FIELD ISSUES

The introduction of national discretions in the BCBS LCR rules gives rise to issues concerning level playing field, which will complicate the implementation and monitoring of the ratio.

LCR rules have now been finalized (or near-final drafts have been published) in several jurisdictions, including the U.S. and the European Union. In some areas, for example, differences are emerging with respect to the definition of liquid assets. In that particular example, the European Union definition is broader than the U.S. version, introducing challenges for global banks that need to manage liquidity positions across different countries and legal entities.

Liquid Assets

High-Quality Liquid Assets (HQLAs) are assets that can be liquidated at any time, including during times of stress, easily and immediately with little or no loss of value. HQLAs exhibit the characteristics shown in Table 11.2.

HQLAs should ideally be eligible at central banks for intraday or overnight liquidity facilities; however, eligibility in itself does not constitute a basis for categorization as a liquid asset.

TABLE 11.2 High-Quality Liquid Assets

Fundamental criteria	Market-related criteria
▪ Low risk, characterized by high issuer rating, low degree of subordination, low duration, low legal risk, low inflation risk, and denomination in a convertible currency. ▪ Ease/certainty of valuation—an asset's liquidity increases if market participants are more likely to agree on its valuation. A liquid asset's pricing formula must be easy to calculate with no strong assumptions and inputs must be publicly available (i.e., no exotic products). ▪ Low correlation with risky assets—high-quality liquid assets should not be subject to wrong-way risk. Assets issued by financial firms are more likely to be illiquid in times of liquidity stress. ▪ Listed on recognized exchange—being listed increases an asset's transparency due to standards in place.	▪ Active/sizeable market (e.g., low bid-ask spreads, high trading volumes, and a large and diverse number of market participants). ▪ Low volatility based on evidence related to price, haircut, and volume at times of stress. ▪ Flight to quality—historically, the market has shown tendencies to move into these types of assets in a systemic crisis.

Source: BCBS, "Basel III: The Liquidity Coverage Ratio and Liquidity Risk Monitoring Tools," January 2013.

HQLAs are classified into three types of assets:

▪ Level 1 assets are cash, central bank reserves, and high-quality government bonds, which can be included without limit in the ratio and are not subject to haircuts.

▪ Level 2A assets are qualifying corporate bonds and covered bonds, which are limited to 40% of the total of HQLAs and are subject to a 15% haircut (see section on Applying the Ratio).

▪ Level 2B assets are qualifying residential mortgage-backed securities (RMBS), corporate debt and common equities and can only comprise up to 15% of the total of HQLAs. Higher haircuts apply to these assets (see section on Applying the Ratio). In addition, the undrawn portion of any contractual committed liquidity facility provided by a central bank, as long as it meets certain conditions, can be included in Level 2B.

Liquid assets are also subject to operational requirements. They should be unencumbered and need to be available to the relevant liquidity risk management function (e.g., Treasury) whenever required. Liquid assets should be turned over on a periodic basis to test their liquidity and to ensure they can be realized during a crisis. And importantly, the BCBS has clearly stated that banks should be permitted by their supervisors to use their liquidity pools in times of stress.

FOCUS ON LIQUID ASSETS

Although banks have increased their holdings of liquid assets over recent years, further increases will be required at some banks in order to meet the LCR, resulting in additional costs for the banking sector.

In addition, due to the high levels of extraordinary central bank support, the cost of liquidity has been much lower in recent years than it necessarily will be in the future. Therefore, any reduction in central bank support will further increase the cost of improving and retaining strong liquidity positions.

Current liquid assets holdings

According to the BCBS Quantitative Impact Study (QIS) data published so far, banks hold the vast majority of their current liquid assets in high-quality government bonds or central bank reserves. A small proportion of the banks' liquid assets are held in corporate bonds and covered bonds. These findings indicate that there may be scope to diversify liquid asset holdings to hold more corporate and covered bonds, thereby reducing the costs of meeting the new rules.

Applying the Ratio

The LCR ratio is applied by running the scenario-based liquidity stress test using prescribed assumptions for runoff rates and liquidation haircuts to assess the net cash outflow over 30 days.

The haircut is a percentage subtracted from the value of the liquid assets, which varies by type:

- Level 1 assets (e.g., cash and high-quality government bonds) are given liquidity credit for their full value.

- Level 2A assets (e.g., qualifying corporate bonds and covered bonds) receive a 15% haircut (i.e., 85% of their value is recognized as part of the determination of liquid assets).
- Level 2B assets receive a larger haircut depending on their nature:
  - Qualifying RMBS that are rated AA or higher, not issued by the bank or its affiliates, which are traded in deep and liquid markets and have not fallen by more than 20% over 30 days in previous stress situations, are subject to a 25% haircut.
  - Corporate debt securities rated between A+ and BBB−, with other conditions similar to RMBS, are subject to a 50% haircut.
  - Common equities that are exchange traded, constituents of a major market index, and with a market history of no more than a 40% decline over 30 days, are subject to a 50% haircut.

The runoff rate refers to the percentage of liabilities due in the next 30 days that are assumed to be withdrawn from the balance sheet in a stressed situation outlined in the LCR scenario.

Key runoff factors are set out in Table 11.3.

In addition, inflow rates that apply to assets maturing in the next 30 days and are outlined in the final LCR rule. There are a number of constraints on offsetting inflows against outflows. Inflows have to be contractual, with no expected defaults, and there is an overall cap on the extent to which inflows can be used in the measure, which is set at 75% of total expected cash outflows.

Managing the LCR

Some business lines and business models are penalized particularly heavily by the new requirements. Please refer to the section on Strategies for Optimizing Business Mix and Balance Sheets in Chapter 12 for a more in-depth discussion.

LCR Design Issues

At the heart of any regulatory measure or risk limit are a number of decisions and trade-offs. One such trade-off is the level of prudence to build into the metric. Calibrating the metric to be overly conservative and the costs to the banking sector (in terms of reduced profitability) and to the real economy (in terms of reduced provision or increased cost of services) will likely be too high. Calibrate the metric to be overly lenient and the banking sector will likely remain susceptible to periods of stress that may impact its ability to provide services to the real economy.

TABLE 11.3 Runoff Rate Factors

Category	Outflow rates
■ Retail deposits and unsecured wholesale funding provided by SMEs (small and medium enterprises)	
■ Stable—only the portion of deposits covered by effective deposit insurance schemes	■ 5% or 3% if the deposit guarantee scheme is pre-funded
■ Non-stable	■ 10%
■ Operational deposits	■ 25%
■ Deposits in networks of co-operative banks	■ 25 or 100%
■ Wholesale unsecured funding provided by non-financial corporate and sovereigns (including central banks and PSEs [public sector entities])	■ 40% or 20% if the deposits are covered by an effective deposit guarantee scheme or public guarantee
■ Secured funding transactions	
■ With a central bank counterparty or backed by Level 1 assets with any counterparty	■ 0%
■ Backed by Level 2A assets, with any counterparty	■ 15%
■ Backed by non-Level 1 or non-Level 2A assets, with domestic sovereigns, multilateral development banks, or domestic PSEs as a counterparty	■ 25%
■ Backed by RMBS eligible for inclusion in Level 2B	■ 25%
■ Backed by other Level 2B assets	■ 50%
■ All other secured funding transactions	■ 100%
■ Currently undrawn committed credit and liquidity facilities provided to:	
■ Retail and small business clients	■ 5%
■ Non-financial corporates, sovereigns and central banks, multilateral development banks, and PSEs	■ 10% for credit, 30% for liquidity

TABLE 11.3   (*Continued*)

Category	Outflow rates
▪ Banks subject to prudential supervision	▪ 40%
▪ Other financial institutions (e.g., securities firms, insurance companies)	▪ 40% for credit, 100% for liquidity
▪ Other legal entity customers, credit and liquidity facilities	▪ 100%
▪ Derivatives	▪ Collateral outflows arising from a 3-notch downgrade ▪ Collateral outflows arising from a financial market shock ▪ Collateral outflows arising from a 20% reduction in the market value of collateral already posted
▪ Specific derivatives risk such as collateral substitution, and excess collateral that the bank is contractually obligated to return/provide if required	▪ 100%
▪ Trade finance–related activities	▪ 0–5% (guidance)

Source: BCBS, "Basel III: The Liquidity Coverage Ratio and Liquidity Risk Monitoring Tools," January 2013.

Another decision concerns the level of complexity in the metric. A simple measure will be easy-to-understand and implement for banks, and will likely be easier to supervise (e.g., there are a limited number of subjective interpretations that it is necessary for banks to make). However, a complex measure is arguably better at capturing the true risks within banks and will likely help to limit distortions that are caused by the metric in financial markets.

Central bank funding   One of the most fundamental design issues with respect to the LCR is how to incorporate the provision of central bank support into the measure. One side of the debate argues that the definition of liquid assets should be equivalent to the list of eligible assets for central bank funding, as the central bank is the only guaranteed provider of funding in times of stress.

The major concern with such a definition of liquid assets is that the central bank would become the lender of first resort in times of stress, rather than the lender of last resort, which has traditionally been the role assumed by central banks in the event of liquidity stress. If one believes this argument, the definition of liquid assets should be defined separately from the list of eligible assets for central bank funding and should, instead, be focused on those assets that are expected to remain liquid in commercial financial markets and provide liquidity without access to the central bank.

The final Basel version of the definition of liquid assets serves to balance these arguments, by primarily focusing on those assets that regulators believe will remain liquid in commercial markets in times of stress, while, following revised guidance issued in January 2014, giving some limited recognition for committed facilities that have been provided by central banks.

Definition of liquid assets   The decision regarding the definition of liquid assets and its link to central bank funding also poses challenges. Broadly speaking, throughout the discussions, two points of view have been put forward on this issue. One point of view supported a narrow definition of liquid assets, focused on Level 1 assets. This was motivated by a desire for a highly prudent and simple measure. A ratio focused on one single definition of liquid assets (i.e., Level 1 assets) would have likely been simple and easy to supervise. The measure would also have provided banks with greater resilience to most stress scenarios given that cash and cash-like instruments (such as available central bank reserves and government bonds) generally tend to be the assets that are most easily liquidated in times of stress.

However, a large number of stakeholders were concerned about such a definition because this would have forced banks to hold a concentrated pool of liquid assets and a large amount of government bonds. In a scenario where the solvency of the government was in question, banks may have incurred large mark-to-market losses arising from falls in the market value of government bonds. And the liquidity of the bonds may have decreased significantly. Of course, the European sovereign crisis lent great credence to this point of view and was a key driver of the final outcome, following the belief that a more diversified pool of liquid assets would provide more effective protection against the full range of financial market shocks that could affect banks' liquidity positions.

There were other arguments for including a wider range of assets. First, a number of stakeholders observed that, at least in developed financial markets, assets other than government bonds, such as high quality corporate bonds and covered bonds, hold liquidity value in times of stress and therefore should receive some recognition in the regulatory measure. Second, there were concerns about whether there is a sufficient supply of Level 1 assets available for banks in aggregate to hold as part of their liquid asset buffers. Third, there were also concerns that the liquidity and value of Level 2 and other assets would be driven artificially lower if these assets were excluded from the regulatory definition (both because of reputational impact and a fall in demand for these assets).

Runoff rates on liabilities There was also a great deal of debate over the runoff rates on various types of liabilities. One of the most significant decisions concerned the proportion of retail deposits that should be assumed to run off. This is a good example of the difficulty of writing a harmonized international regulatory standard when such significant differences exist between national financial markets. In this case, there are very significant differences between the deposit guarantees that exist in different countries, both in terms of the level of coverage, the speed of pay-out, and the method of funding (in particular whether the scheme is pre-funded or not). This was the prompt for the introduction of a new 3% runoff category in January 2013 and is also the reason why there remains significant scope for national supervisors to apply judgment in determining the outflow rates attached to certain types of deposits (e.g., in whether to apply 5% or 10% and how to define deposits that should be subject to a higher outflow rate than 10%).

Another item over which there was significant debate was the runoff rate for off-balance sheet commitments provided to non-financial corporates as backup lines for their commercial paper programs. This was particularly important to the U.S. firms, where such backup lines are a crucial part of the financial market support given to the corporate sector. Originally, such commitments were subject to a 100% outflow rate. This was reduced to 30% in the January 2014 standard.

LCR Technical Challenges

There are a number of key technical challenges associated with the interpretation of the LCR rules, described in more detail below.

Liquidity transfer restrictions The LCR is a consolidated ratio, but firms will have to assess impediments to transferring liquidity across individual entities. Analysis will be required to determine the potential transferability of assets and committed intercompany facilities for inclusion in the LCR. Furthermore, policy, operating model, and technology changes will be required.

Operational deposits: definition, distinctions and treatment A working level definition for distinguishing operational versus non-operational deposits (which impacts the cash outflow runoff rates) will need to be established.

Clear internal policy guidelines are required to classify wholesale deposits. Flagging deposits may require significant changes to a bank's systems and data architecture.

Differentiating between liquidity and credit facilities As explained earlier, for certain categories of counterparties, different outflow rates apply to undrawn committed facilities, depending on whether they qualify as liquidity or credit facilities. Although the Basel III rules have been clarified in the final rule, it is not easy to allocate these facilities to one category, as contracts usually do not prevent creditors from using general working capital facilities (which would qualify as credit facilities) for liquidity purposes. It is therefore likely that contractual terms of such facilities will have to change to allow for the application of the LCR rules.

Collateral allocation and eligibility The LCR rules require a clear linkage between collateral for derivative positions and the underlying securities. For example, there is a requirement to identify reverse repo and collateral swap trades that are short covering trades (which also raises allocation methodology challenges, particularly where collateral positions are managed on a pooled basis). Data model and systems changes to introduce the necessary linkages could be difficult to implement. Policy and operating model changes may also be required (e.g., to define the collateral allocation methodology).

Other The lack of clear guidance regarding the treatment of certain products, such as brokered deposits, and intragroup transactions in the LCR is a concern for firms and could lead to differences in interpretation. In addition, reporting derivatives, particularly with respect to netting, still differs between banks.

LCR Implementation Issues

The LCR is in the process of being translated into national regulations (so that it is legally binding on firms) and implemented by supervisors. While the LCR has been finalized by the BCBS, a number of choices remain for national supervisors with respect to how to implement the ratio.

First, and most importantly, supervisors have a choice with respect to how quickly to introduce the LCR and at what level. The BCBS has set out a minimum standard that the LCR should be introduced at 60% in January 2015, rising by 10% each year to become fully binding at 100% in

January 2019. National supervisors can implement more stringent require-ments earlier if they so desire. For example, the European timeline for the LCR moves firms to 100% compliance one year early in 2018 (with a 20% increase from 2017 to 2018).

There are also likely to be differences in the way in which national super-visors apply the ratio to different types of firms. Some countries such as the U.S. will choose to apply the Basel LCR standard only to the largest inter-national banks within their jurisdiction (this is the type of bank for whom the Basel standards are explicitly written) with different liquidity rules or a different version of the LCR applied to smaller and/or domestic banks. Some jurisdictions, such as Europe, are also debating how the standard should be applied to investment firms, or smaller firms that are focused on a particular type of business.

One key issue that the BCBS has debated over recent years is what the reaction of supervisors should be in the event that a bank falls beneath the 100% minimum level of the LCR. In January 2014, the BCBS published some guidance concerning the circumstances under which a firm would be allowed to slip beneath the minimum standard and what the regulatory requirements should be in the event that this happens (e.g., the requirement to submit a contingency plan outlining how full compliance will be restored). This is helpful and clarifies supervisory expectations. However, the guidance is still high-level and there remains anxiety in the market amongst banks that they will be penalized very heavily (or even shut down) if they were to fall below the minimum. More detail is needed from supervisors if this challenge is to be overcome.

Finally, the national implementation of the LCR is inevitably going to lead to some differences between the standard that international banks need to comply with in one country compared with that in another country. This increases costs in terms of putting into place the data and reporting solutions that allow banks to report these standards to regulators and to the market. It also makes it more difficult for an international bank to manage its liq-uidity on a common global basis if the regulatory standards to which it is measured differ across countries (e.g., in terms of the outflows attached to a particular liability). To manage differences in regulation and ambiguity in interpretation, banks need to establish where judgement might be required and formalize associated governance arrangements. Regulatory differences also create an ongoing challenge for the BCBS in terms of monitoring these differences and trying to reduce the number and size of differences. The work that the BCBS has started, in terms of monitoring the implementation of the Basel III rules, is a step in the right direction.

NSFR

Definition

The second measure of liquidity risk proposed by the BCBS is the NSFR. The aim of this measure is to ensure that banks are sufficiently strong from a funding and liquidity profile perspective (i.e., that they have sufficient long-term or stable funding to fund less liquid and longer-term assets on their balance sheet).

The ratio achieves this by calculating a bank's available stable funding (ASF) and required stable funding (RSF). ASF is a measure of the capital and liabilities expected to be reliable over the one-year time period. For example, a bank can be confident that its capital and long-term wholesale funding (which cannot be withdrawn ahead of its contractual maturity) along with a significant proportion of its retail deposits will be retained. By contrast, the experience of the crisis suggests that short-term wholesale funding is less reliable, and therefore this can only count partially towards the definition of stable funding.

RSF is a measure of the liquidity and maturity of the assets of a bank, linked to its ability or willingness to sell or repo those assets over a one-year time period. For example, a bank is less likely to be able to sell the majority of its long-term retail loans such as mortgages when compared with liquid financial market securities. Additionally, as the recent financial crisis illustrated, certain financial market securities, while moderately liquid in normal times, can become illiquid in certain circumstances, and cannot be sold or funded through repo without taking a significant haircut.

The requirement is described by the following inequality:

$$\frac{ASF}{RSF} \geq 100\%$$

While the NSFR is a measure originally designed by the BCBS, the concept is very similar to other measures (e.g., the cash capital ratio) that were used in the industry ahead of the crisis, albeit with a tighter definition to address some of the weaknesses identified during the financial crisis. It also bears strong similarities to the loan-deposit ratio used by many retail-focused banks.

There were a number of concerns with the balance sheet structures of banks before and during the crisis that led to the introduction of the ratio and influenced its design and calibration. At the forefront of the BCBS's concerns were the numerous banks that funded a large proportion of their long-term loan books through short-term wholesale funding such as interbank deposits, certificates of deposit, or commercial paper. The use of short-term repo markets to fund trading book investments in assets that turned out to be relatively illiquid during the crisis was also a concern. While the introduction of the LCR was viewed as a potential solution to problems identified at the very short end of the maturity spectrum, it did not address problems beyond that initial one-month period. In fact, a number of members of the BCBS felt that the introduction of the LCR could exacerbate weaknesses in the medium-term structural balance sheet strength of institutions because the cost of the LCR would encourage firms to lower the average maturity of their funding outside of the initial one-month period. In this regard, the NSFR is an important complement to the LCR.

Available Stable Funding and Required Stable Funding

Available stable funding As introduced earlier, ASF is a measure of the capital and liabilities that a bank expects to be stable over the one-year time period. Every on-balance liability is classified into one of five possible categories. The on-balance sheet value (usually using the accounting treatment) of that liability is multiplied by the ASF factor and all the amounts are aggregated into a total available stable funding number.

A summary of the ASF factors is included in Table 11.4.[6]

While the ASF factors are described in terms of the amount of funding that is retained over the one-year period of stress, it might be informative to consider them as outflow assumptions, particularly for readers more familiar with short-term stress testing measures such as the LCR. For example, we can describe the assumptions concerning retail deposits as being equivalent to losing 5% (for stable deposits) and 10% (for less stable deposits) over the one-year period. Extending that point, the ratio assumes that firms lose 50% of their funding from non-financial corporates.

Required stable funding RSF is a measure of the liquidity and maturity of the assets of a bank, and pays consideration to the bank's ability or willingness to sell or repo those assets over a one-year time period. Every on-balance asset is classified into one of eight possible categories. Off-balance sheet commitments are classified into one of two categories. The value (estimated using accounting treatment) of that asset is multiplied by the RSF factor, and all the amounts are aggregated into a total required stable funding number.

A summary of the RSF factors is set out in Table 11.5.[7]

---

[6]Basel Committee on Banking Supervision, "Basel III: The Net Stable Funding Ratio," p. 6.
[7]Basel Committee on Banking Supervision, "Basel III: The Net Stable Funding Ratio," p. 11.

TABLE 11.4 ASF Factors

Category	ASF factor
▪ Capital and funding with a contractual maturity of greater than one year	▪ 100%
▪ Stable retail deposits* with maturity less than one year	▪ 95%
▪ Less stable retail deposits* with maturity less than one year	▪ 90%
▪ Wholesale unsecured funding provided by non-financial corporate and sovereigns with maturity of less than one year ▪ Operational deposits ▪ Other funding with residual maturity of not less than six months and less than one year not included in the above categories, including funding from central banks and financial institutions	▪ 50%
▪ All other liabilities ▪ NSFR derivative liabilities net of NSFR derivative assets (if positive) ▪ "Trade date" payables	▪ 0%

*The definition of stable and less stable retail deposits is the same as the definition used in the LCR.

High-quality mortgages only require stable funding equivalent to 65% of their balance sheet value on the assumption that securitization markets will be open at some point over the one-year horizon, even if mortgage-backed securities require higher collateralization than in normal times. The scenario assumes that a small amount of credit and liquidity facilities are drawn over the horizon.

The NSFR assumes that the bank retains its long-term assets and is also unable (or unwilling) to sell or repo its marketable assets at their previous market value. The size of the haircut taken on marketable assets depends on the underlying liquidity of the asset. With respect to the bank's short-term assets, the factors vary depending on the type of business. Short-term loans to financial institutions can largely be assumed to mature and the bank can benefit from the inflow. However, it is assumed that the bank wants to roll over (or write new business equivalent to) half of its maturing lending to non-financial corporates and retail customers. This makes sense within the context of a measure that assumes that a bank wants to continue to fund its core businesses and write new business.

TABLE 11.5 RSF Factors

Category	RSF factor
■ Cash, central bank reserves, short-term (less than six months) claims on central banks and "trade date" receivables	■ 0%
■ High quality government bonds	■ 5%
■ **Unencumbered loans** to financial institutions with maturity less than six months, where the loan is secured against high-quality government bonds and where the bank has rehypothecation rights against those bonds	■ 10%
■ High-quality corporate and covered bonds and lower quality government bonds ■ Unencumbered loans to financial institutions with maturity less than six months (not included in the above categories)	■ 15%
■ Equities and lower quality corporate bonds ■ Liquid assets encumbered for a period of between six months and one year ■ Loans to financial institutions of maturity between six months and one year ■ All other assets with a maturity of less than one year ■ Operational deposits	■ 50%
■ High quality mortgages (and other unsecured loans) with maturity of greater than one year	■ 65%
■ Other unencumbered performing loans, securities, equities, and commodities ■ Assets posted as initial margin for derivative contracts and assets provided to contribute to the default fund of a CCP	■ 85%
■ Other on-balance sheet assets (including assets encumbered for a period greater than one year and non-performing loans) ■ NSFR derivative assets net of NSFR derivative liabilities (if positive) ■ 20% of derivative liabilities (as per the NSFR definition)	■ 100%
■ Irrevocable or conditionally revocable credit and liquidity facilities	■ 5%
■ Other off-balance sheet items	■ National supervisor discretion

Managing the NSFR

As with the LCR, some business lines and business models are penalized heavily by the new requirements. Please refer to the section titled *Strategies for Optimizing Business Mix and Balance Sheets* in Chapter 12 for a more in-depth discussion of those.

Design Issues

Just as with the LCR, in the design of the NSFR, the BCBS was required to make a judgment call on a number of decisions and trade-offs. As highlighted previously, there are some concerns that the NSFR may constrain the ability of banks to provide services to the real economy. For retail banks, these concerns appear to have been eased with the 2014 revisions, in particular with the increase in ASF factors for retail deposits. For investment firms, concerns remain over the treatment of certain instruments, including equities, and derivatives, for example.

In terms of the level of complexity desired in the measure, the 2010 version of the NSFR is a relatively simple measure. The 2014 version of the NSFR is slightly more complex (although still simple when compared with the LCR) due to the inclusion of a more granular approach to the maturity buckets of the NSFR, namely a six-month bucket to sit alongside the one-year bucket.

In addition, some supervisors are concerned that the NSFR is too crude to be able to cope with the vast diversity of different business models that exist within the banking sector. For example, all other things equal, the ability of investment banks to access financial markets and liquidate holdings of investments could be seen as inherently greater than that of retail banks. This could warrant a lower RSF factor for marketable assets for these institutions compared with retail banks. Similarly, a bank with an established presence in mortgage-backed securities (MBS) markets and a long track record of successful issuances could perhaps be more confident than the average bank in its ability to securitize assets in times of stress. Again this could lead to those assets benefitting from a lower RSF factor.

NSFR Technical Issues

A number of NSFR technical issues are similar to those of the LCR as a significant number of the NSFR definitions and categorizations have been drawn from the LCR's detail. There are a couple of specific examples that are worth highlighting here.

First, in determining the maturity of a liability, firms need to take into account any optionality that exists.[8] If the investor has a put option, then the liability should be assumed to mature at the date of the call option rather than the contractual maturity date (based on the assumption that the investor will put the debt if it is revealed that the issuing firm is under stress). This is relatively simple to implement, as long as firms have methods of identifying and analyzing the optionality that exists in debt they have issued. It is more complex in the event that the call option is under the control of the issuer. In this case, because it is under the control of the firm, it would be easy to assume that the debt will not be called and hence its maturity can be assumed to be the contractual maturity rather than until the call date. However, the standard requires firms to consider the reputational and market pressures that might be present in times of stress. For example, if a bank is under market stress, it may wish to exercise the callable feature so that it can demonstrate to the market that it has adequate funding and liquidity.

Another complex technical issue concerns repo and encumbered assets. The NSFR requires firms to identify which assets are encumbered against which liabilities, e.g., which assets have been used to secure repo funding contracts. This includes identifying the type of asset, the period for which it is encumbered, and the firm's need to take into consideration assets that have been borrowed as well as those assets that are on the firm's balance sheet.

Implementation Issues

It remains early days in terms of implementing the NSFR, as it will not be introduced before 2018. However, there are two specific issues that are worth considering here. First, it seems possible, given the relative simplicity of the current version of the NSFR, that supervisors will want to embed some additional risk-sensitive assumptions into the metric for individual institutions, which would be equivalent to the imposition of Pillar 2 add-ons.

Another important implementation issue that should be considered is the behavior of the measure under stress and the reaction of supervisors if a bank was to fail to meet the 100% requirement when under stress. The same issue applies to the LCR and has been considered by the BCBS in recent years, as illustrated in the revised, more detailed guidance. That guidance indicates that in the event that a bank fails the 100% requirement, supervisors should give that institution a period of time to rectify the problem.

---

[8]This issue is also applicable to the LCR, but it is arguably more important for the NSFR which is focused on a longer time horizon.

A similar approach could be warranted on the NSFR, but thought needs to be given to the type of stress that may warrant such an allowance and the length of time that should be given to banks if there is a problem.

QUALITATIVE REQUIREMENTS AND MONITORING TOOLS

In addition to the quantitative standards, the BCBS has introduced a suite of monitoring tools to capture information related to cash flows, balance sheet structure, available unencumbered assets, and certain market indicators, which are as follows:

- **Contractual maturity mismatch.** The contractual maturity mismatch profile identifies the gaps between the contractual inflows and outflows of liquidity for defined time bands. No behavioral assumptions are applied, which will allow supervisors to apply their own assumptions and perform analysis across the market.
- **Concentration of funding.** This measure aims to identify funding concentrations by counterparty or type of instrument/product in relation to wholesale funding across material currencies (accounting for 5% or more of the bank's total liabilities).
- **Available unencumbered assets.** This measure relates to the amount and key characteristics of unencumbered assets, including currency denomination and location. Banks should also provide expected haircuts required on the secondary market or by the central bank and the expected monetized value of the collateral.
- **Market-related monitoring tools.** These will be broken down into market-wide, financial sector, and bank-specific information and will be used by supervisors to monitor potential liquidity difficulties at banks.
- **LCR by material currencies.** Supervisors will require firms with a significant proportion of their balance sheet in different currencies to report information on the LCR in single currencies.

TACKLING THE PRACTICAL IMPLEMENTATION CHALLENGES

The new rules have a significant impact on data requirements, IT systems, reporting processes, strategic funding decisions, and the overall liquidity management framework.

These impacts will likely provide challenges particularly for treasury, risk management, and finance. Firms will likely be faced with the need to find adequate internal resources to address the issues and challenges. In addition, consideration should be given to the trade-off between tactical and strategic solutions with respect to cost savings and implications, particularly in terms of liquidity buffer levels and the expectation by regulators of the need for robust systems and controls.

No firm will likely find the impact of these new requirements easy. However, institutions that understand the implications and fully embed liquidity considerations into their business decisions should come through stronger.

As a result of the implementation of these liquidity standards, many banks will need to undertake a review of their funding and business strategies and a significant upgrade of reporting systems. Well-informed and proactive banks should be able to identify ways in which to reduce the impact of the new rules and fund their businesses in a more cost-efficient manner. They can also develop a much sharper picture of what business is viable and how it should be appropriately priced.

The following sections provide an overview of key considerations that firms should consider when implementing the new liquidity ratios.

Updating System and Data Solutions in a Short Time Frame

From an operational and systems perspective, the banks have prepared to be in a position to report the LCR to their supervisors as of January 1, 2015 (and reporting started earlier in some regions, such as the European Union, from the first quarter of 2014). In order to avoid any unpleasant surprises, banks have had to work on their infrastructure for the past months or years. In addition, the banks needed to make any adjustments to their balance sheets in good time (recognizing that the phase-in arrangements will give more time to make adjustments to meet the 100% minimum requirements), and resolve the inevitable data issues that the new reporting requirements will uncover. The level of reporting detail, in particular the need to be able to report on individual legal entities and overseas branches, where required, as well as tailoring to meet home and host supervisory requirements, should not be underestimated. For EU banks, the updated Capital Requirements Directive requires greater granularity than Basel III.

In most jurisdictions, it is not yet confirmed when the NSFR will have to be reported (although in some, e.g., the European Union, reporting started in early 2014). For some banks this is less of an immediate concern. Additionally, in its current calibration, the NSFR appears to be simpler to report than the LCR, with far fewer lines and less areas of uncertainty and correspondingly less need for technical interpretation.

While the short timetable for introduction of new reporting forms will force some banks to adopt a tactical solution in the short-term, in the long-term the demands associated with this new reporting will require implementation of a fully developed strategic solution. In part this is driven by the huge increase in detailed data that will be required, the frequency with which reports may have to be produced (daily in times of stress), and the strengthened governance arrangements that regulators are now demanding. In addition, the supervisors' demand for data and desire to quantitatively assess the banks' risk positions is increasing.

The task to put in place a strategic solution is complicated by the constant changes to the reporting requirements:

- **EBA.** Current remodeling of the LCR and LR templates; remodeling of the NSFR templates to be expected when the EU NSFR is finalized
- **UK PRA.** Possibility of bespoke reporting forms on liquidity
- **U.S. FRB.** Fifth Generation ("5-G") and 2052-a and -b reporting requirements

Disclosing the LCR

In summary, firms will be required to disclose the LCR on a consolidated basis with details of the underlying data and assumptions used. This is a significant change from current practice and has prompted a great deal of debate over the merits of such disclosures. The regulatory community has argued that greater disclosure of numbers on liquidity risk will help to strengthen the role of market discipline in ensuring that banks do not take too much liquidity risk. However, concerns have been raised by the industry, in particular because of the possible negative reaction of markets when LCR numbers are disclosed in times of stress and reveal deteriorating positions: If counterparties observe that a bank is losing funding and having to use its pool of liquid assets, this may prompt more counterparties to withdraw funds, creating a vicious circle.

To mitigate the effects of this cycle, firms will be required to publish numbers based on average positions over the appropriate period (rather than at a point in time). This will help to mask any problems that were short-term and operational.

Conclusion

The Basel III ratios and monitoring tools will play an important role in influencing the shape of the capital and liquidity management framework and associated systems and controls. They will need to be embedded at the highest levels of the organization and across the overall governance framework.

The introduction of the new ratios will further increase the role of the board and senior management in managing liquidity and assessing whether any change in strategy, business model, and/or funding is required.

Outlined below are examples of areas where the Basel III ratios will impact on the existing liquidity risk management framework:

- A financial institution will need to update its liquidity risk appetite to take account of the liquidity ratios. The Basel III ratios and monitoring tools are likely to lead to the implementation of additional limits to cover all aspects of liquidity management. Examples include the funding concentration with limits such as proportion of secured funding versus unsecured funding; maximum exposure to one single repo counterparty or maturity profile for intragroup funding and secured funding. In addition, the impact of new products and new types of transactions on these ratios should be modelled and monitored to make sure the bank stays within its risk appetite and also properly takes into account the total cost of the product/transaction.

- Contingency funding plans need to be considered in light of the new ratios (e.g., the manner in which firms should respond to deteriorating positions, and whether contingency plans should be automatically triggered when ratios are breached).

- In terms of stress testing, the Basel III requirements present another set of assumptions and parameters, which banks should align with existing liquidity stress scenarios.

- The Basel III ratios also introduce an additional control on how the cost of liquidity is allocated to the business and how funding plans are developed. Embedding the LCR and the NSFR into funds transfer pricing is a key challenge, but also an opportunity to reflect the cost associated with liquidity requirements of different instruments. This will help banks to reflect the true cost of different business strategies, and thereby achieve a more optimal position over the longer term. It will also help to reflect the new constraints in performance measures and incentives.

- The LCR poses a number of challenges in relation to collateral management, e.g., the ability to move securities and cash across borders, knowing the exact location of securities at any one time, and having a better understanding of how specific pieces of collateral are being used to hedge positions or collateralize trades.

- Liquidity risk management frameworks also need to incorporate specific provisions for the liquid asset buffer: defining, establishing, and maintaining operational control of a liquidity buffer, including periodic testing.

- Finally, banks should review the management of liquidity across jurisdictions and whether to book specific products in some jurisdictions where liquidity treatment is more favorable.

The key to bringing this all together is a clear and comprehensive enterprise-wide view of capital and liquidity risk, consistent with the regulatory rules. It is also important to make sure capital and liquidity risk management are closely embedded into the broader risk appetite and risk management framework of the group. This in turn requires close cooperation between the trading desks and credit teams in the front office and the finance, risk management, and systems teams that support them.

Three

Optimizing Business Practices

Strategic and Tactical Implications of the New Requirements

Hortense Huez[1]

INTRODUCTION

This chapter specifically focuses on the impact of the Liquidity Coverage Ratio (LCR), the Net Stable Funding Ratio (NSFR), and the Leverage Ratio (LR) on different types of banks. It looks at strategies to tackle regulatory change, including suggestions for how to sustain profitability while meeting these new demands.

STRATEGIC IMPACT OF THE NEW RATIOS

This section analyzes the combined impact of the LCR, NSFR, and LR on business models for retail banks, building societies, universal banks, and investment banks. While most types of banks, particularly the large institutions in the UK, Europe, and U.S., would meet the LCR ratio without major problems, the NSFR is more of a challenge for investment banks. The LR will also prove challenging for banks with lower RWAs.

A closer analysis of the impact of these three ratios on hypothetical models of a retail bank, an investment bank, a universal bank, and a building society help to form a clearer picture of the comparative impact of the new liquidity ratios on different business models. When undertaking the analysis, one can draw on actual data from existing institutions that represent each business model, but there is also the need to make informed assumptions concerning the composition of liquid assets, repo/reverse repo books,

---

[1] Hortense Huez is a director in PwC's London office.

derivative positions, amount of operational deposits, and quality of retail deposits, given the lack of data publicly available on these items.

A look at the public disclosures of banks confirms that most institutions have yet to fully disclose their leverage and liquidity ratios at the time of this book's printing. Those that did release data in 2014 generally appear to be well on their way to meeting the new requirements. However, while the best prepared banks are also the most likely to disclose their ratios, it is still not possible to infer that all banks will be equally ready for the new requirements by their respective effective dates. Additionally, the lack of explanatory notes to accompany the ratios makes it difficult to ascertain if the calculation methods are comparable.

Banks on Course for LCR

Overall, banks of all types appear to be ready to meet the LCR demands. This reflects the buildup of liquid asset buffers following the financial crisis, with the UK leading the way in implementing a regulatory regime that has actually set a higher bar than the LCR.

Absent uniform disclosures across the banking industry and different jurisdictions, analytical and anecdotal evidence suggests that institutions with investment and universal bank business models tend to have slightly higher LCRs due to the relatively higher amount of High-Quality Liquid Assets (HQLAs) they hold, especially when using the European Union (EU) definition of the LCR. This obviously depends on the types of business they are in: fixed income asset inventories providing a bigger pool of potential HQLA than commodity asset inventories, for instance.

However, it is worth noting that retail banks derive a large proportion of their funding from retail deposits, which have a significant advantage in meeting LCR requirements given the low cash outflow rate associated with such liabilities.

Retail Deposits Give Clear NSFR Advantage

Given the regulatory incentives for long-term funding and preference for retail unsecured funding rather than short-term secured funding, it is unsurprising that retail and even universal banks are better able to contend with the NSFR requirements than their investment bank counterparts.

The differences in NSFR generally stem from the treatment of liabilities. Investment banks are heavily wholesale funded, with greater reliance on the shorter maturities associated which such funding. Given the less favorable treatment of short-term wholesale funding, especially repo funding, the NSFR is likely to be the more binding requirement for investment banks.

Investment banks are also affected by the high Required Stable Funding (RSF) impact on their derivative assets, while net derivative liabilities do not provide Available Stable Funding (ASF), with an RSF for 20% of those. This treatment, combined with the high outflow rates in the LCR for derivative positions not collateralized by HQLA, and more broadly the increase of margin requirements due to the push for central clearing, will put pressure on the profitability of investment banks' derivatives businesses. By contrast, retail banks and building societies tend to have funding bases which provide higher ASF.

Universal banks in the UK present an interesting case. In the past, they could take advantage of the synergies and cross-funding opportunities between their retail and investment divisions. However, ring-fencing may now place their investment banking arms in a similar situation to pure investment banks, with comparable NSFR and LCR implications.

Figure 12.1 outlines the impact of the LCR and NSFR on different business models. The results are intended to be indicative on relative positions rather than actual levels.

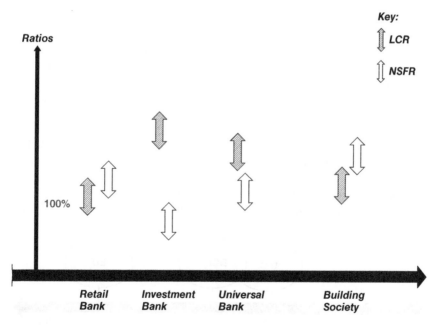

FIGURE 12.1 Illustrative Relative Ranges for LCR and NSFR Levels for Different Business Models
Source: PwC analysis

Balancing Riskiness with Leverage

Rather than varying by business model, the key influence on the LR requirement appears to be the riskiness of assets as this ratio has a bigger adverse impact on low risk-weighted activities, which attract lower risk-based capital requirements.

Although investment banks have seen a big increase in their RWAs as a result of the introduction of Basel 2.5/3, the use of internal models has reduced this effect, resulting in lower risk-weights and lower regulatory capital requirements. This means a non-risk weighted capital requirement is likely to hit them harder. Repo funding also increases balance sheet size and therefore imposes leverage ratio requirements.

The LR framework could also be a binding constraint for building societies. This would reflect the low average risk weighting in their asset portfolios, which consist mainly of retail loans and mortgages. However, a consistent pattern has yet to emerge across banks and building societies that have high balance sheet concentrations in these types of assets.

Managing across Jurisdictions—the LCR Example

One particular challenge for large and well-diversified international banks is how to manage their regulatory requirements across many different jurisdictions and legal entities, many of which have different rules and binding ratios. Each country tends to adopt a version of the international standards that is adapted to the specifics of its banking system.

While the NSFR has not yet been translated into national legislations, these differences are notable for LCR requirements. Figure 12.2 sets out the LCR for a hypothetical investment bank under the U.S., European Banking Authority (EBA) and Basel Committee on Banking Supervision (BCBS) approaches. The LCR ratio is higher in Europe because the definition of permissible HQLA is far wider and includes more covered bonds, auto-loans, and consumer credit backed-securities. By contrast, the U.S. version of the LCR is stricter than the BCBS recommendations. The U.S. LCR is based

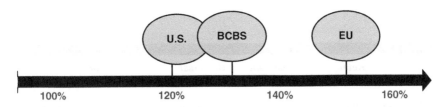

FIGURE 12.2 Relative Ranges for LCR Levels under Different Local Rules.
Source: PwC analysis

on the highest occurrence of cumulative net outflows during the 30-day period vs. the outflow over the 30-day period in Europe. The U.S. LCR regulation also adopts a narrower definition of permissible HQLA, excluding covered bonds and other securities by financial institutions, auto-loans, and consumer credit backed securities.

It is also worth highlighting that even where the LCR is applied in a consistent manner, there can be cross-jurisdictional differences. For example, sovereign bonds could be counted as HQLA when issued in the country where a bank is headquartered. However, these assets may not be deemed to be highly liquid in foreign jurisdictions. Similarly, the classification of liabilities between stable and less stable might differ by jurisdiction.

While this could give opportunities to optimize the location of different types of assets and liabilities with changes in booking models, it will also create inefficiencies because excess sources of liquidity in third country currencies may not provide much benefit for the group-level calculation of the ratio. These limitations are due to LCR requirements for operational control, restrictions on the fungibility of cross-border liquidity, and differences in HQLA eligibility rules.

STRATEGIES FOR OPTIMIZING BUSINESS MIX AND BALANCE SHEETS

The regulatory response to the financial crisis created a separate ratio for each problem identified: excessive leverage, over-reliance on short-term funding, and inappropriate management of liquidity risk. Some of the intended consequences are already visible: significantly lower risk reflected in balance sheets since 2007–08, overall reduction of bank leverage, and decrease in repo funding.

However, the layering of regulation results in an overall framework that can have contradictory consequences. As Table 12.1 highlights, the new ratios have potentially contrasting impacts on various bank business models. The ratios can also encourage behaviors that could impinge on the real economy. For example, increasing the liquid asset buffer for the LCR might leave less room for lending, given the LR constraints. And the upcoming requirement to hold a minimum amount of total loss absorbing capacity (TLAC) for systemic institutions adds even more complexity to the mix. As such, while retail funding is encouraged by the BCBS NSFR, and the U.S. GSIB capital surcharge rules include de facto considerations for reliance on short-term wholesale funding, the TLAC requires a minimum amount of long-term wholesale debt to be issued. For some banks, TLAC might even become the most binding constraint, as it is a hard requirement with a direct impact on the funding mix.

TABLE 12.1 Summary Table of the New Ratios

	Ratio's objective	Differences between jurisdictions	Key implications
LCR	■ Requires banks to maintain a buffer of HQLA against net cash outflows to survive a liquidity stress lasting 30 days.	■ U.S. interpretation more stringent on banks ■ BCBS and U.S. implementation in January 2015. EU implementation in October 2015.	■ Overall, most banks are on course to meet the new requirements, although investment and universal banks could have a slightly higher LCR than retail banks due to the relatively higher amount of HQLA they hold.
NSFR	■ Aims to reduce liquidity risk over a longer time horizon by requiring banks to fund long-term activities with stable resources.	■ The EBA and U.S. were due to report on NSFR implementation in 2015, with a likely "go live" date in 2018. ■ U.S. GSIB rules include a short term wholesale funding capital surcharge.	■ Retail banks and building societies seem to be better prepared for the NSFR as they tend to have funding bases that deliver higher ASF. Investment banks did not fare as well on the liability side as they hold more short-term wholesale funding.
LR	■ Ratio of a bank's Tier 1 capital to total assets to assess the risk of excessive leverage in financial institutions.	■ The finalized EU version of LR came out in 2014. The U.S. finalized the Enhanced Supplementary Leverage Ratio (ESLR) in 2014, which seeks to harmonize it with European guidance, although it still has elements that go beyond the Basel III LR. ■ Expected implementation is in 2018. ■ The Bank of England recommends a 3% minimum leverage ratio with implementation in 2016 for G-SIBs and other major UK banks. ■ The U.S. ESLR includes a 2% buffer at the bank holding company of U.S. G-SIBs as well as a 6% SLR requirement for their insured depositary institutions to be classified as well capitalized.	■ Banks with low-risk but high-volume activities are most impacted.

Seeing the Big Picture

In this new, perplexing, and potentially conflicting regulatory environment, modeling the impact of the changes as a whole requires a firm to identify:

- The impact of each requirement and the overall impact of all requirements assessed together
- Shortfalls for one or more requirements and how these can be addressed while maintaining profitability without causing a deterioration in the other ratios
- Headroom for one or more requirements and how these can be addressed in a manner that is consistent with risk appetite, market expectations, and revenue targets

Effective modeling would enable banks to perform scenario and sensitivity analysis on the impact on new products, new funding sources, and, more broadly, of any change in the strategic business planning of the bank.

There is also a range of strategies that banks can deploy to optimize their balance sheet management.

Options for Optimization

High level options include:

- **Review funding mix.** Retail funding offers greater stability. However, the type of funding is often linked to the nature of activity on the asset side, so adjustments could probably only be of a marginal nature.
- **Be proactive in identifying future funding needs.** Act promptly, taking the opportunity to build up funding when conditions are favorable.
- **Optimize use of repo to minimize encumbrance.**

More specific options to optimize the liability side of the balance sheet include:

- **Extend the maturity of liabilities.** This can be achieved by securing the optimal mix of funding tenor to avoid spikes in redemptions and reduce NSFR volatility. Given the step change at the one-year maturity bucket, and the inclusion by the BCBS of a six-month maturity bucket to sit alongside the one-year bucket, banks need to proactively monitor their funding maturity mix to take into account those new constraints on an ongoing basis. Possible options include extending funding to ensure maturities stretch out beyond one year. However, the potential advantages of longer-term funding would need to be weighed up against the cost and impact on returns.

- **Incorporate new regulatory costs in deposit pricing.** It is important to review and, where necessary, restructure the choice of fixed-term deposits offered to retail and corporate clients by optimizing their relative pricing, taking account of their NSFR and LCR impacts. For example, banks could incentivize clients to adopt deposit products with 31-day notice periods, or charge additional fees for non-operational deposits.

Options to optimize the asset side include:

- **To manage liquidity, optimize the mix between Level 1 and Level 2 assets.** Particular considerations include the balance between the cost and relative liquidity of assets across sovereign and covered bonds. This will be especially relevant when central banks eventually scale back quantitative easing and liquidity levels decrease, increasing the overall cost of liquidity. The LCR could also be improved by using repo to exchange level 2B assets with a high haircut for cash/government bonds. For example, equity holdings (with a 50% haircut in the HQLA ratio) could be exchanged for cash/treasuries.
- **Use collateral transformation.** This provides firms that have excess liquidity reserves with an opportunity to pick up additional yield. At the same time, firms short of scarce HQLA collateral can use collateral upgrade transactions to manage potential bottlenecks and ensure LCR compliance.
- **Explore options for netting more effectively by:**
  - Increasing the use of clearing houses for derivatives: This would have the added advantage of assisting with European Market Infrastructure Regulation (EMIR) compliance.
  - Working with clients and counterparties to simplify bilateral collateral arrangements and identify ways to reduce derivative exposures, e.g., by simplifying derivative exposures across a range of counterparties where risk or market value may offset.
  - Decreasing balance sheet size by derecognizing client collateral: meeting certain accounting criteria about strict non-use of client collateral can allow to take the client collateral off-balance sheet.
- **Use maturity-matched repo and reverse repo where feasible.** While the consistency in netting rules between the LR and the NSFR will help banks in managing the new rules, the maturity of the netted exposure will have an impact on the NSFR calculation, with net repo positions over six months yielding an ASF benefit.

■ **Look for opportunities to shorten the duration of some lending products.** Creative restructuring could help to lower RSF for long-term lending such as project, aircraft, or shipping finance, which traditionally requires costly long-term funding.

Banks also need to build the capabilities to identify interdependent assets and liabilities to prove to regulators that transactions are directly linked and should therefore be assigned 0% ASF and RSF. For example, total return swaps, equity swaps and futures could meet a lot of the criteria laid out in the Basel NSFR recommendations (See Table 12.2).

TABLE 12.2 Summary of Impact by Ratio

	Action	LCR	NSFR	LR
Liability-side optimization	Extend the maturity of liabilities	●	●	■
	Review funding mix	●	●	■
	Be proactive in identifying future funding needs	■	●	■
	Incorporate new regulatory costs in deposit pricing	●	●	■
Asset-side optimization	Optimize the mix between Level 1 and Level 2 assets	●	●	■
	Netting			
	■ Increasing use of clearing houses for derivatives	■	●	●
	■ Simplify bilateral collateral arrangements	■	●	●
	■ Derecognizing client collateral	◆	●	●
	Optimize use of repo to minimize encumbrance	●	●	●
	Use maturity matched repo and reverse repo where feasible	■	●	■
	Reduce (sub AA-) corporate bond exposure	●	■	■
	Shorten the duration of some lending products	●	●	■

Keys
PwC
● *Positive*
◆ *Negative*
■ *Neutral*

TABLE 12.3 Selected Industry Insight

	Investment banks	Retail and commercial banks

Examples of impacts	■ Depending on the firms, LCR, NSFR or leverage ratios are the main constraints
	
	  ■ Where LCR is a constraint, firms are focusing on beefing up their liquid assets buffer and getting rid of riskier assets. Some mention concerns around liquid assets supply and market liquidity
	
	  ■ Where LR is a constraint, firms work on increasing capital or reducing balance sheet size, for example via reduction of intercompany transactions. Some firms "take advantage" of headroom in their RWAs to re-risk their balance sheet
	
	  ■ Enhancing the NSFR is seen as particularly challenging, especially given the uncertainty around the rules and the complexity of the businesses involved (e.g., derivatives)
	
	  ■ TLAC is seen as a threat by some banks, and a key constraint over and above LCR, NSFR and LR
		■ LCR tends to be the main constraints. Several firms are under 100% but this can be a conscious business decision and these firms have clear plans to reach this level in the next few years

Examples of actions taken	■ Some banks have large B/S implementation programmes to manage regulatory constraints; however, constraints tend to be dealt with tactically and independently from each other
	
	  ■ Product innovation (e.g., 31 day rolling deposits)
	
	  ■ Legal entity restructuring
	
	  ■ Booking model simplification (mainly driven by RRP)
	
	  ■ Cost of capital and liquidity allocated on a trade by trade basis and reflected in product pricing
		■ Focus on embedding the right behaviour in the business through FTP or risk/reward mechanisms

Since actions that banks take to optimize their position may adversely affect the liquidity that is available to clients, a key aspect of this calculus will be to weigh the business impact across product lines and against total capital and liquidity consumption. This will help to optimize the business mix, understanding how regulatory requirements impact segment value and reallocating product spending, pricing, and sales team loads accordingly. For example, in the context of the LCR, wholesale deposits from clients attracting a 100% runoff assumption could be managed out while clients who have predominantly operational deposit accounts will be competed for more aggressively.

Table 12.3 offers some insights into what banking institutions have been doing to manage the new constraints.

CONCLUSION

Multiple capital and liquidity ratios are now a fact of life. It is important to look at the impact in a holistic manner and develop sustainable structures and strategies to build these new realities into business-as-usual.

Each business model is going to be affected differently, depending on the ratios (investment banks impacted more by NSFR, mixed impact for the LR) due to the specific asset (e.g., repo, derivatives) and liability (e.g., short-term wholesale funding) mix. But all banks will have to assess the implications as a whole, adding in the mix other constraints such as risk-weighted capital ratios, bail-in-able debt, ring-fencing, or bank levy, and work out how to optimize their balance sheets.

First, banks should review the combined impact of the regulatory requirements on the profitability of various business lines. Drawing on the results of this assessment, banks can then look at their asset and liability mix to identify opportunities to improve their ratios while preserving their overall business strategy, franchise, and profitability.

Banks should also need to factor in the implementation and operational costs, not only with regards to reporting but also areas such as the need to redesign their funds transfer pricing to appropriately balance the liquidity costs of providing new business.

Banks that get this overall calculus correct will likely be able to take these new demands in their stride, safeguarding their businesses and ensuring compliance, while delivering an optimized offering to their clients.

CHAPTER 13

Funds Transfer Pricing and the Basel III Framework

Stephen Baird, Bruce Choy, and Daniel Delean[1]

The basic objective of funds transfer pricing (FTP) is to create an internal management accounting framework that attributes or credits "funding revenues" to business units or activities (such as deposit taking) that generate sources of funds for the institution and allocates or charges "funding costs" to business units or activities (such as lending) that use those funds. This framework also transfers away market risks (e.g., interest rate, basis, convexity, currency) from the asset- and liability-originating businesses into a central treasury function that is best equipped to manage these risks for the enterprise as a whole. This transfer mechanism allows the asset and liability originating units to focus on their areas of primary competency (e.g., originating loans or offering deposit products) while leaving the treasury function to address the risk management considerations inherent in interest income and interest expense arising from asset-liability mismatches in tenors, rates, and liquidity. In addition to administering the FTP framework, the treasury function also hedges those same market risks with counterparties in the wider financial markets and is generally accountable for ensuring that the bank is able to meet going concern cash flow obligations regardless of market conditions. As such, the focus of most FTP frameworks has traditionally been on both mitigating and reflecting the impact of changing market rates on the bank's asset and liability positions.

The financial crisis of 2007–08 highlighted two fundamental shortcomings in approaches banks were taking to FTP. First, liquidity risk frameworks—themselves generally underdeveloped in the industry prior to the crisis—were not adequately (if at all) reflected in FTP. With pre-crisis term credit spreads relatively low and banks willingly accepting high levels of short-term wholesale funding risk, the cost of extending (and the value of receiving) liquidity risk in the business lines was not adequately recognized.

---

[1]Stephen Baird is a director in PwC's Chicago office, Bruce Choy is a director in PwC's New York office, and Daniel Delean is a director in PwC's McLean office.

Secondly, the strategic objective of FTP—to serve as a management decision making framework that would drive value-creating decision-making within the business lines—was often absent with FTP all too often serving as a broad-brush, top-of-the-house internal accounting mechanism. Line management, with minimal visibility into the principles driving FTP, pursued other financial objectives such as loan volumes and revenues without regard to the financing or liquidity costs associated with generating these revenues.

The transformation of liquidity risk management since the financial crisis is driving banks to take a fresh look at their FTP frameworks, and in particular, the mechanisms for capturing and transferring the cost of liquidity risk beyond just the cost of financing. As we will discuss in this chapter, these overhauls go beyond basic (though certainly challenging) enhancements to FTP, such as more granular segmentation, improvements in underlying behavioral models, more consistent application across the enterprise, and better risk governance. The Basel III Liquidity Coverage Ratio (LCR), and its requirement that banking institutions maintain a liquidity buffer to cover unanticipated net cash outflows, provides a core principle for how banks should manage liquidity risk. As such, the approach to attributing the cost of liquidity risk to the business units within the institution must be closely aligned to the size and composition of the liquidity buffer.

The years since the financial crisis have witnessed a fundamental transformation in the approach to FTP, with enhancements addressing a spectrum of challenges. In this chapter, we shall focus on the specific question of how should FTP, and liquidity transfer pricing (LTP) in particular, be structured to properly transfer the liquidity costs and benefits implied by the sizing of the bank's liquidity buffer.

OVERVIEW OF FUNDS TRANSFER PRICING OBJECTIVES AND APPROACHES

The overarching objectives of the FTP framework are to centralize market risk for the banking book while insulating the business units and supporting performance measurement. Meeting these objectives in turn enables a bank to:

- Optimize and allocate the financing costs of managing the balance sheet
- Determine fully loaded, net interest income contributions from the bank's product offerings
- Support market-sensitive and competitive product pricing decisions

Several principles should guide the process of maintaining an FTP framework that meets these objectives:

1. **Complete balance sheet and off-balance sheet coverage.** The framework should account for total exposure, including both on- and off-balance sheet, to ensure that the franchise costs of maintaining the safety net of term funding and liquid assets are attributed to all business units and constituents.
2. **Matched maturity marginal market rate.** Transfer prices should be built from independent, "arms-length" market rates. Assets are assumed to be backed by funding that precisely matches the length of the commitment. The applicable market rate should be assigned at origination whereby the marginal transaction's vintage/cohort is used to determine the historical rate that is applied to the asset.
3. **Complete risk coverage.** All forms of market risk should be accounted for in the framework, including interest rate, repricing, basis, optionality, currency, term liquidity, and contingent liquidity risk. The central treasury provides this evaluation and risk attribution/mitigation service with no profit margin.
4. **Fair to all business units.** All banking units should be treated equally and consistently in the framework. Centralization of funding and liquidity should show no favoritism to the various users of the funds.

In practice, there are three basic approaches to determining the FTP rate applied to business units and the funding center—the single pool approach, the multiple-pool approach, and the matched-maturity approach. In the single pool approach, the treasury center simply nets the net interest margin excesses and deficits across business units. This approach is fundamentally flawed as it does not recognize differences in interest rate and liquidity risk characteristics across lines of business. The multiple-pool approach moves in the right direction by creating pools, for example at the product category level, and assigning FTP based on pool averages.

The most sophisticated of these approaches—matched maturity— charges FTP rates for the use of funds and credits rates for sourcing funds by matching the rates on the marginal funding curve to the maturity of the asset or the liability instrument (Figure 13.1). While the level of precision in implementing this approach varies among institutions, it has become the industry standard, and is the typical starting point when considering appropriate adjustments to reflect the Basel liquidity framework.

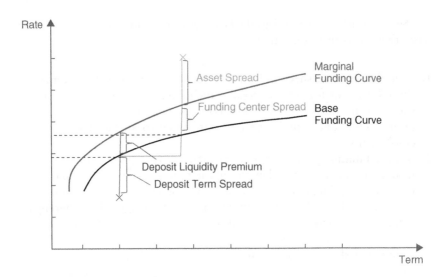

FIGURE 13.1   Matched Funding Funds Transfer Pricing Model

Calculating FTP under the matched-maturity framework has traditionally required addressing the following components:

Base rate. The rate that reflects the estimated duration of each balance sheet item, using a base-funding curve typically derived from
LIBOR/swap rates

Term liquidity premium/charge. The rate that reflects the institution's
liquidity premium, i.e., the spread between actual borrowing costs
(or marginal funding curve) and the base rate, based on the estimated liquidity life of the balance sheet item

Option costs. A charge to capture the optionality of certain balance sheet
items (e.g., mortgages)

Capital. A charge to reflect the equity capital component of any funding
required for the balance sheet item

Example 1: A bank accepts a retail checking deposit. To calculate the
base rate, the institution first estimates (based on historical experience) that
the deposit will have a life of a certain number of years, even though the
customer has a legal right to withdraw the funds at any time. The bank also
estimates (also based on historical experience) that the deposit has a "beta"
of 0.8, i.e., the change in the rate the bank will have to pay on the deposit to
retain it will match 80% of market rate moves. To calculate the base rate, the
bank assigns an overnight base rate on the 80% rate-sensitive portion of the

deposit. The bank further assigns a long-term base rate on the 20% non-rate sensitive portion. To calculate the term liquidity premium, the bank assigns long-term spread differential between the marginal funding curve and the base funding curve. Option charges are not applicable.

CAPTURING VOLATILITY

If the bank's duration and repricing estimates are correct, and the institution is funding at the margin (i.e., not holding excess liquidity), the approach illustrated above will perfectly capture the incremental funding value provided by the deposit relative to accessing wholesale funding markets. However, this approach does not capture the fact that while the overall life of the deposit could be expected to be, for example, 10 years, there could be significant volatility of the actual balance levels. This fact led many banks, even before the 2007–08 financial crisis, to include a "volatile" component in their liabilities to capture this risk in FTP.

Example 2: A bank accepts a commercial demand deposit. To calculate the base rate, the bank applies the same approach described in Example 1—assigning a rate based on the beta and expected liquidity life. However, in assigning the term liquidity premium, the institution applies this credit only to the 70% of the deposit it believes to be stable (based on historical volatility and trend analysis of the deposit type). The remaining 30% of the deposit is held to be "volatile" and does not receive the credit.

In designing the FTP structure and assigning rates to each component, it is helpful to imagine a theoretical matched balance sheet that assigns equivalent investment end points for each funding pool. Figure 13.2 illustrates a typical four-component structure.

While this traditional matched-maturity FTP approach works well in attributing funding and liquidity characteristics to banking activities in a business-as-usual (BAU) environment, it was not explicitly designed to capture stressed liquidity impacts. As we shall see, the recent increase in focus on liquidity risk is leading banks to rethink their approaches to capture this key component.

A NEW FOCUS ON LIQUIDITY RISK AND FTP

Following the 2007–08 crisis and the subsequent buildup in deposits that occurred at many U.S. institutions in particular, treasury centers have become increasingly concerned that pre-crisis approaches to assigning liquidity life and determining the volatile component of deposits may

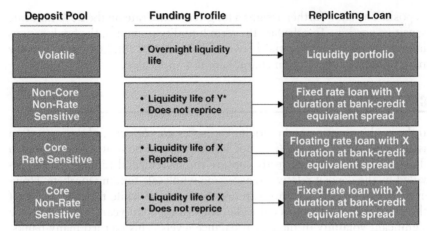

*Applicable where bank wishes to set a non-rate sensitive pool with Y duration that is less than X

FIGURE 13.2 Illustrative Matched Maturity Balance Sheet

overstate the stability of these liabilities. In practice, many banks have chosen to simply invest deposits—particularly those from large clients—in liquidity portfolios or even in excess central bank reserves. With this concern in mind, as well as the fact that for many banks incremental deposit funding is unable to be repositioned to loans in a weakened lending environment, treasury centers have assigned term liquidity premia to a shrinking proportion of the deposit portfolio.

At the same time, financial industry regulatory reform has brought a sharp focus on the liquidity risk inherent in indeterminate liabilities and unfunded commitments. The Basel III Liquidity Coverage Ratio in particular explicitly requires cash buffers to protect against unanticipated deposit outflows, which can be as high as 100% for certain categories. At the supervisory level, examination teams are increasingly scrutinizing banks' abilities to appropriately capture the stressed liquidity risk inherent in deposits and unfunded commitments in stress testing models to ensure the liquidity buffer is sized appropriately to cover these risks.

With this liquidity risk transformation as the backdrop, regulators have increased the focus on FTP frameworks in particular. The need to appropriately capture the liquidity cost of products has been embedded in U.S. regulatory guidance since the Federal Reserve's SR 10-6 Interagency Policy Statement on Funding and Liquidity Risk Management (2010) and is a formal requirement under the Dodd-Frank Enhanced Prudential Standards for U.S.-based institutions, effective since the beginning of 2015. Meanwhile, examination teams are carefully reviewing FTP frameworks to ensure they provide the right strategic incentives to line of business lending and deposit gathering activities.

As a result of these developments, FTP is undergoing its first overhaul in well over a decade. These overhauls of FTP are being driven by the need to upgrade several aspects of the framework, including:

- Enhancing methodologies for delineating core from non-core balances (e.g., utilizing multivariate regression approaches) and estimating duration
- Expanding sources of data for constructing the wholesale funding curve where issuances are limited or nonexistent
- Explicitly linking the cost of contingent liquidity to both on- and off-balance-sheet accounts, through better alignment with Basel III LCR and/or internal stress testing
- Improving the level of segmentation to adequately reflect differences between products, business lines, markets, balance tiers, and other behavioral factors
- Improving FTP efficiency through automated analytics and integration with core systems
- Meeting increasingly strenuous model risk governance requirements

APPROACHES FOR INTEGRATING CONTINGENT LIQUIDITY COSTS AND FTP

The objective of integrating contingent liquidity costs into FTP is to capture the opportunity cost of any liquidity buffer that must be held to support unanticipated outflows (liabilities) or funding (undrawn commitments) under stress. Approaches to achieving this goal vary among institutions, but an effective strategy can be summarized as follows:

1. **Determine the binding constraint that is driving the minimum liquidity buffer size.** For many banks the binding constraint is the LCR over a 30-day period. Alternatively, it may be a specific governing internal liquidity stress test that may run longer than 30 days into several months and may be specified as such within the institution's board-approved risk appetite statement.
2. **Determine segmented runoff pools.** For example, deposit and off-balance-sheet commitments should be segmented into the various runoff pools developed for LCR monitoring.

3. **Map the runoff pools into the FTP pools.** Ideally, there should be little distinction between runoff pools and the FTP structure, and better practice is to seek as full an alignment as possible. In practice, full alignment is a challenge. For example, if the FTP system is configured to process at the chart of account and cost center level, there will be misalignment between the very granular LCR pools and what is currently possible under FTP. In those instances an approach must be developed (e.g., taking an existing FTP pool like commercial analysis checking and developing a composite LCR runoff profile).

4. **Determine core/volatile.** The core/volatile delineations should be determined assuming a non-stressed, BAU environment. Methodologies for making this determination vary, but it is important to avoid arbitrary assumptions that often are overly conservative and instead reflect a mix of both stressed and non-stressed considerations. Alternatively, assigning core deposit balances based on behavior during the post-crisis liquidity buildup is unlikely to capture possible impacts of rising rates. Leading practices, such as utilizing econometric models, should be considered.

5. **Determine rate sensitivity betas** based on accepted methodologies such as regression analysis.

6. **Assign term liquidity premia** based on the BAU core duration assumptions and the wholesale funding curve.

7. **Attribute the incremental liquidity buffer.** For each FTP pool, determine the liquidity buffer required based on composite LCR or internal stress testing assumptions.

8. **Determine the buffer charge.** For example, the term liquidity premium credited under the BAU duration could be reversed as a charge.

9. **Incorporate additional components** such as option charges, capital charge, and miscellaneous charges.

10. **Determine the final FTP based on the previous components.**

Example 3: A bank accepts a commercial demand deposit. The bank calculates the BAU FTP, though taking care to ensure that the 30% volatile determination does not include a stressed assumption (e.g., by considering volatility observed during the financial crisis or otherwise considering "fear factors" under subjective assumptions). The bank then determines that this deposit, which contains a mix of operational and non-operational deposits, reflects a blended LCR runoff factor of 35%. The FTP is then charged for a 5% (representing the difference between the 35% buffer requirement and the 30% already assigned to volatile) incremental liquidity buffer based on the spread between the wholesale funding curve and the yield on high quality liquid assets.

SOME PRACTICAL CONSIDERATIONS

The aforementioned approach outlines a high-level roadmap to incorporating contingent liquidity into the FTP framework. However, banks are likely to encounter a number of practical issues as they implement the necessary changes to their frameworks:

- **One step vs. two steps.** An alternative approach is to capture both the non-stressed and stressed FTP components in a blended approach when delineating core/volatile funding. For example, for a deposit pool that receives 100% runoff under LCR, it may seem redundant to calculate the BAU FTP and then apply a liquidity charge, as the end result will certainly not include any term liquidity or term funding component. While this approach is theoretically possible, it is recommended to delineate between non-stressed and stressed FTP assumptions to ensure transparency and a conceptually sound approach to developing assumptions. See Figure 13.3 for a more detailed comparison of these two approaches.
- **Addressing stressed runoff and FTP misalignment.** A significant challenge in integrating contingent liquidity and FTP is misalignment between LCR/stress testing pools and the FTP structure. In implementing methodology changes it is preferable to consider practical approaches such as developing a composite assumption where the level of potential inaccuracy is within acceptable bounds (e.g., a retail deposit product type may be assumed to contain a mix of insured and uninsured balances that maps approximately well to a blended LCR assumption). On the other hand, workarounds may be required where, for example, the impact of high-runoff LCR pools in a commercial product/cost center must be tracked separately for FTP purposes to avoid unacceptable distortion.
- **Pushing down liquidity charges to the business.** While a well-structured FTP approach is a critical first step to appropriately aligning business line incentives and decision making with liquidity costs, the institution should not stop there. Customer profitability and pricing frameworks should also be enhanced to reflect the extent to which granular customer segments, individual products, and even individual clients are contributors to or users of liquidity. Implementing these enhancements will ensure that individual clients and products are not over- or undercharged relative to the more blunt segmentation structure likely to be required for FTP.
- **Charging out the liquidity buffer.** In theory, the contingent liquidity charge will fully and perfectly allocate the carrying cost of the enterprise liquidity buffer. In reality, this is unlikely to be the case. For example,

Business as usual behavioral life should determine the duration assumptions for FTP purposes. Stressed runoff modeling should determine the required liquidity buffer and buffer charges included in FTP. Robust segmentation should enable precision treatments.

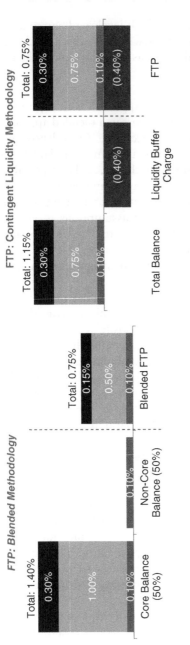

FTP: Blended Methodology

- ■ Overnight Funding Rate ■ Matched Funding Rate
- ■ Term Liquidity Premium

- Core balance is assumed to be stable and receives matched funding rate and term liquidity premium based on liquidity life
- Non-core balance is assumed to have no liquidity life and receives overnight funding rate
- FTP is understated when non-core liquidity life is realized such as under a non-stressed scenario
- FTP is overstated if core portion is subject to run-off, such as under a stressed scenario

FTP: Contingent Liquidity Methodology

- ■ Overnight Funding Rate ■ Matched Funding Rate
- ■ Term Liquidity Premium ■ Liquidity Buffer Charge

- The total balance is assigned a liquidity life under non-stressed assumptions, receiving matched funding and term liquidity premium
- Required contingent liquidity is estimated based on stressed scenario modeling (or regulatory requirements), resulting in a liquidity buffer charge

FIGURE 13.3 Blended vs. Contingent Liquidity Methodologies

treasury may choose to maintain a balanced portfolio of short-term maturities that earns a higher rate than the overnight funding assumptions used for FTP buffer charge purposes.

■ **Accounting for countermeasures.** For banks that set their liquidity buffer based on internal stress testing outcomes (as opposed to the LCR limit) the assumption of any countermeasures will serve to offset the required buffer and should in theory reduce the buffer charged out to the line of business. Arguably, the impact of the countermeasure should be attributed to each FTP pool (i.e., based on which line of business/product line executes the countermeasure). The institution should develop a practical but sound approach to addressing this problem.

■ **The problem of excess liquidity.** As a result of the 2007–08 financial crisis liquidity buildup, many banks now hold more liquidity than is required for LCR or liquidity risk limit purposes. This mismatch can create a conceptual challenge to marginal funding-driven FTP methodologies, which may have the unintended consequence of over-incenting deposit gathering (in an environment where deposits are unneeded) and overpricing loans (in an environment where more loan generation is needed). The bank will need to develop an approach to addressing this issue systematically rather than, as has too often been the case, through arbitrary FTP adjustments. For example, the central treasury function may determine that excess cash should be considered in the context of broader capital structure considerations and should be addressed through share repurchases or otherwise absorbed by the treasury center. Alternatively, the bank may choose to charge back the excess liquidity cost through adjustments to the wholesale funding curve.

CONCLUSION

Long considered a "solved science," the FTP framework has become an important component of the bank's liquidity risk framework and, following the financial crisis, has been increasingly scrutinized by regulators and other stakeholders. While nearly all financial institutions of significant size have an FTP framework in place that delineates asset and liability matched-funding characteristics at a basic level, there are usually several areas for potential improvement. In particular, the liquidity risk framework inherent in Basel III— supporting the liquidity risk associated with liabilities through carefully measured cash buffers—is not aligned to the traditional components of core/volatile funding sources and costs that underpin most FTP frameworks. By building in a contingent liquidity component to the FTP rate that appropriately captures the impact of business line activities on the size and composition of the liquidity pool, an institution can ensure a closer linkage between transaction-level activities and enterprise-level financial performance.

CHAPTER 14

Liquidity and Funding Disclosures

Alejandro Johnston[1]

This chapter examines the current state of banks' liquidity and funding disclosures. The section immediately following provides the perspective of the banks (disclosure preparers). Thereafter, we discuss the perspective of investors (disclosure users). Finally, the last section provides a summary of leading industry practices in the area of liquidity and funding risk disclosures.

In the years after the recent financial crisis, policy makers, regulators, and investors have focused on the transparency of the risk profiles of large international banks. As a result of various regulatory and private sector efforts, and in no small part to respond to expectations of funding providers, there has been an improvement in the quality of risk disclosures in recent years. Moreover, there has been increased collaboration between preparers and users of risk disclosures in defining specific areas for enhancement. Investors continue to push for additional and clearer disclosure in this area, prompting banks to continuously reevaluate their approach.

The events of 2007–08 and failures or near failures of many large financial institutions exposed weaknesses in the liquidity risk management capabilities of large international banks. The regulatory response to these events has been to significantly increase the expectations of banks in areas such as liquidity stress testing and stability of funding sources, which are reflected in the Liquidity Coverage Ratio (LCR) and Net Stable Funding Ratio (NSFR) components of the Basel III framework. Similarly, expectations on the part of regulators and investors concerning the transparency of liquidity and funding risks and how banks manage them have also increased. Regulators and investors have paid particular attention to liquidity and funding disclosures in recent years. Both the Securities and Exchange Commission (SEC) and International Accounting Standards Board (IASB) have specific requirements for liquidity and funding disclosures which have become a focal point in their ongoing discussions with banks. Table 14.1 summarizes the disclosure requirements currently in place. At a high level, these requirements fall

---

[1] Alejandro Johnston is a principal in PwC's New York office.

TABLE 14.1   Regulatory Requirements for Liquidity and Funding Disclosures

	SEC	IASB
Liquidity Disclosure Requirements	■ Provide the average amount of liquid assets available during the period in addition to the amounts and sources of liquidity as of the balance sheet date.[2]	■ Include a description of the approach to liquidity risk management.[3]
Funding Disclosure Requirements	■ Disclose the existence and timing of commitments for capital expenditures and other known and reasonably likely cash requirements.[4] ■ Provide a tabular disclosure of contractual obligations.[5] ■ Enhance disclosures about a registrant's primary sources of liquidity, impact of credit downgrades on funding and liquidity, collateral requirements, and borrowing arrangements.[6] ■ Disclose a description of expected changes in the mix and relative cost of capital resources.[7] ■ Describe internal and external sources of funding, including any material unused sources of liquid assets.[8]	■ Provide an analysis of contractual maturities of financial liabilities.[9] ■ Provide contractually committed amounts for acquisition of property, plant, and equipment.[10] ■ Provide amounts contractually committed to buying, building, or developing investment properties, or amounts contractually committed to repairing, maintaining, or improving investment properties.[11]

[2] PwC. "SEC Comment Letter Themes." September 2011.

[3] IFRS Foundation. "International Financial Reporting Standard 7–Financial Instruments: Disclosures," http://eifrs.ifrs.org/eifrs/bnstandards/en/2014/ifrs7.pdf. August 2005. Viewed January 16, 2014.

[4] Securities and Exchange Commission. "Interpretation: Commission Guidance Regarding Management's Discussion and Analysis of Financial Condition and Results of Operations," Securities Act Rel. No. 33-8350, Exchange Act Rel. No. 34-48960, Financial Reporting Rel. No. FR-72, http://www.sec.gov/rules/interp/33-8350.htm. December 19, 2003. Viewed January 16, 2014.

[5] Securities and Exchange Commission. "Interpretation: Disclosure in Management's Discussion and Analysis About Off-Balance Sheet Arrangements and Aggregate Contractual Obligations," Securities Act Rel. No. 33-8182, Exchange Act Rel. No. 34-47264, Financial Reporting Rel. No. FR-67, http://www.sec.gov/rules/final/33-8182.htm. February 5, 2003. Viewed January 16, 2014.

[6] PwC. "SEC Comment Letter Themes." September 2011.

[7] See footnote 3 above.

[8] See footnote 3 above.

[9] See footnote 2 above.

[10] IFRS Foundation. "International Accounting Standard 16 – Property, Plant and Equipment," http://eifrs.ifrs.org/eifrs/bnstandards/en/2014/ias16.pdf. December 18, 2003. Viewed January 16, 2014.

[11] IFRS Foundation. "International Accounting Standard 40–Investment Property," http://eifrs.ifrs.org/eifrs/bnstandards/en/2014/ias40.pdf. December 18, 2003. Viewed January 16, 2014.

into the following key areas: (1) descriptions of the approach to liquidity risk management and the overall funding strategy, (2) quantitative detail related to the liquidity reserve in place and the primary sources of liquidity and funding, and (3) maturity breakdown for key liabilities and contractual obligations.

There is debate among banks over the applicability and usefulness of certain disclosure requirements. Banks generally agree that most liquidity and funding disclosure requirements by the SEC and IASB can be useful to investors. However, some banks are of the view that a few of these requirements provide limited information about an institution's liquidity or funding profile. Specifically, the SEC requirement related to contractual cash obligations and the IASB requirement pertaining to contractual maturities of liabilities have been highlighted as items of limited value in a liquidity and funding context. A similar view is shared by banks, and some investors, with respect to the EDTF's recommendation concerning the contractual maturities of assets and liabilities. Some banks find this type of information to have limited value in describing funding mismatches given that contractual maturities are, in many cases, significantly different from maturities that reflect behavioral patterns.

While existing liquidity and disclosure requirements can be helpful, there is consensus among regulators and investors that disclosures can be improved to provide additional transparency of the banks' risk profiles and risk management practices. Thus, there continues to be ongoing dialogue between banks, regulators, and investors around the quality of risk disclosures. This dialogue has become more structured since May 2012 due to the establishment of the EDTF.[12] The EDTF is a private sector group of preparers and users of risk disclosures established by the FSB to recommend enhancements to existing disclosures. In October 2012, the EDTF released a report detailing 32 disclosure recommendations that banks could make across seven key risk areas, including liquidity and funding.[13] In 2013, subsequent to this report, the EDTF conducted a study to examine the extent to which banks had adopted these recommendations in their 2012 annual reports.[14] The results of the study were positive in terms of

---

[12]The EDTF was formed by the Financial Stability Board in May 2012. It is an independent group consisting of bank representatives, investors and analysts, credit rating agencies, and external auditors.

[13]Enhanced Disclosure Task Force. "EDTF Principles and Recommendations for Enhancing the Risk Disclosures of Banks," http://www.financialstabilityboard.org/2012/10/r_121029/. October 29, 2012. Viewed January 18, 2014.

[14]Enhanced Disclosure Task Force. "2013 Progress Report on Implementation of the EDTF Principles and Recommendations," http://www.financialstabilityboard.org/2013/08/r_130821a/. August 21, 2013. Viewed January 18, 2014.

progress, but they also indicated gaps between what investors expected to see and what banks were providing. This was particularly true in the area of liquidity and funding disclosures, where there were two recommendations for which banks indicated a much higher implementation rate than investors perceived.[15]

THE BANK VIEW

The majority of banks have enhanced their risk disclosures in the wake of the financial crisis. The enhancement of these disclosures has been particularly evident in the area of liquidity and funding, which was not always given the same emphasis in the years leading up to the crisis. Most banks have increased the granularity of disclosed information with respect to the liquidity buffer, the maturity profile of assets and liabilities, and the general funding strategy. However, investors and regulators, primarily across Europe and North America, continue to request further enhancements and are increasingly maintaining a dialogue with banks in this regard.

Banks have been responsive to investors' requests and have acknowledged there is room for improvement despite having a fundamentally different view on disclosures than investors in certain areas. These differences may explain some of the discrepancies between investor expectations and bank disclosures.

From a quantitative perspective, preparers usually focus on providing a breakdown of resources available to face liquidity needs. In addition, preparers tend to place considerable importance on qualitative disclosures and narrative that provides context to quantitative information and describes how management understands and manages liquidity and funding risks. In particular, banks' liquidity and funding disclosures tend to focus on four key areas:

- Quality and amount of liquidity buffer components available to cover liquidity events
- Stress testing framework and types of stress testing analysis performed
- Funding sources and concentrations
- Liquidity risk management framework coverage and application

---

[15]The study included a self-assessment by each bank of whether they had implemented each of the 32 recommendations. For eight of the recommendations, the EDTF conducted a user (investor) review where users were asked to assess whether the banks disclosures address the recommendation.

From the perspective of the banks, regulators play an important role in the monitoring of liquidity and funding risks using information in regulatory reports. For this, regulators in the United States, and increasingly in other jurisdictions, collect large amounts of liquidity information on a daily basis. For example, in the United States, the largest organizations are required to provide daily reports of their liquidity position to the Federal Reserve. These reports require a detailed breakdown of assets, liabilities, and potential claims.

While all of this information is not publicly available, it is the banks' view that investors can have some level of comfort from the oversight that regulators provide. However, many users place little weight on the regulators' oversight activities when making investment decisions and prefer to do their own analysis.

Disclosure Development and Production

In providing liquidity and funding disclosures, banks target a wide audience that includes not only sophisticated fixed income and equity analysts but also a wide range of stakeholders such as the press and individual investors. This translates into liquidity and funding disclosures that are meant to be easy to understand by the average user, who may not have a deep understanding of liquidity and funding concepts. Banks also pay close attention to the way in which disclosures could be interpreted by the financial press, a group that also includes users with varying levels of sophistication, in ways that could increase headline risk. Finally, banks take into consideration the demands of more sophisticated sell-side and buy-side analysts by including additional information in investor presentations and targeted supplements.

From a preparer perspective, providing effective disclosures is a delicate balancing act between transparency to the target audience and protection of sensitive information. Banks aim to be responsive to investors' requests for risk information while also focusing on providing information they consider useful to the market. At the same time, banks look to protect information that can be sensitive and/or harmful to the franchise. From the preparer's view there are four primary elements that are balanced against transparency objectives in the development of liquidity and funding disclosures:

■ **Complexity of information.** Certain information is not suitable for general market consumption without extensive explanations and supporting analysis. For example, banks make assumptions about the maturity behavior of assets and liabilities for internal risk management purposes, which in many cases are different from the contractual maturities of these instruments. These assumptions are made using complex models and analysis that would be difficult to disclose without revealing trade secrets and would require extensive explanations to prevent confusion on the part of users and protect the bank from franchise risk.

- **Level of sophistication of users.** Certain liquidity and funding information is prone to misinterpretation, which can result in an inaccurate view of a bank's liquidity profile and trigger adverse market responses. For instance, an LCR value of 95%, which is lower than the required 100%, may be misinterpreted by uneducated users as a sign of imminent liquidity problems, when in fact the bank may have adequate resources to cover its liquidity needs.
- **Focus on critical areas.** Disclosure requirements and the need to manage legal risk have led banks to produce annual reports and periodic filings that span hundreds of pages, which make it difficult for users to find risk information and differentiate between critical and marginally important data. Banks generally look to focus on providing information for a few key areas rather than adding disclosures that may distract users from the more important messages.
- **Alignment with internal practices.** The level of granularity, metrics, and presentation of disclosures is highly influenced by the bank's internal approaches for liquidity and funding risk management and reporting. Disclosures included in periodic filings tend to closely resemble internal practices. However, banks usually produce customized disclosures in the form of investor presentations that aim to respond to specific requests by users.

The production of risk disclosures requires close and active collaboration among various groups within the bank, most importantly treasury, risk management, financial reporting, and investor relations. Most banks have formal disclosure committees that review and approve the information that is made available to the public.

As owners of liquidity and funding information, the bank's treasury group usually has a primary role in developing the narrative and quantitative information to be disclosed. Once these draft disclosures are developed, they are reviewed by the risk management and financial reporting teams to fine-tune the content and messages in the disclosures. Internal audit is also involved in reviewing the disclosures for alignment with the bank's internal policies. Similarly, the legal teams review disclosures for compliance with regulations but also to manage the bank's exposure to legal risk. Finally, the investor relations department plays an important role in suggesting enhancements and new disclosures based on questions and feedback received from investors.

Areas of Disclosure Enhancement

While many large international banks in different jurisdictions have enhanced liquidity and funding disclosures in recent years, they acknowledge that there is room to improve, particularly in these three areas:

- **Comparability.** There are still significant differences in the way banks break down their liquidity and funding information. Some of these differences result from the different standards and regulatory requirements applicable to banks across multiple jurisdictions. For instance, banks use a variety of different table structures, approaches and definitions to present the liquidity buffer and its components. While some banks have tried to conform to standard definitions such as those in the LCR framework, which hasn't yet been adopted in many G20 jurisdictions, other institutions present this information using customized internal definitions of liquid assets.
- **Consistency of definitions and metrics.** There are also significant differences in definitions for liquid assets and/or the metrics used to monitor liquidity risk. For instance, some banks have adopted high-quality liquid assets (HQLA) categorizations provided by regulators, while other institutions rely on internal liquid asset criteria. Further, banks use different metrics and ratios to monitor liquidity risk internally. Additional enhancements can be made by preparers in better defining the terms and metrics used to provide users with the level of understanding required to make appropriate comparisons.
- **Information overload.** The quantity of liquidity and funding information disclosed by large international banks varies greatly among institutions. In some cases, the amount of information provided can make it more difficult for users to differentiate between what is important and what is not. Some banks perceive this to be the case and are of the view that providing details about areas that can be immaterial or that are not well understood by users may in fact defeat the purpose enhancing their disclosures and create confusion rather than provide clarity.

THE INVESTOR VIEW

Large institutional investors as well as sell-side analysts have played a key role in the effort to enhance banks' risk disclosures in recent years, providing ongoing feedback to banks regarding additional disclosures that can be made and how existing disclosures can be refined. Although many investors acknowledge the improvements made in recent years, they continue to request additional granularity and transparency of risk information. In the area of liquidity and funding disclosures, investors see significant room for improvement and have noted that only a limited number of institutions have adopted leading practices.

Investors rely on risk disclosures to perform analysis that ultimately supports investment decisions or buy/hold/sell recommendations. Information about the liquidity and funding profile of an institution is used as an input to assign money market and long-term internal credit ratings, to run stress testing analysis, and to evaluate the performance of each institution against peers under different adverse scenarios. Analysts evaluate whether the market price of a security is attractive given their view of the risk profile of the issuer and structural features of the debt or equity.

For investors, it is critical to understand the funding profile of the bank and how well management demonstrates an understanding of the bank's balance sheet and its vulnerabilities. In particular, investors are focused on answering the following questions:

- How are the bank's assets funded by currency and line of business?
- Where does the bank have funding mismatches and how would those mismatches change under stress conditions?
- How conservative is management's approach to managing funding mismatches?
- How do new debt or equity issues affect the funding profile of the organization?
- How concentrated and sustainable are funding sources and strategies?
- To what extent can available assets meet liquidity and funding needs?
- What process and tools does the bank use to manage liquidity risk?

Liquidity and funding disclosures are a primary source of information investors use to answer these questions. Analysts complement their analysis through discussions with management that aim to provide further details concerning management's approach in areas such as funding limits, funds transfer pricing (FTP) process, and approach to modeling the maturity of deposits.

It is important to note that fixed-income and equity investors have different analytical objectives and focus on different data points in performing their analysis. For fixed-income investors, the funding and liquidity profile of an institution and the way the bank manages these risks drives the ability of the bank to honor its debt service, as agreed, under situations where default is unlikely. Thus, liquidity and funding risk analysis is critical regardless of the situation of the bank at the time of the analysis. Equity investors, on the other hand, tend to pay less attention to liquidity and funding considerations for institutions considered to be of high credit quality. For this group, however, the bank's liquidity and funding profile becomes critical when an institution shows signs of weakness that may affect revenue streams or expected returns, and hence its valuation.

In achieving their objectives, investors are interested in obtaining granular liquidity and funding information presented in tabular form that is easy to locate and understand. For example, in evaluating the funding profile of an institution, investors are interested in the breakdown of liabilities and how those serve to fund assets by currency and line of business. Investors are interested in determining whether or not a bank could be subject to a shortfall of funding in a particular jurisdiction due to local adverse economic or political events.

When it comes to liquidity and funding disclosures, investors are interested in both quantitative detail and a qualitative discussion. Quantitative metrics are a critical input into the investor's analysis and serve as the basis to understand, for example, funding mismatches and size of the liquidity buffer vis-à-vis expected outflows. However, investors also look for a narrative that explains the story behind the numbers, main drivers of change and management's perspective of the bank's liquidity and funding profile. Without this type of qualitative support, quantitative disclosures can leave unanswered questions and limit the analyst's ability to appropriately interpret the information. Examples of qualitative information that are valuable to investors include:

- A description of bank's overall funding strategy, including a description of key sources and uses of funds
- A discussion of recent changes in funding profile and underlying drivers (e.g., regulatory, management decision)
- A discussion of the bank's approach to funding different business lines, including the FTP process
- A description of the process for stress testing liquidity inflows and outflows
- A discussion of the liquidity buffer components and how they are appropriate to address liquidity needs

The transparency of risk information may influence an investor's appetite or willingness to invest in a particular security in a nonlinear fashion. While investors make investment decisions primarily on the basis of their internal estimates and the prevailing market price, investors tend to have a larger appetite for institutions that demonstrate sound management judgment over time. While transparency influences the analyst's perception of an institution, disclosure is no substitute for sound business strategy.

However, all else being equal, greater transparency increases an investor's willingness to lend and should ultimately be reflected in a somewhat lower funding cost. In addition, investors tend to be more willing to lend, and for longer durations, to institutions that are perceived to be more transparent about their liquidity and funding risk profile. While many analysts qualitatively indicate an inverse relationship between disclosure quality and funding cost, this impact is hard to measure given the number of factors that drive investment decisions.

LEADING PRACTICES FOR LIQUIDITY AND FUNDING DISCLOSURE

As mentioned previously, liquidity and funding disclosures vary across institutions. During the years after the crisis, the granularity and quality of liquidity and funding disclosures had been driven in part by the need of banks in certain jurisdictions to be more transparent due to investor or regulatory demands. For example, some UK, Swedish, and Norwegian banks provided granular, quantitative disclosures of liquidity reserve and funding prior to the existence of the EDTF. Japanese banks have done a comparatively better job in identifying and explaining asset-liability mismatches, tabulating maturity of assets and liabilities and breaking down the liquidity reserve and its components[16]. After the release of the EDTF report in October 2012 and the EDTF progress report in 2013, many large international banks have made improvements to their liquidity and funding disclosures to align to the EDTF recommendations. Currently, many leading practices in the area of liquidity and funding disclosure align with the EDTF recommendations.

Liquidity Buffer

The amount and type of liquid assets available to a bank (i.e., liquidity buffer) is an important risk measure as it indicates the bank's ability to withstand short-term market stresses. Leading institutions provide both a quantitative breakdown of their available liquidity as well as a supporting narrative that describes the key sources of liquidity and how they are managed. From a quantitative standpoint, the leading practice is to disclose the following items:

- Detailed breakdown of liquidity buffer by asset type with separate columns or views if liquidity is measured under different regulatory regimes and/or currencies
  - Separate views for year-end and average balances
- Summary of stress test results (e.g., LCR) and excess liquidity (surplus)

---

[16]Enhanced Disclosure Task Force. "EDTF Principles and Recommendations for Enhancing the Risk Disclosures of Banks," http://www.financialstabilityboard.org/2012/10/r_121029/. October 29, 2012. Viewed January 18, 2014.

In terms of a supporting narrative, leading practice includes providing the following information:

- Description of the components of liquidity buffer (e.g., unencumbered assets, central bank eligible assets)
- Brief description of the drivers of the overall level and specific composition of the liquidity buffer (e.g., wholesale liability movement, interest cost considerations)
- Brief description of the current composition of the liquidity reserve and its changes over the past year
- Types of stress tests against which the liquidity reserve is tested
- Brief discussion of any significant (%) portion of liquidity reserve maintained in restricted subsidiaries or in different currencies

Review of Encumbered and Unencumbered Assets

Encumbered assets reduce the pool of assets available to unsecured creditors, and are regarded as being a particularly important area of risk disclosure. The overall balance of secured and unsecured funding, the extent to which assets are encumbered, and the amount of unencumbered assets available to support liquidity are all important factors to investors. Leading practice in this area is to provide a schedule(s) of encumbered and unencumbered assets that detail the following:

- Encumbered vs. unencumbered assets by key asset category (e.g., trading, derivatives)
- Collateral pledged (unavailable) vs. collateral received (available for re-hypothecation or re-deployment) and how much collateral received remains available
- The ratio of encumbered assets to total assets
- Summary of on-balance sheet vs. off-balance sheet assets that can meet funding needs

Maturity Analysis of Financial Assets and Liabilities

Many banks provide maturity information for their key assets and liabilities, or liabilities only; however, there are notable differences in terms of the number of maturity buckets and the granularity of asset and liability categories used. Leading banks provide sufficient line item detail and other information for investors to understand the nature of the bank's funding needs over time, including:

- Table summarizing all key assets and liabilities broken down by maturity "bucket"

- Assets and liabilities broken out, at a minimum, by primary balance sheet categories
- At least eight maturity "buckets" (e.g., less than 1 month, 1–3 months)
- Borrowings broken down by level of seniority (unsecured, secured, subordinated) and by maturity "bucket"
- Off-balance sheet commitments broken down by maturity "bucket"

Funding profile and management

Leading institutions provide a qualitative description of the bank's funding profile, including key funding sources as well as a discussion of how funding is managed. Specifically, those banks leading in this area provide descriptions of the following:

- Key funding sources and level of access under baseline and stress conditions
- Material concentrations in funding sources, with specific attention to wholesale funding and its distribution across different jurisdictions and currencies
- Changes in funding sources over time
- Approach to managing funding on an ongoing basis (e.g., funding spreads, diversification of funding sources)

Leading banks also provide the following information in supporting tables and charts:

- Amount of funding by source (e.g., repurchase agreements, deposits, long-term debt)
- Deposit-to-loan coverage (customer deposits as % of loans)
- Breakdown of any key asset—liability match funding

Other Qualitative Disclosures

In addition to providing qualitative descriptions related to funding strategy (noted before), leading institutions provide meaningful qualitative disclosures in each of the following areas:

- **Stress testing.** Leading banks provide a narrative explanation of their liquidity and funding stress testing practices and linkage to the bank's broader liquidity and funding management framework.
- **Basel III liquidity ratios.** Leading banks provide a narrative discussion of plans to comply with proposed Basel III ratios.
- **Currency liquidity and funding profile.** Leading banks provide a narrative discussion of the breakdown of liquid assets maintained in any material currency and funding profile in each major currency.

CONCLUSION

In the wake of the 2008 financial crisis, banks have faced increased expectations from both regulators and funding providers with respect to the stability of their liquidity and funding profile. One area of focus for both regulators and investor groups has been on improving the quality of banks' liquidity and funding disclosures such that end users have an accurate picture of the bank's stability. During the ongoing collaboration with investors to enhance disclosures more broadly, liquidity- and funding-related disclosures have been one of the key discussion topics.

As a result of this dialogue and heightened regulatory expectations, banks have made marked improvements in the quality of liquidity and funding disclosures. Nonetheless, investors continue to push for enhancements with respect to the granularity and breadth of banks' disclosures. As a result, the discussion remains ongoing, with banks trying to strike a balance between being responsive and disclosing too much information. Banks generally acknowledge that their liquidity and funding disclosures can be enhanced, in particular as it relates to the comparability of disclosures across banks and the consistency of liquidity-related definitions. However, banks also emphasize that these enhancements need to be weighed against other considerations—for instance, the potentially sensitive nature of information or the level of sophistication of the average investor. In addition, banks highlight that regulators collect large amounts of liquidity-related data on a daily basis and that investors should take some level of comfort from the oversight provided by these regulators. Investors, for their part, acknowledge the recent improvement in banks' liquidity and funding. However, investors still highlight the need for more granularity, especially in terms of the bank's liabilities and how those liabilities fund assets by currency and line of business. In addition, investors emphasize the need for more meaningful qualitative narratives discussing the bank's funding strategy, its approach to funding different business lines, and its process for stress testing.

Biographies

Shyam Venkat

Shyam is a principal in PwC's U.S. Financial Services Advisory practice and is based in New York. Over the course of his 30 years' experience, Shyam has been advising clients on a broad spectrum of risk management, treasury, capital, liquidity, and finance matters impacting strategy and operations. His expertise has enabled him to advise and implement solutions in the areas of risk management strategy and policy; governance and organization structure; asset valuation; market, liquidity, and credit risk management and measurement; asset-liability management; performance measurement; operations; and management information systems. His clients include leading global and domestic banks; insurance companies; asset managers and pension funds; government sponsored enterprises; non-bank financial institutions; multilateral financial institutions; and Fortune 500 industrial, consumer products, and energy companies.

Stephen Baird

Stephen is a director in PwC's U.S. Financial Services Advisory practice and is based in Chicago. Stephen specializes in the area of liquidity optimization for financial institutions. With over 15 years' experience as a treasury practitioner and consultant, Stephen focuses on helping financial institutions optimize performance through enhanced liquidity risk management practices, funds transfer pricing frameworks, customer deposit rate optimization, and liquidity product strategies. His client work has also focused on wholesale client transaction services such as treasury management, trade, and securities services.

PwC U.S. Financial Services Advisory

With more than 2,500 professionals in over 20 U.S. markets, PricewaterhouseCoopers' U.S. Financial Services Advisory (FS Advisory) practice believes in putting clients first by providing innovative solutions for the financial world's evolving and most challenging needs. Organized with knowledgeable and highly credentialed staff whose subject matter expertise and experience mirror the trends in the market, the practice comprises strategy, finance, risk, operations, and technology specialists that seamlessly deliver custom, practical, and sustainable solutions to clients. PwC's FS Advisory consultants are problem-solvers that consistently strive to add value from strategy through execution, whether they're helping clients adapt to dynamically changing industry models, navigate the complexity of regulatory reform, or elevate the customer's digital experience.

PwC's UK Financial Services Risk and Regulatory Practice

Composed of over 60 partners and 1,000 professional staff, PwC's UK Financial Services Risk and Regulatory (FSRR) practice works with clients to provide high quality advice and assurance to the financial sector. PwC's UK FSRR practice helps clients anticipate and understand regulatory and policy change and make the necessary adjustments to their businesses to manage this change. Where it is too late to prevent failure, the practice works with clients to investigate the source of the problem, deal with the impacts, and help to establish controls to support compliance going forward.

Index

and risk disclosures, 268
and risk management governance, 9, 10,
    142, 204

universal banks, 239, 240, 241
user acceptance test (UAT) for source data,
    170, 171, 179–180

value transfer network (VTN), 77
volatility
    of asset prices, 63
    of bank cash flows, 63
    and funds transfer pricing, 255
    of markets, 15, 86, 133
Volcker, Paul, 55

Washington Mutual, 28–29, 38, 42
wholesale funding
    bank reliance on, 22, 203, 214, 240, 243,
        275
    as early warning indicator, 107
    monitoring of, 146
    as recovery plan trigger, 186
    vs. retail, 49
    unsecured, 43
wholesale funding curve, 257, 261
wire transfers, and intraday liquidity,
    60, 61
working capital, 14, 224

yield curve, 52–53
yield vs. portfolio liquidity, 48–49

Printed and bound by CPI Group (UK) Ltd, Croydon, CR0 4YY

23/04/2025

14660927-0001